THE POSITIVE HERO

in Russian Literature

The
POSITIVE HERO
in Russian Literature

RUFUS W. MATHEWSON, Jr.

Columbia University Press

NEW YORK   1958

For Murray, Tommy, and Kevin

This study, prepared under the Graduate Faculties of Columbia University, was selected by a committee of those Faculties to receive one of the Clarke F. Ansley awards given annually by Columbia University Press.

PREFACE

Early in the planning of this book I decided not to go beyond 1946, when Georgi Zhdanov published his draconian "Report on the Journals *Zvezda* and *Leningrad*." One must stop somewhere, if only to withstand the headlines with their nagging demand for accountings and further accountings, but the choice was not entirely arbitrary. Zhdanov's article, with its many echoes of prescriptions set and hardened throughout a century, is an apt and consistent stopping place. Perhaps the greatest pressure to alter this decision in the course of writing came with Stalin's death and the subsequent literary "thaw." If there had been then a true liberation in Soviet literature, the continuities and traditions I have traced here would have appeared less enduring than I have maintained. However, it was, in fact, not a real thaw at all. The ice has held—and for reasons which I hope will be evident to the reader of this study.

Take, for example, Vladimir Dudintsev's novel, *Not by Bread Alone*, which seemed to promise a sharp change of course in Soviet literary affairs. It is not a first-rate novel, lacking Babel's intensity, Sholokhov's range, or Leonov's depth, and Dudintsev has made his job more difficult by working within some of the more deadening conventions of standard Soviet fiction—the setting of industrial production, the simplified moral spectrum, the primitive view of human needs and aspirations. What is new in the novel is the expression of Dudintsev's feeling that the rigors of dialectical materialism have given way to a "materialism" of new cars, private dressmakers, and comfortable apartments, which are won and held onto in savage bureaucratic warfare, and that there exists, as a counterweight, a Party of the Good, made up of "idealists" and dreamers who live and work outside official institutions and often at odds with them. Apart from their accuracy as social disclosures, these attitudes in a novel seemed to offer the possibility that the writer might break the individual out of his political casing and treat him apart from it, a significant departure from the literary doctrine prevailing since Zhdanov's "Report" in 1946, and a real gain for the literary profession, if allowed to stand. Unhappily it was not: the most significant thing about this novel is that it was suppressed, and its author forced to recant.

Dudintsev's ill-fortune permits us to conclude, in a general way, that though much has happened since 1946, little has really changed. There has been much evidence of unrest among writers, but none of it has led to important changes in the theories that confine the literary imagination, nor to any significant release from the controls that enforce adherence to them.

One cannot say that change will never come. The classical Russian tradition, always present on school curricula and publishers' lists, must exercise a strong influence on literary preferences. It is difficult to imagine that a literature that is not literature can continue its imposture indefinitely, or that an audience brought up on Pushkin, Gogol, Tolstoy, Dostoevsky, and Chekhov can fail forever to make its wants known. Nor is it inconceivable that a series of brilliant new literary works, provided they were allowed to see daylight, might suddenly render the entire structure of socialist realism obsolete, another monument to Russia's agony and servitude. But piece-by-piece dismantling, if that is the only way change can come, would not be a short or a simple task. Socialist realism has the weight of two traditions behind it— Lenin's activist version of Marxism, and the utilitarian aesthetic developed by Russian revolutionary movements over a century—as well as the vested interests of a unitary state, unused to criticism, hostile to pluralism, and untroubled about the larger ends of existence.

I have thought of this study as a contribution to the extensive current effort by specialists to explore the continuities and discontinuities between the two worlds of Russian intellectual history that are separated by the October Revolution. It was clear to me from the outset that the whole story as I hoped to tell it, from Belinsky to Zhdanov, could not be compressed to book length, that I was obliged, therefore, to find a workable principle of selectivity or abridgment. One authoritative version of this continuity has already been established: Soviet critics, scholars, and politicians have defined their own tradition in recent years, and have traced it back in detail to the first half of the nineteenth century. In a culture where the history of ideas is at the mercy of the social mythmakers, traditions can be made more easily than in a culture where the evolution of ideas is undirected and where the formulators of a tradition must defend the validity of what they choose to value in the past. The imposed tradition is nonetheless real, in the sense that it may exert a powerful influence on the minds of men who have no choice but to accept it. A critique of the selection Soviet theorists have made from the past, and of the values that underlie it, would provide, it seemed to me, both a valid limiting principle and a valuable new approach to the subject. I would concentrate on the men, the works, and the ideas that have been incorporated in this tradition, and would record as well some of the voices that opposed it while it was being made.

Whatever the Soviet theorists have left out of their account of the living Russian moral and literary tradition has been forgotten, misrepresented, or defamed. This, of course, is another story. If one were to record fully the development of the image of the Russian revolutionary type, thorough inquiries would have to be made into the view of the moral personality held by the Narodnik movement with its special cult of the hero, into Georgi Plekhanov's attitudes toward a whole range of problems concerning the relations between literature and revolutionary politics, into biographical material on the early Bolsheviks, and into many more of the deviant heroes in Soviet literature of the twenties.

As I have passed over this rich material in pursuit of my Soviet guides, I have been aware of the price one must pay in order to cover a century. Since I have not been able to tell the full, sequential story, I have limited my objectives accordingly. I shall be content, finally, if I can suggest lines of connection, in the hope that denser, more localized studies will bear out my hypotheses.

I have also hoped that this book would introduce certain truths about Russian literature to the broad community of critics and scholars in America. I have tried, therefore, to share my sources with non-Russian-speaking readers by citing English translations whenever possible. I must ask the indulgence of my colleagues on this score.

Many people have helped me in a great variety of ways while I was compiling, writing, and rewriting this book. It would require more space than I have to acknowledge the particular quality of each kindness which was shown me. To Professor Ernest J. Simmons of Columbia University, who has accompanied me, as it were, from the beginning stages of my work on this subject, I owe a very large debt of gratitude. As director of the stimulating seminar in which the idea to write it first occurred to me, and as chairman of the committee which directed this work when it was a dissertation, he was an inexhaustible source of discriminating editorial advice and warm personal support. I owe much, too, to the other members of my committee—to the late Manfred Kridl, whose astringent mind and generous heart often helped me on my way, and to Leon Stilman, whose encouragement and judgment I particularly value. I must also express my thanks to Lionel Trilling, whose counsel helped me at the critical moment when I began to transform the dissertation into a book.

Special acknowledgment must be made of my debt to Robert Hankin, who set aside his own work in order to translate the appendix at a time of great work pressure for me. I have been helped by the librarians of Columbia and Harvard universities, of the New York Public Library, and of the Institut d'Études Slaves in Paris. Two typists, Robert Dunham of New York, and Mrs. Helen E. Leighton of Blue Hill, Maine, gave invaluable assistance.

To my wife, who worked tirelessly as editor, critic, typist, and collaborator in all senses except that of actual authorship (for which I alone am responsible), I owe a debt of gratitude that cannot be adequately expressed.

I received important financial assistance during the period of research from the American Council of Learned Societies, in the form of two consecutive year-long grants, for which I express my profound thanks herewith.

The following firms have been kind enough to permit me to quote at length from books they have published: Alfred A. Knopf, Inc., from Alexei Tolstoy's *The Road to Calvary* and from Mikhail Sholokhov's *Seeds of Tomorrow* (published in England by Putnam and Co., Ltd., as *Virgin Soil Upturned*); A. A. Wyn, Inc., from Leonid Leonov's *Road to the Ocean* (copyright 1944, by A. A. Wyn, Inc., originally published by L. B. Fischer Publishing Corp., New York); the Citadel Press, from Maxim Gorky's *Mother*; Henry Holt and Company, Inc., from Ilya Ehrenburg's *Out of Chaos*; Random House, Inc., from Louis Fischer's *Machines and Men in Russia*; Hutchinson and Co., Ltd., from Yuri Olesha's *Envy*; and International Publishers Co., Inc., from Karl Marx and Friedrich Engels's *Selected Correspondence* and *Literature and Art*, Engels's *Anti-Dühring*, V. I. Lenin's *"Left-Wing" Communism*, and Fedor Gladkov's *Cement*.

RUFUS W. MATHEWSON, JR.

Paris, 1958

CONTENTS

THE POSITIVE HERO
in Russian Literature

1
INTRODUCTION

Perhaps it is a commonplace, by now, to mention the unique
intimacy of politics, morality, and literature in the Russian
tradition. We know that in the nineteenth century, where
this study begins, writers were constantly enjoined to treat
political issues; that literature was charged in very specific
ways with the responsibility to oppose serfdom and the autocracy and to further political measures which challenged
the status quo. The writers themselves often shared the
social and economic grievances of the politically-minded,
while differing as to methods. Moreover, the very assertion
of a free literature's right to exist was a kind of political act
and further grounds for identification with radicalism. The
radicals, in their turn, made heavy demands on literature
because they saw it as one of the few outlets of expression,
"Aesopian" or not, for the great social issues.

These relationships are well established. Less can be taken
for granted, however, about the durable compatibilities such
shared sympathies might suggest. The conventional view,
echoed by Edmund Wilson, for example, in his essay "The
Historical Interpretation of Literature," that writer and radical critic in Russia coexisted in some form of loose, untroubled alliance based on their shared opposition to the
status quo, must yield to a new understanding of what
bound them together and what finally separated them. Their
association more nearly resembles an alliance in which the
grounds for communion between them were undermined

by deeper disagreements, under stresses which have now, through acquaintance with other kinds of "Popular Fronts," become familiar to us. In 1860 there was a crucial separation, which established a fundamental polarity in thinking about literature. Other conventional formulations of the division —"pure" vs. "utilitarian" as these terms were used in the nineteenth century, or "sociological" vs. "aesthetic," or "Marxist" vs. "formalist" as it is sometimes described in the USSR—do not comprehend the real terms of the opposition which has existed largely, as it seems to me, within the realm of realist fiction. We shall find, too, that after the revolution, these contentions were waged inside the confines of Marxism, and that each faction found ammunition in that armory.

In this debate, and in the continued association, free or enforced, of art and politics in the Soviet era, there is a clear continuity of tradition across the October Revolution. It is manifested particularly in the reappearance in the Soviet era of the nineteenth-century concept of "positive" literary heroes, that is, of emblematically virtuous images of political men. Since 1932 there has prevailed in the USSR a cult of heroism embracing education, psychology, literature, and the fine arts. It has become one of the principal means of indoctrination and exhortation throughout the society, and one of the most important propaganda instruments of Party and government. It is, of course, an obvious propaganda technique, and if it were only that, if the Soviet hero was represented only in the newspaper portraits of Stakhanovites, or the statues of war heroes in public squares, there would be little to say on the subject. But the Soviet cult goes far beyond such conventional instances of iconology. The new Soviet hero rests upon a theory which is both intricate and ancient. From this fund of ideas he has been fitted out with the rudimentary elements of an inner life, and with an ethical code which guides him surely and inflexibly.

Literature has a key role in publicizing this fabricated individual, who may or may not exist in Soviet life, but who, when he is treated by writers, tends to conform to the lineaments drawn by the official moralists. The writer is told where he will find him, what his loyalties will be, and the destiny he will have. The writer is then expected to document this blueprint, to discover bright, persuasive instances of the prescribed type.

My interest in the subject of this book was not at first directed toward the problem of continuity, although I was aware of it from the outset. I had thought, rather, to concentrate on the Soviet version of the positive hero, hoping, first, to gain insight into the moral condition of the Soviet Communist and, second, to define one of the literary archetypes of our time. It soon became apparent that these lines of investigation were barren. The Soviet positive hero is too much the instrument of Party policy and too little a product of the literary imagination to bear comparison with the hero-types of other literatures. These problems were not dropped entirely, but were made a part of the main effort.

It became clear to me that the central ideas on the hero in literature had been transmitted very nearly intact, in the form of a continuous controversy, from the middle decades of the nineteenth century to the Soviet present. Finally, it became clear that the concept of the positive hero had been developed as a weapon of argument in the pivotal debate in the 1860s about the nature and function of literature. The debaters were, on the one hand, political radicals who advanced a systematic aesthetic in which the positive hero was central; and on the other, the classical writers who rejected any suggestion that they devote themselves merely to the celebration of political virtue in literature, and who defended their art as an autonomous kind of exploration, concerned with politics but finally independent of any political claims made upon it. The essential conflict in the debate—between a free and a controlled art—conducted sometimes in the open, sometimes not—endured for nearly a century. On later occasions the participants were not always aware of the sources of their ideas. A Soviet novel which slipped by the censors might suddenly revive the argument by evoking central ideas from the classical heritage. But sometimes in the ensuing argument neither the writer nor the critics would recognize that they were repeating the basic terms of the argument between Turgenev and Chernyshevsky. When Stalin coined his repellent description of the writer as "an engineer of the human soul," he may not have known of its origins in the manipulative aesthetic theory of the radical democratic critics in the mid-nineteenth century.

The positive hero, then, is important as a characteristic element in the thinking of one group of contestants in the long war for control of Russian realism. The debate has ended in complete victory for the political utilitarians and the partisans of positive heroes, with A. A. Zhdanov's assertion in 1946 of total Party dominion over the literary imagination. This melancholy conclusion may prompt the student of literature to wonder what profit he may expect to draw from this account of the decline of a great national tradition. Too often it may seem that we are concerned with attitudes bleakly hostile to the literary imagination, or with the thankless critical task of explaining why bad novels are, indeed, bad. It should be pointed out, however, that the whole strand of continuity we are following is a controversy about the nature of literature itself, and it is to be hoped that we will touch repeatedly on questions of general interest.

If the art form under discussion were the icon we should not be so apologetic. But the novelist's obligation to reveal the whole of man in all his meaningful relations runs full tilt against any pressure to advocate or to celebrate virtue in fiction. For this reason we shall frequently be involved with assumptions about the very nature of human experience. Can it be believed that man can live wholly, successfully, in an exemplary way, within such a rigid code of political virtue? Or would it not be better to accept a commitment from the outset, in company with the great Russian writers, to the proposition that one of the distinguishing marks of man's humanity is his fallibility, that weakness, compromise, and defeat are elements of all men's lives, and that a novelist's failure to say so represents a degrading kind of falsification?

II

These political attitudes, literary ideas, and moral values are, of course, not peculiar to Russia, although the intensity with which they were expressed, the particular emphases put on them, and the final configuration they were to assume have not been duplicated elsewhere. Western European, North American, and other cultures have known moments of economic crisis and political urgency as great as Russia's, and have at times been called upon to deal with fanatical codes of political virtue and obnoxious doctrines for the "proper" uses of literature. Since the Renaissance the West has generally rejected them or outgrown them, or contained them within a pluralist framework. Russia's inability to rid herself of them has its sources deep in her history, and may be seen more recently as the outcome of a bitter, complex struggle in Russian thought between Western and Eastern, between libertarian and authoritarian approaches to man and society.

The two antagonistic traditions measure the value and efficacy of ideas in sharply contrasting ways. It may be said, in general, that the Western tradition is more used to consider ideas for their larger applications, as they relate man's momentary needs to his permanent condition. The Eastern European tradition tends to value ideas for their local utility (against a background of dogmatic absolutism) as defined by the governors (or the subverters) of the society, usually in a situation of extreme social tension. When the critic Belinsky steeped himself in the Hegelian system, its most important consequence for him was the effect it had on his attitude toward the Tsarist regime. Intoxicated by the formula "what is, is what ought to be," Belinsky lived at perfect peace with the autocracy. But when the left-Hegelians showed him the contrary tendency in Hegel's thought, that "what is" is constantly evolving into "what ought to be," that history never stands still, he became a revolutionary overnight. Belinsky's conversion illustrates an attitude toward ideas which is both passionate and myopic, which responds to them on the basis of their immediate relevances alone, and inevitably reduces them to tools. Belinsky's reading of Hegel is certainly duplicated in Lenin's reading of Marx.

This habit of reduction is partly to be explained by Russia's special situation on the fringe of Europe, and by the enormous appetites stimulated in the one who lags behind. The contradictory needs to exclude Europe and to become like her have again and again generated a spirit of urgency that is hostile to the free exercise of thought and imagination. Earlier iron curtains, we remember, excluded every great movement of European thought before 1700 in the name of national integrity and a sterile Byzantine orthodoxy. It might be said that Russia has never recovered from her success in excluding the "harmful" effects of the Renaissance in the name of the "Third Rome." But Western ideas could not be permanently kept out. The governors of the regime needed technology, military skills, administrative techniques; the opponents of the regime needed arguments to support their cry for social justice. Once begun, the flood could not be turned back. But the opposition between the Western and Eastern approaches reproduced itself in the interpretation of these imported ideas. Much of the intellectual history of the nineteenth century may be read in the light of the struggle between those who were concerned with the larger implications of the ideas and those who would convert them immediately into social levers. Here investigation, speculation, and experiment stand in opposition to rationalization, persuasion, and exhortation. Wonder confronts certainty. Theory and ideology challenge each other as mutually exclusive modes of thought.

The situation of literature in this contest is clear, I think. The major writers found and staked out an area of leisure and equilibrium in which they could examine the deeper meanings of their countrymen's suffering. It was a troubled, precarious kind of leisure, to be sure, encroached upon by the government censor from one side and by the revolutionary critic from the other, and kept clear, as it sometimes seemed, only as a kind of no-man's land in the savage war between the two forces. Tolstoy deserted this position and organized his own campaign to harness the free imagination. More than once the area appeared to have been engulfed, only to manifest itself again in the form of new and compelling works of art. At the risk of simplifying a very complex process, it might be said that the struggle ended, on the level of critical theory, when Soviet Marxists established the devastating proposition—as Marx never did—that literature

is a form of class consciousness, and ended, in fact, when
Zhdanov converted the proposition into an enforceable statute in 1946. His victory over the creative imagination may
be read as the formal, and perhaps the final, defeat in Russia
of the Western way of taking experience.

Utility as a criterion of artistic value is not unknown, of
course, in other societies, including our own. Extraneous
claims on literature have taken many forms: writers have
been asked to refrain from undermining many kinds of de-
corum, many views of morality, many attitudes of belief.
When Flaubert is dragged into court by the French police,
when books are banned in Jersey City or Boston, when
Pushkin's work is put under the surveillance of the Tsar,
when Dickens reports the enormous pressure on him of Victorian expectations, we are in the presence of the police
sergeant's fear of literature as a profound disturber of the
peace. This kind of negative claim is more common than
the step beyond it which solicits the writer's active support
of a given code of values. Albert Camus has noted both attitudes in a brief review of the question in *The Rebel*,[1] but
he does not distinguish sufficiently, I believe, between the
ignorant hostility toward art which would tame it or silence
it, and the more sophisticated contempt for art which would
keep it alive in order to use it. He cites extreme examples
of the censorious attitude among the Russians: Tolstoy in
the mood of *What Is Art?* and Pisarev, the nihilist, who
advocated the abolition of literature. In the West he names
the Saint-Simonians and Victor Hugo as advocates of an art
that would serve progress by stimulating healthy social forces.
Actually there are many more of both kinds in both East
and West, but no one, I think, has duplicated the effort

[1] Albert Camus, *The Rebel* (New York, 1954), pp. 222–24.

made by the Russian radicals to gain control of the literary imagination. Successive generations sought to establish a definition of literature's function and value that would proclaim as good writing only those works that advocated *their* program of social change, and would proscribe all else. In the West, partisan claims on literature from all species of bigot to produce "edifying" works have somehow been resisted; literature survives, at least, if it does not always flourish. But in Russia the claims were so urgent, backed, as it often seemed to the guilt-ridden intellectuals and writers, by the massive grievances of the Russian populace; and the habits of thought resisting them were so precariously grounded, that the eventual victory of the utilitarians seems foreordained. Art was frivolous, many Russians, including Tolstoy, were prepared to agree, unless it humbled itself before the needs and expectations of the disinherited majority and actively set forth models of behavior that promised a better life in the future for the entire nation.

We return finally to the question of the hero and of his place in literature. Today, in the West, the French are most preoccupied with this problem. Discussing our chances for survival, André Malraux has said in a recent interview: "It is not certain that our civilization can rediscover the heroes and found on them its exemplary image of man."[2] Apart from the roles heroes do or do not play in the fate of cultures, it seems pertinent to inquire whether or not it is proper for the "exemplary image" to appear in literary works. Camus may be completing Malraux's thought when he says that the aim of the world's great literature

seems to be to create a closed universe or a perfect type. The West, in its great creative works, does not limit itself to retrac-

[2] "Man's Quest," *Time*, LXVI, No. 3 (July 18, 1955), 29.

ing the steps of its daily life. It ceaselessly presents magnificently conceived images which inflame its imagination and sets off, hot foot, in pursuit of them.[3]

It is important to ask what is meant here. Has this really been the function of Western literature in the past? In what sense are Lear, Ahab, Julien Sorel, Emma Bovary, or Kyo Gisors "exemplary," that is to say, serving as a pattern or deserving imitation? What do we do when we overtake them in our "hot foot" pursuit? How do we identify with them? Do we admire them, pity them, learn from them, emulate them? Obviously there is no simple answer. The reader's identification with the hero may take many forms, but it must not, it seems to me, be complete nor blindly subordinate. Reader and hero must meet in some sense as equals, and yet an essential distance between them must be maintained. It is this remove, preserved by Aristotle's catharsis, that permits tragedy, and frees the reader of the terrible burden of the hero's suffering. And it is precisely this remove that is absent from "official" Soviet writing. Even when the hero dies, no provision is made for the spectator's disengagement. The heroes of the world's great literature are not edifying in the copybook sense; homilies cannot be drawn from the examples of their lives. The Soviet hero, on the contrary, is primarily a model whose example is expected to give rise to admiration and emulation. He stands in an authoritarian relationship to the reader. He is the representative of official virtue, and the certified model for behavior.

Homo sovieticus and his ancestor, the Russian revolutionary, considered as human types for a moment, not as literary constructs, must be recognized as members of the family of man—of a special and exotic branch, perhaps—and not as agents of the devil. He has an historical pedigree, and he is

[3] Camus, *The Rebel*, p. 228.

not the first of his kind to plague mankind. Roundheads, Jacobins, and Abolitionists, to name only his most familiar relatives, knew as surely as the Bolsheviks did that their version of the truth was the only one that could save mankind. The Russian differs from his predecessors, however, in one important particular: power to impose his truth on a nation fell into his hands and he managed to hold onto it. The earlier political brotherhoods, for all the mark they left on history, were kept from the prolonged exercise of power. The societies that nurtured them found slower, less direct, and less painful ways to move toward the goals which the absolutists hoped to reach without delay, compromise, or pausing to count the costs. In many ways the Russian revolutionary is a tougher, deadlier specimen. Bred over a century in a world of absolute denial and absolute assertion, he was psychically armed for no-quarter struggle, prepared for expediency, deception, and violence, and well equipped with ideologies and strategies.

He might seem at first glance to make a poor candidate for literary portraiture. But Turgenev, Dostoevsky, Conrad, and others have found, on the contrary, that he was indeed an excellent subject, provided he was kept at a distance, and shown in all his dimensions. He had energy, passion, courage, and principle, he lived dangerously, and his life was full of pain, deprivation, and defeat. He was often disfigured in his collisions with life, and was, as a result, badly flawed in a human or moral sense. As such he became a fitting subject for tragic investigation, as Dostoevsky, above all others, found out. But when the artist's detachment is lost, when, in effect, the hero writes immodestly about himself, pity is impossible; his tragic appeal is blotted out by his oppressive sense of his mission. This, in general, is the situation in Soviet literature.

Malraux's heroes in *Man's Fate* use the Shanghai workers'

insurrection as an occasion to confront, in a total way, their condition as men. Though they remain true to their vision of the cause throughout, and though they hope that the example of their deaths will be efficacious, will, as Malraux says, create "the bloody legends from which the golden legends are made," [4] in their moment of heroic agony they rise above the political scene and come face to face with the mystery of their presence on earth. They endeavor, in their extremity, to transcend the knowledge that men live in untouchable solitude, that life, itself, is empty and absurd, without love or meaning. Such questions are not allowed to trouble the Soviet hero. It is incidental to Malraux's novel that his revolutionaries rise to heroism in the act of defying Party orders, but in a Soviet novel such a contingency is unthinkable. Doctrinal truths contain the universe. All things are declared to be known, including history's final outcome, and the mysteries of existence are kept by the society's Grand Inquisitors from troubling their subjects.

[4] André Malraux, *Man's Fate* (New York, 1936), p. 323.

2

THE HERO AND THE HERITAGE

Russian imaginative literature—perhaps more than any of the world's great literatures—has been concerned with the celebration of emblematic literary heroes. The source of this tradition is lost in remote antiquity. Early Russian literature, both oral and written, has held up numerous images of virtuous men, for the comfort, instruction, or inspiration of its audience: the *bogatyr* (hero of the oral epic), the martyred saint, the Cossack bandit-revolutionary, the peasant-fool, the neoclassic *raisonneur*, and the benevolent (or terrible) tsardespot have served at various times as symbols which were intended to give meaning and purpose to experience. The propagation of the image of virtue, too, whatever its human guise, has served many interests, religious, social, moral, and political—and in all these areas, tendencies both conformist and subversive.

Of course, similar types have served similar purposes in other literatures. What really distinguishes the Russian tradition before the nineteenth century is the absence of other approaches, notably of the indirect, exploratory mode of tragedy. In general, Russian literary heroes were conceived as attractive and uncomplicated representatives of specific points of view, that is, as teachers by their beneficent—rather than by their terrible or pitiable—example.[1]

[1] *The Lay of the Host of Igor*, the first great work of Russian literature, written, it is now believed, at the end of the twelfth century, contains elements of a primitive tragic drama. The hero, Prince Igor, in search of personal glory, endangers the security of Kievan society by

In the shift to a more recognizable human type during the nineteenth century, the requirements of realism reduced the hero's dimensions, and the writers' predominantly tragic view of experience muted the note of affirmation which had prevailed in the earlier, less sophisticated literary forms. The search for hero images continued, nevertheless. The question of the nature and the destiny of the literary protagonist was foremost among the thematic preoccupations of the century. And the degree to which nineteenth-century Russians read their own spiritual history in the lives of their literary heroes is a unique feature of the whole national literary experience.

The solemn Russian novel of character, with its rudimentary plot structure, was peculiarly well designed to focus attention on the moral responsibilities of individuals. Russian literature was hero-centered, if not heroic in the conventional sense, from the earliest moments of the realist epoch. Pushkin's Onegin, the hero of his novel in verse, *Eugene Onegin*, and Lermontov's Pechorin, the central figure of his novel, A *Hero of Our Time*, established a pedigree for the literary protagonist in the early decades of the nineteenth century which persisted to the point of becoming a stereotype. Dostoevsky's Myshkin, Raskolnikov, the Karamazovs, Tolstoy's Pierre, Prince Andrei, Levin, Turgenev's gallery of faltering heroes—to name only the most prominent—all demonstrate an intensive effort to center the novelists' moral quest in the figure of the protagonist. In his fate are contained the novelist's generalizations—hopeful or despairing —about human experience.

---

leading an irresponsible attack on neighboring pagan nomads. He is thoroughly beaten by them, but then is miraculously rescued from the consequences of his vain and unpatriotic acts, and is brought home in triumph.

Of the critical controversies that nourished the literature
of the century none was more intense than discussion about
the *kind* of significance that should be invested in the figure
of the literary hero. The politically-minded critics, Belinsky,
Dobrolyubov, and Chernyshevsky, who made specific, in-
sistent, and programmatic demands on literature, devoted a
large part of their energies to the matter of effecting a fundamental change in the image of the hero. In calling for a
literature which would serve social change they had first to
isolate and define the characteristics of the hero they wanted
to replace. In generalizations they made about "Oblomovism" [2] and "the superfluous man" they attacked the single
characteristic of the dominant hero-type which they most
hoped to change—his overwhelming predilection for defeat.
The reasons for the emphasis on failure might be sought,
they felt, in various hypotheses: that life offered no other
significant types; that tragedy was somehow rooted in the
nature of the novel form; that the celebration of fallibility,
the "worship of sorrow," were basic to the tradition of European literature and to the world-view of the writers themselves. None of these justifications seemed to the radical
critics to be valid deterrents to the creation of a more effective and more successful literary hero.

Seen as a type which dominated Russian literature for a
century, the kind of hero they opposed is a complex figure,
apart from his habit of failure. The men without hope—
Pechorin, Stavrogin (Dostoevsky's *The Possessed*), and
Prince Andrei (Tolstoy's *War and Peace*)—are successful

[2] See N. A. Dobrolyubov, "What Is Oblomovshchina?" in *Selected
Philosophical Essays* (Moscow, 1948), pp. 174–217. This article, which
first appeared in *Otechestvennyie zapiski*, Nos. I–IV, 1859, is the most
striking effort to find a lowest common denominator in the behavior
and the destinies of Russian literary heroes. Although this is not the
first discussion of the subject, it may be said to have initiated the major
phase of the hero controversy.

in their rebellious search for annihilation. The men of hope and good intentions fail, in spite of themselves, to live as they plan to, or to fulfill the apparent promise of their lives. Such are Turgenev's ego-centered heroes *manqués*, each with his special personality failure—Rudin's fatal eloquence, Lavretsky's weakness disguised as scruple, Bazarov's narcissistic arrogance.[3] Both these types are characterized by a disastrous alienation from other human beings and from purposeful activity. For the radical critics it was the inactivity resulting from this maladjustment which linked all these figures, disparate though they were in character and in motivation.

These types were given a label, "the superfluous men," taken from Turgenev's short story "The Diary of a Superfluous Man" (1850). Though it became one of the most durable clichés of Russian literary criticism, there is a curious ambiguity about the term's actual meaning. It is not clear in many cases to whom the superfluous man is unnecessary nor by whom he is unwanted, nor, indeed, that it is he who has been rejected. Lermontov's Pechorin, for example, cannot be considered a pathetic castoff from society; he himself took the initiative, with some foreknowledge of its tragic consequences, in revolting against a way of life he considered contemptible. The modern concept of "the alienated man" accounts more comprehensively and more precisely for the process of interaction between individual and society which resulted in the individual's final condition of aloneness, defeat, or death. In flat contrast, then, we may speak of the revolutionary hero sought by the radicals as the "integrated man"—integrated, that is, with the "scientific" promises and the ethical sanctions of his ideology of dissent, or, after 1917,

[3] Rudin is the hero of *Rudin* (1856), Lavretsky of *A Nest of Gentlefolk* (1859), and Bazarov of *Fathers and Sons* (1862).

with the values and goals of the new society. The superfluous man, it must be kept in mind, does not represent retrogressive values; rather, he opposes them inadequately; he is their victim, not their advocate.

Scattered references throughout the century suggest that the need to develop affirmative ideological heroes was deeply felt by others, but that the obstacles to its imaginative realization were enormous. The Decembrists, the most authentic and dramatic symbols of political protest, apparently defied artistic re-creation. Pushkin, in a variant conclusion to *Eugene Onegin*, considered having his hero join the Decembrist conspiracy at the end of the novel.[4] With the Eugene Onegin we know, the artistic cost of such a conversion seems exorbitant; Pushkin, we must assume, had the good taste, as well as the political prudence, not to attempt it. The long detour Tolstoy made around the same problem—that of incorporating the Decembrist movement in fiction—when he was beginning *War and Peace*, suggests the strength and the multiplicity of the pressures opposing the representation of this kind of political virtue in art.[5] There is no doubt that a good part of the difficulty lay in the creative problems attendant on the reproduction of a plausible, active, and successful image of ideological virtue.

It might seem that Tolstoy's "blundering" heroes, Pierre Bezukhov in *War and Peace* and Levin in *Anna Karenina*, qualify as affirmative figures. But the modest lesson they affirm—that life, defined in terms of love, family, and work, is somehow preferable to death—lacks the combative spirit and the specifically social orientation sought by the radical critics. Apart from these dogmatic objections there are literary grounds, as well, on which to question the success with

[4] See Ernest J. Simmons, *Pushkin* (Cambridge, 1937), p. 327.
[5] See Ernest J. Simmons, *Leo Tolstoy* (Boston, 1946), p. 259.

which this Tolstoyan truth is presented. E. M. Forster, for example, offers a persuasive interpretation of the concluding mood of *War and Peace* which casts doubt on the modest note of affirmation that seems to have been intended:

Tolstoy, like Bennett, has the courage to show us people getting old—the partial decay of Nicolay and Natasha is really more sinister than the complete decay of Constance and Sophia [in Arnold Bennett's *The Old Wives' Tale*]: more of our own youth seems to have perished in it.[6]

The same sense of the destructive effect of time's passage surrounds Levin's final discovery of "the meaning of life," which has the quality of a desperate assertion shot through with uncertainty, not of a statement of unqualified belief. Hindsight, of course, confirms these impressions: to the extent that Bezukhov and Levin are autobiographical figures, they must be presumed to contain the seeds of Tolstoy's impending spiritual crisis, in the course of which despair at the approach of death came close to gaining supremacy in his system of values.

Gogol had made an earlier effort to personify a specific concept of virtue in Volume II of *Dead Souls*. In the confusion of the last few pages of the novel, two shadowy figures suddenly appear, the wise and forgiving man of wealth, Murazov, and the unnamed Prince, a high bureaucrat of great pride and rectitude.[7] It is their joint function to restore order and morality after the unrelieved wickedness that has gone before. The magnitude of their task—which includes the reform of Chichikov—is too much for them, and, inferentially, for Gogol's unique imaginative powers. He was clearly unable to solve the moral problem by persuasive literary means, arbitrarily, that is, to alter the vividly established

[6] E. M. Forster, *Aspects of the Novel* (New York, 1927), p. 63.
[7] See Nikolai Gogol, *Dead Souls* (New York, 1936), pp. 229–65.

moral nature of his central character, or abruptly to assume a tone of high moral earnestness, in contrast to the sly and ribald cynicism which dominated the earlier sections of the novel. Actually Gogol has turned to an earlier tradition for his affirmative spokesmen. The images of his dual heroes, and their *ex machina* appearance on the scene, are reminiscent of the *raisonneurs* of neoclassic drama, the omniscient representatives of virtue who correct the malefactors and draw the moral for the spectators. This abstract personification of good, it should be pointed out, was no more satisfactory to the radical critics of the nineteenth century than it is to the modern reader or, if we may judge by his attempt to destroy the manuscript, than it was to Gogol himself.[8]

In Dostoevsky's work the problem of the hero, as it reflects the controversies of the sixties, assumes an importance which invites a more extensive investigation than is possible here. Dostoevsky reacted strongly, at first, against the radical prescription for the hero, then attempted to adapt the purely literary formula to his own diametrically opposite views about politics and society. The "antihero" of *Notes from Underground* (1864) is intended as a polemical counterstatement to the roseate vision of heroism in Nikolai Chernyshevsky's *What Is to Be Done?*[9] The attack on his radical position is thorough and deadly. Dostoevsky's view of human

[8] Gogol's concern with the virtuous moral agent receives a quite different statement in one of his comments on his comedy, *The Inspector-General:* "I regret that no one noticed the honorable person who was in my play. Yes, there was one honorable, noble person acting in it through its entire length. This honorable, noble person was laughter." (N. V. Gogol, *Polnoe sobranie sochinenii* [Moscow, 1949], IV, 169.)

[9] Dostoevsky was quite explicit about his intention. See Ernest J. Simmons, *Dostoevski; the Making of a Novelist* (New York, 1940), p. 137, for a discussion of his state of mind at the time he planned the work. Both novels are primary documents in the great cultural crisis that split the liberals and the radicals during the years immediately preceding and following the emancipation of the serfs in 1861.

nature as weak, unstable, governed by caprice, given to irrational acts of rebellion, is used to challenge the radicals' untroubled identification of reason with progress, and of happiness with the satisfaction of material needs.

Having ridiculed the concept of the rationally virtuous revolutionary hero, and every premise on which he stood, Dostoevsky set about in *Crime and Punishment,* two years later, to convert him. Raskolnikov is the first Dostoevskyan version of the revolutionary "new man," the proud, active, Western-oriented rationalist who imagines that he is independent of all codes of morality. Raskolnikov acts decisively —by committing two murders—and his act is shown to have symbolic meaning in many spheres of human activity and belief. It is then Dostoevsky's intention to strip away successive layers of rationalization and show that in all spheres this kind of "reasoned" act is evil and insane. Raskolnikov's controversial conversion in Siberia to Sonya's ethic of submissive and limitless love for mankind, although it strains credibility to the limit, is meant to conclude his journey from evil to good, from a rebellious individualism in which "all is permitted," to a pious acquiescence in the way things are, however painful and unjust.

Dostoevsky's difficulties with the stubborn Raskolnikov suggest that the active, emblematic man was generally hard to handle in literary terms—as difficult to reclaim from his evil ways as he was to present sympathetically. Dostoevsky's solution invites comparison with Turgenev's treatment of Bazarov in *Fathers and Sons.* These two outsiders' views of the radical personality have much in common: both writers, the liberal Turgenev and the conservative Dostoevsky, admire his strength and fear his violence and irresponsibility. But while Turgenev pities his hero and allows him to die defeated but unreconstructed, Dostoevsky apparently felt that his must be brought to a complete reversal of attitude, however implausible it might seem in terms of character and motivation. While he was writing the novel, he considered suicide as an alternative end for Raskolnikov. It would have been neater, perhaps, and easier to bring off, but apparently it did not fulfill Dostoevsky's moral intention. In any case, it is not to be wondered at that the radicals, who, like most of their contemporaries, read the imaginative literature of their own time as a more or less literal transcript of experience, were pleased with neither portrait of their champion.

The only area open to reform is the individual human soul which, though fallible and perverse, is not immune to the example of selfless, all-forgiving love, as enacted by Dostoevsky's men of virtue. To act in any other sphere is to engage in self-centered and presumptuous lawlessness. Thus the radical challenge to society is contained, whether it proceeds from egocentric defiance or from an unselfish desire for social change. This, at least, is the *political* relevance Dostoevsky's novels bore to the contemporary scene.

In *The Idiot* (1868–69) and *The Brothers Karamazov* (1880) Dostoevsky tried to create a "conservative" positive hero. In the Christlike figure of Prince Myshkin a major note of affirmation was intended, although his personal defeat at the end of the novel is complete. Here the doctrine by which Myshkin tries to live is inadequately tested, since Myshkin certainly is a special case, unworldly and unwell, and not equipped to cope with the crushing knowledge of evil.

Myshkin's final madness is instructive, nevertheless, as a view of the destiny that awaits the saintly individual who is at the same time an incomplete, emasculated man. As though profiting by his experiment in *The Idiot*, Dostoevsky evolved a more robust standard-bearer a decade later in the figure of Alyosha Karamazov. He came closer, too, to solving the difficult problem of creating an active spokesman for an attitude which was passive toward many of the acknowledged causes of human maladjustment and suffering. Since the flaws in the social and political environment were excluded from the sphere of remedial action because man's reason is powerless to change them and he risks his moral integrity in daring to try, Alyosha relies on his belief in the responsiveness of the human heart to sustain him in his positive acts. Thus armed, he intervenes at many points in the passionate human entanglements around him, always in behalf of kindness, forgiveness, and a sense of personal justice between individuals. In his most impressive success he is instrumental in teaching Dmitri to respond to the regenerative forces in his own character. But final and complete vindication of his approach in the central conflict of values between Ivan, the unreclaimed rationalist, and himself, the Christian humanist, is denied him. His victory is permanently deferred because the destiny of his opponent, on which his own destiny finally depends, remains forever unresolved in the mists of Ivan's brain fever.

With Alyosha, Dostoevsky came as close to a successful image of the affirmative hero as any of the major writers of the century. Yet it is certain that the radical democrats, had they been active at the time, would have had less patience with Alyosha Karamazov than with his brother Ivan, who might have been catalogued as another in the long list of well-intentioned failures. Failure to validate an ideology of dissent would, we may be sure, have been preferred by Dobrolyubov or Chernyshevsky to the celebration of any attitude which seemed to counsel acquiescence in the social, political, and economic status quo.[10]

[10] M. A. Antonovich, who continued to apply the principles of the revolutionary democrats to literary matters in the seventies and eighties,

II

How can we begin to distinguish those aspects of this complicated hero-quest which are relevant to the Soviet period?

An overall dependence on the views of the radical democrats may be asserted from the outset. This borrowing includes definitions of the nature and function of literature, of the proper relationship between literature and society, of the nature of value in literary judgment, and of the moral and social obligations of the writer. In this conglomerate, the positive hero is a focal point, where theory is translated into literary practice. Although they were held in respect, the radical democrats' influence is diffuse in the years just after the revolution and is seldom acknowledged. But the importance of the radical democrats was to receive more and more explicit statement in critical pronouncements after the First All-Union Congress of Soviet Writers in 1934, and to receive ultimate official sanction in the declaration of literary policy made by A. A. Zhdanov in his 1946 "Report on the Journals *Zvezda* and *Leningrad.*" In it he establishes them as primary legislators of Soviet literary theory:

It follows that the finest aspect of Soviet literature is its carrying on of the best traditions of nineteenth-century Russian literature, traditions established by our great revolutionary demo-

---

tends to confirm this hypothesis in his angrily unfavorable review of *The Brothers Karamazov*, "Mistiko-asketicheski roman" (*Izbrannye stati* [Leningrad, 1938], pp. 243–97), first published in 1881. Antonovich says of Alyosha: "The personality of Alyosha . . . is extremely pale, unnatural, undefined, and incomprehensible, it is simply an invention of the author, a fantasy" (*ibid.*, p. 252). Ivan, too, is "undefined, untypical, and unclear," but "his poem, 'The Grand Inquisitor,' presents the only poetic pages in the entire novel" and the "form" in which Ivan's doubts are expressed is "truly artistic" (*ibid.*, pp. 266–67). Translating from the critical idiom of this school which identifies the "poetic" and the "artistic" with the true, and the true with the socially desirable, it is not difficult to read these opinions as judgments about the political significance of the two characters.

crats, Belinsky, Dobrolyubov, Chernyshevsky, and Saltykov-Shchedrin, continued by Plekhanov, and scientifically elaborated by Lenin and Stalin.[11]

Zhdanov's remarks might be read simply as a glib summoning of native Russia in the search for non-Western sources for Soviet attitudes, or a casual theft of ideas in the face of a widespread shortage. But they represent more than that. His report marks the culmination of a long process of intellectual development, the movement toward final ascendancy in the Soviet consciousness of the nineteenth-century utilitarian aesthetic. The tradition's continuity was eclipsed twice by other leftist theories of literature. The Narodniks' Mikhailovski and the early Marxist, Plekhanov, developed distinctive approaches to problems of literary analysis and judgment. But a direct line of inheritance can be established nevertheless.

The relation of contemporary Soviet theorists to the Russian past is simplified by their abrupt rejection of all but a handful of men, and all but one body of ideas. Given this simplified view of cultural history, it is not surprising to find

[11] A. A. Zhdanov, "Doklad o zhurnalakh *Zvezda i Leningrad,*" *Literaturnaya gazeta,* No. 39 (September 21, 1946), p. 3. In this legislative statement the names of Belinsky, Chernyshevsky, and Dobrolyubov are mentioned nineteen times, Lenin's seven times, Stalin's six times, and Marx's not at all. The only reference to Marxism further confirms the importance of the Russian radicals' ideas: "Marxist literary criticism, which carries on the great traditions of Belinsky, Chernyshevsky, and Dobrolyubov, has always supported realistic art with a social stand" (p. 3). Marxism still supplies the formal *arrière-plan* for most thinking about cultural matters. But the radical democrats have become primary authorities on all specifically literary matters. One of the most authoritative recent books on Soviet Marxism (F. V. Konstantinov, ed., *Istoricheski materializm* [Moscow, 1950]) admits the Russian radicals into the tiny group of thinkers who are credited with designing the official cosmology. L. I. Timofeev's *Teoriya literatury* (Moscow, 1938) sets forth the Soviet position in the terms of traditional aesthetic theory. Though Timofeev does not always acknowledge his debt, this book makes it clear that the radical democrats' ideas pervade all aspects of Soviet thinking about literature.

them siding with their champions in the decisive break between liberals and radicals in 1861. The split occurred along
a basic fault in the uneasy alliance between the two groups
which had had its origin in Belinsky's overbearing defense of
Gogol during the forties, and ended in the wholesale rupture
that accompanied the publication of *Fathers and Sons* in
1862. The occasion of the break was a disagreement about
the means, the tempo, and the goals of social change, notably in the matter of freeing the serfs. But the break was so
profound, so complete, and so clean that it divided them
on a score of related issues—including most phases of art's
relationship to life. In the forefront of the battle between
the two factions stood the two competing hero images, the
"new" and the "superfluous" men, who crystallized in the
contrast between them most of the underlying doctrinal
issues.

Soviet criticism has taken sides in this century-old conflict
because of the radicals' uncompromising stand on social and
economic matters, not because of the intrinsic validity of
their views on art. In the Soviet view, the value of the second
flows from the correctness of the first. For this reason, any
follower of the radical approach is bound to find himself
committed to the defense of a number of exposed positions
which raise very awkward questions of literary judgment. As
a result of their politically motivated assault the radicals
managed to alienate every major writer of the century, with
the exception of Nekrasov and Saltykov, from their own
extreme position.[12] Soviet literary scholarship has inherited,
and has had to make the most of, this costly distinction,
which since 1932 has excluded Turgenev, Tolstoy, Dostoevsky, and others as a source of primary guidance for their own

[12] Nekrasov and Saltykov, it is worth noting, are the only two nineteenth-century writers who are favorably mentioned by Zhdanov in his
report.

writers. The scholars and critics have rationalized their choice by arranging the competing idea-systems in an evolutionary sequence, maintaining that the radical theory is a "higher," that is, a more advanced, a more profound, and a more useful, approach to the understanding of the literary process, because it represents a later and "higher" stage of economic development. Terminology has been devised to account for this sweeping judgment: the intellectual assumptions and the literary practice—"world-view" and "method" in the Soviet vocabulary—of all the great classical writers have been classified under the heading "critical realism," and the theory that replaced it, first sketched out by the radical democrats, has, since 1932, been given the permanent designation "socialist realism," which Timofeev says flatly "is the highest stage in the development of art," "the fulfillment" of the history "of all art and literature." [13] Critical realism, although it was based on an imperfect understanding of society, served a beneficial function by exposing human suffering in Russia, and by challenging, however indirectly, the Tsarist status quo. But it was inferior (arrested, that is, on a lower level of the evolutionary scale) because it refused or was unable to point the way toward a better future in

[13] Timofeev, *Teoriya literatury*, p. 7. Critical realism, which came into being under conditions of unresolved contradiction between objective, social reality and man's aspirations toward a better life, "set itself the task of revealing life's imperfections, the depiction of the crisis man and society were living through," hence its negative designation (*ibid.*, p. 306). Though the "most important step forward" is the transition from critical to socialist realism, one or more intermediate phases are distinguished in what Timofeev calls the literary "movement of liberation" (*ibid.*). The article "Realism" in the *Literary Encyclopedia* identifies them as "radical democratic realism" and "proletarian realism," citing Gorky's *Mother* as the outstanding example of the latter school (*Literturnaya entsiklopediya*, IX, 573). Timofeev, more recently, names "radical democratic realism" as a progressive mutation within the movement of critical realism but absorbs proletarian realism, and, with it, Gorky's *Mother*, into socialist realism.

which the human agony the classical writers described so well would be done away with. The new literature, because of its doctrine of active intervention in the processes of social change, and because it reflects a new and higher form of social organization, deserves, according to the Soviet formula, *a priori* recognition as a qualitatively superior order of creation. The distinction between the two literatures is not made to exclude or suppress the older literature. Heeding Lenin's injunction to repossess the classical heritage for all, the Soviet leadership has made the work of the classical writers (with exceptions) available to readers on an enormous scale. But when guidance from the past is sought by Soviet writers and critics today, they are sent directly to the precepts of the radical democrats, as Zhdanov's "Report" clearly indicates.

The problem of the hero is at the heart of the Soviet system of classification. Thus critical realism is distinguished by its unsuccessful effort to create a credible human spokesman for its positive moral content: "The search for him . . . was expressed in the creation of heroes whose positive traits were limited, incomplete, or Utopian." [14]

Revolutionary democratic realism, by identifying itself with the "people's interests," "expressed itself in a much sharper criticism of the bases of bourgeois landowner society, and in the formation of the images of revolutionaries fighting against this order." [15] The "correct" representation of heroism, we are told today, is the first task of socialist realism and the surest measure of its superiority over all the literature that has preceded it.

Following Soviet historians back to the starting point of this absurdly simple, unilinear "dialectic process," through the hectic decade 1855–65, the trail ends finally with Belin-

[14] Timofeev, *Teoriya literatury*, p. 307.   [15] *Ibid.*, p. 308.

sky. In the course of his "furious" career he laid down a number of operating principles that Soviet critics have made part of their own theories. The central notions that good literature exerts a kind of beneficent leverage in the process of social change and is good for that reason were his. The later assertion—that the emblematically virtuous hero was the most effective of literary levers—issued from Belinsky's premises.

3

BELINSKY
"My Heroes Are the Destroyers"

*I cannot live without beliefs,
warm and fanatical.* BELINSKY

The history of Vissarion Belinsky's (1811–48) reputation in Russia is an immense subject, touching on nearly all major currents of thought and of imagination. He offered guidance and inspiration to successive generations of radical thinkers and activists, and his unquestioned purity of purpose won the respect of many who were indifferent or hostile to his ideas. Certainly for the past twenty years in Soviet literary councils his has been a most authoritative voice from the Russian past. The Soviet version of Belinsky's legacy is by no means true to the original on all counts. Soviet critics have drawn almost exclusively on his later (the post-Hegelian) period, and in deriving a coherent aesthetic from the whole body of his work have ignored all that does not serve their own needs.

It can be fairly said, I think, that to discover consistency in Belinsky is to distort him. Herbert Bowman has recently said of his role in Russian literature: "He came not so much as its systematic analyst, but rather as its evangelist. His contribution to Russian criticism was less a gift of mind than a gift of soul." [1] It was a saving grace—and a characteristic

[1] Herbert E. Bowman, *Vissarion Belinski, 1811–1848; a Study in the Origins of Social Criticism in Russia* (Cambridge, 1954), p. 14. This careful, literate study of Belinsky's thought proved indispensable as background to a study of the uses his successors have made of him.

of Belinsky's "method"—that by blurring distinctions, by entertaining ambiguities on crucial points, or simply by contradicting himself, he was able to escape the toils of his theory before it really became a system. But in the hands of less passionate, more orderly men—"men of far duller and cruder minds," as Isaiah Berlin has characterized the generation of radical intellectuals which followed his [2]—who do not share his underlying reverence for literature itself, Belinsky's thought has been given the value of codified legislative utterance. This is not to say that what later interpreters, including contemporary Soviet commentators, claim to find there is not there. It is, but it is not all that is there. And by selecting only what they need, they have identified Belinsky with attitudes, values, and policies he very probably would have refused to endorse. He has been narrowed, rigidified, and made into a spokesman for a literature not of service to human welfare, which he advocated vigorously if intermittently, but of subservience to political dictatorship.

The key to the Soviet use of Belinsky is contained in a half-serious judgment Trotsky made in 1925:

Belinsky was not a literary critic; he was a socially-minded leader of his epoch. And if Vissarion could be transported alive into our time, he probably would be . . . a member of the Politburo.[3]

Trotsky, of course, knew the difference between a literary critic and a social theorist, an essential difference which has been forgotten by later Soviet commentators. His designation of Belinsky as a political forebear, an initiator of movements that culminated in the October Revolution, has been repeated by so many Soviet voices that it has become a

[2] Isaiah Berlin, "A Marvellous Decade," *Encounter*, IV, No. 6 (June, 1955), 37.
[3] Leon Trotsky, *Literature and Revolution*, trans. Rose Strunsky (New York, 1925), p. 210.

permanent article of faith. Unquestionably this attitude is
the real source of Belinsky's authority in the USSR, and
literature is inevitably diminished in any such interpretation
of Belinsky's legacy. Trotsky made his own contribution to
this tendency when he wrote:

The historic role of the Belinskys was to open up a breathing-hole
into social life by means of literature. Literary criticism took the
place of politics and was a preparation for it. But that which
was merely a hint for Belinsky and for the later representatives
of radical publicism, has taken on in our day the flesh and blood
of October and has become Soviet reality.[4]

In this view the line of descent includes a transition, it
would appear, from a lower to a higher kind of concern.
If literary criticism is but "a preparation for" political activity is it not subordinate to politics, is it not considered to
have identical aims? For less cultivated men than Trotsky,
who apparently knew that "radical publicism" was not really
concerned with literary criticism at all, the temptation to
demean literature was overwhelming. When it became necessary to subject imaginative literature to the purposes of the
Soviet state, the literary magistrates turned to their politically certified ancestor and found the elements of a theory
which unmistakably justified literature's subordination to
social concerns. The Soviet reading of Belinsky, selective as
it is, is not entirely implausible. The prescriptive aspect of
Belinsky's thought is there for all to see. Its quality and the
terms of its translation into Soviet doctrine is what engages
our attention now.

Belinsky was in solicitous attendance at the birth of Russian realism. He welcomed it, nurtured it, and defended it
against its detractors. In the course of this devoted work he
expressed a number of attitudes toward literature, incorpo-

[4] *Ibid.*, p. 209.

rating much that foreign philosophies had taught him, and much that social reformers and political radicals could find no other way to say in the Russia of Nicholas I. His defense of the new realism rested on larger notions about the nature of society and of history, which exerted constant pressure on his aesthetic theory and insistently shaped it to his extra-literary purposes. Having officiated at the birth of this promising new phenomenon, realism, he felt at times that it was a part of his own philosophy, and ventured to legislate its scope, function, and purpose and to chart its future development. These contradictory tendencies in his thought—toward the liberalizing of old standards and toward a new orthodoxy of his own making—characterize (and confuse) all he had to say about art.

As the champion of a new kind of writing Belinsky had first to challenge the attitudes he hoped to replace. Initially he set out to justify the use of subjects which were forbidden under the canons of neoclassicism and romanticism: in this he performed a service acknowledged by his friends and his enemies, opening literature to include the vulgar, the average, the topical, and the unpleasant, to make possible the candid exploration of the lives of average men. The new "truthfulness" of literature was an important step forward: in this light Belinsky's questionable judgment about Gogol, that he was "the first who looked boldly and directly at Russian reality," [5] has relevance as an historical judgment which it lacks as a description of Gogol's imaginative vision. Similarly, Belinsky's enthusiastic description of *Eugene Onegin* as an "encyclopaedia of Russian life" was meant as high praise in

[5] V. G. Belinsky, *Selected Philosophical Works*, ed. M. T. Yovchuk (Moscow, 1948), p. 182. This recent selection of his work for export, designed, according to a publisher's note, to show Belinsky's role as "a predecessor of Russian social democracy," is the only edition of his work in English.

its time, though it rings strangely to a modern reader who does not read the poem for the information it contains. These judgments, however, arise logically from his premise that Russian literature, henceforth, must concern itself with the contemporary, the topical, and the national, all of which he discovered in abundance in *Onegin* and *Dead Souls*.

His efforts to broaden the scope of fiction worked at the same time to reduce to life-size whatever, in the earlier genres, had been larger than life. In this leveling process the heroic stereotypes of the past were swept away with everything else that seemed to him false, conventional, lifeless, or overblown. So drastic was the purge that the heroic mold itself seemed at times to have been destroyed. But the contrary tendency in his thought, the prescriptive phase of his theory of realism, exerted a strong pressure in the opposite direction. Moving beyond his general injunction that literature engage itself with reality, Belinsky devised an intricate set of commitments within which literature, in his view, must function in order to acquire value. It is at this point that he engages the attention of his future disciples. His views of progress, of human nature, of the function of ideas, of the nature of society, of the relations between the individual and society, were brought to bear on the literary imagination in later years. They are essential ingredients of the literature of positive heroes.

II

It was the extra work literature was asked to perform that created the conditions of its servitude. In Belinsky's view, great works of art were freighted with intellectual and moral significance. When he repudiated neoclassicism he did not mean that art's obligation to convey moral ideas was abolished nor that art was to become simply a recording apparatus. The special conditions of Russian intellectual life which tended to channel many extraliterary concerns into forms of imaginative expression influenced Belinsky's fundamental definition of the nature of art: "Art," he wrote, "is the immediate contemplation of truth, or a thinking in images." [6] Literature was thus broadly and carelessly linked with any and all activities of the human mind, and the way was open for literature to serve as the vehicle for a whole range of ideas which were denied other outlets. It is easy to see how one proceeds from this close equivalence between the products of the literary imagination and of abstract thought to a condition in which art's truth is subordinated to other intellectual disciplines, to the truths of philosophy or social science, or to the half-truths of political ideology. Sometimes Belinsky seems to be saying that literature was intended to serve *primarily* as a means of transmitting ideas: "In it, and it alone, is contained the whole of our intellectual life." [7] And, further, "it is the vital spring from which all human sentiments and conceptions percolate into society." [8]

In assuming a responsibility to crystallize and disseminate

[6] *Ibid.*, p. 186. This formulation has survived to the present. Plekhanov welcomed it as the most profound concept developed by the radical critics. Konstantinov cites a similar definition by Belinsky as an amplification of the Marxian definition of art as "a form of social consciousness." It is worth quoting in full:

"The philosopher speaks in syllogisms, the poet in images and pictures, and they both say the same thing. The political economist armed with statistics, *proves*, by acting on the reason of his readers or listeners, that the condition of a certain class in society has greatly improved or worsened, as a result of certain causes. The poet, armed with a clear, living representation of reality, *shows* in a faithful picture, by acting on the imagination of his readers, that the condition of a certain class has improved or worsened for certain reasons. One *proves*, the other *shows*, and both *convince*, one by logical means, the other by pictures." (Quoted by F. V. Konstantinov, ed., *Istoricheski materializm* [Moscow, 1950], pp. 591–92; Belinsky, *Selected Philosophical Works*, p. 432.)

[7] Belinsky, *Selected Philosophical Works*, p. 333.

[8] *Ibid.*, p. 339.

all the fruits of his society's intellectual life, the writer is invited to derive comfort from the fact that he is a primary agent in a process of progressive historical change. "Life consists only in progress," Belinsky wrote, and progress is a steady movement in the minds of men, of nations, of humanity toward "self-cognizance." [9] Thus the importance of the "encyclopaedic" *Eugene Onegin* lay in the fact that it was "an act of consciousness for Russian society . . . a great step forward . . . after which there could no longer be any question of standing still." [10]

The national self-cognizance toward which history moves is only partly concerned with the search for the unique national identity, the nation's "soul," that is the usual preoccupation of theories of nationalism. It moves rather toward a double awareness: on the one hand, of correct and healthy principles of social justice, including full recognition of the inalienable rights of man, and on the other hand, of their daily violation, by serfdom and autocracy, in contemporary Russia. The goal was a nation in which the natural rights of man were to be recognized by all and the individual human personality would be freed thereby of indignity and injustice. Then, presumably, Russia would be free to realize its unique identity. These are the terms of social morality, and in the Russian setting of that time they were controversial—even subversive—ideas. Literature is thus committed to an educational function which automatically places it in an advanced position of advocacy and partisanship.

The writer describes and forwards this process which goes on unceasingly in the world of ideas and in the minds of men. The form of advance is conflict in the familiar Hegelian pattern of forward movement through the clash of oppo-

[9] *Ibid.*, p. 308. The Hegelian source of this notion is obvious.
[10] *Ibid.*, p. 276.

sites, between progressive and retrogressive forces. These contending forces are not given fixed labels by Belinsky, but the definitions that emerge resemble the eighteenth-century opposition between reason and prejudice. Belinsky, after Hegel, has made the static opposition between good and evil a dynamic one, has given the process "lawful" regularity and set it in motion toward an assured goal. In the war for control of the society's governing moral ideas, eventual victory for the forces of progress is assured, but before that moment the issue is always in doubt, and the full collaboration of the already-convinced is the only means to its achievement.

Generally in this climate of conflict the obligation is as binding on the writer as it is on anyone else. It is on this point, of course, in all varieties of this approach, that literature's subordination to extraliterary concerns begins. The writer's enlistment in the service of a demanding but ultimately beneficent dialectical process, which he accelerates by reporting accurately, represents a crucial act of surrender. This definition of literature's obligatory service in the cause of human welfare needed to be changed only in particulars as it passed from the hands of one radical literary theorist to another, from Belinsky, finally to Zhdanov. The definition of the warring forces in the universe may be drastically and continuously altered without releasing literature from its fundamental obligation to serve the progressive current in history.

Belinsky has given his own version of the *terms* of its service in a sequence of definitions. He began, as we have seen, by opening literature to direct observation of everyday Russian experience. But the writer's entanglement in the dialectic of history introduces important restrictions affecting the selection and treatment of material. In order to focus the writer's perceptions, Belinsky paid particular attention to the standards of selectivity. In his optimistic view of the universe, with its implication that the contest between truth and error would, in the end, go well, the writer could not be indifferent toward experience nor was he free to write about any random or insignificant aspect of Russian life. Objectivity did not necessarily imply neutrality, nor did realism mean that the writer was freed of his obligation to select and evaluate his material. On the contrary, the writer could not fail to be passionate and committed—in Belinsky's term, "subjective"—about the world he lived in.

His essential connection with experience took place under the wholesome influence of a "vital idea," one which is close to the secret of the unfolding universe and is engaged therefore in mortal combat with the outworn regime of superstition and prejudice. In this way art performs its function of interpreting reality purposefully and, in effect, takes sides in the master conflict,

[Art] is no longer confined to a passive role—to mirror nature faithfully and dispassionately—but it brings into its reasonings a living, personal idea that imparts to them design and meaning.[11]

The writer's lively personal engagement with experience—the continuous action of his "subjectivity"—is a matter of the emotions and the nerves, an intuitive relationship with the dominant idea that gives meaning to the experience. Art might be a "thinking in images," but the transition from abstraction to image did not take place within the mind of the writer. His attachment to the "vital idea" depended not on its compelling logic but on its emotional power and its moral radiance. By its action on his imagination the moral idea automatically imparted a "healthy" tendency to all the material that passed through it. The reader presumably would

[11] *Ibid.*, p. 287.

respond to the tendency by feeling and thinking, and finally by acting differently. When this didactic function was properly performed some aspects of Belinsky's own social morality were certain to be transmitted. Literature, though it depended on life in all essentials ("poetry is life first and art afterward"), achieved in its concentrated and selective reproduction of experience a clarity and a power of evaluation that raw experience never offered: "A poetical conception is shorn of all the accidental and extraneous and depicts only the necessary and the significant." [12]

Selectivity raises the problem of literature's capacity to generalize. How does a purposive, realistic literature achieve a level of general statement and preserve the liveliness of the particular image and the full effect of the didactic ingredient at the same time? Belinsky's solution was contained in the concept of "typicality." [13] The typical character and the typical circumstance, recorded in all their detail and color—their "realness"—would not, if they were properly selected, lose any of their broader meanings in the particularity of their representation. Belinsky thought that the genuinely typical character was endowed with energy, individuality, and significance by the same "vital idea" that informed the writer's view of experience. Writing of Gogol, who, he felt, had achieved a notably sound fusion of the particular and the general without falsely idealizing his characters, he said:

Here the crux of the matter is types, the ideal being understood not as an adornment (consequently a falsehood) but as the relations in which the author places the types he creates, in conformity with the idea which his work is intended to develop.[14]

[12] *Ibid.*, p. 292.
[13] *Ibid.*, p. 413. This notion is not original, of course, with Belinsky.
[14] *Ibid.*

The danger that the new realism would lose its verisimili-tude and degenerate into a literature of moralistic abstrac-tions preoccupied Belinsky, who sometimes sensed the con-tradictory tendencies in his own thought. To keep the general significance of the typical character from engulfing his concrete identity, Belinsky insisted on the wholeness and integrity of personal motivation within the narrative. Only in this way could the literary images of men achieve the unmistakable semblance of life. The documentation of their personal traits and of their public attitudes must be precise and voluminous, because literature had first of all to seem real. It must not be a clever fabrication but a representation of experience subject to verification by the reader. Only in this way could generalization, tendency, and instruction re-ceive persuasive fictional statement. The highest value—indeed, the *sine qua non*—of literature, Belinsky never ceased to proclaim, was its "truthfulness." Any conflict between truth and instruction must be resolved in the light of this injunction. But the contradictory tendencies in his thought remain to plague him and all his followers, and the resolu-tion is more often in the other direction. Belinsky never forgot that the documentation of an *a priori* attitude is not the same thing as the naked wrestling with experience that produces great works of art, but he was able at the same time to entertain ideas which were quite incompatible with the practice of a free art.[15] It is the prescriptive phase of his thinking which has been emphasized here because it is the source of the three principal concepts—optimism, service, and typicality—which constitute the legacy Soviet critics claim to inherit from Belinsky. They have had to set aside

[15] Bowman shows how Belinsky contradicted himself on these essen-tial points until the end of his life (see Bowman, *Vissarion Belinski*, pp. 178–79 and p. 199).

all that he said in favor of art's and the artist's independence.
The real tragedy of Belinsky's legacy is that in his passionate
volte-faces he managed to blur certain essential distinctions
—notably between art and life, and between the language
of art and the language of science and of doctrine—which
made it easier for his successors to use him for purposes it is
hard to imagine he could have supported. It is *not* easy,
finally, to picture Belinsky as a member of the Politburo.

III

Two important questions arise for a literature which heeds
Belinsky's direction to select, distill, and generalize. How
does it render its service to human welfare within the system
of the dialectic? And who, if anyone, is to play the role of
virtue's conscious agent?

The radical critics devised two general answers to the first
question: literature might hasten the disintegration of the
old, retrogressive tendency by exposé or ridicule, or it might
accelerate the progressive tendency by indicating its presence
and by giving it favorable publicity. Belinsky was aware of
these two possibilities, but all that he found in Russian life
and literature persuaded him that the affirmative note would
have to be postponed indefinitely in favor of a literature of
criticism and negation. In this reluctant choice are found the
answers to the second question, and the key to Belinsky's
basic attitudes toward heroism.

In the contest between value systems the actual combat-
ants in the field are individual men, and the partisans of
truth are the virtuous agents of progress. Belinsky felt sure
that they must exist—had their not always been heroes in the
past?—but their identity, their function, and their relationship to literature in his time raised questions that were not
easily answered. He found it easier to excoriate his enemies

than to celebrate his allies, and in this pugnacious, destructive mood his deepest attitudes toward heroes were formed. "My heroes," he wrote in a letter to Botkin, "are the destroyers of the old, Luther, Voltaire, the Encyclopaedists, the Terrorists, Byron . . . and so on." [16]

In his own time Belinsky sought these exposers and destroyers among the men of thought and imagination; in Russia the likeliest candidates were the writers whose critique of the reigning order seemed to him to be doing history's work. The critic—in this case himself—could make his own contribution. In apologizing to Botkin for an article which he described as a "clumsy patchwork" of his own and Katkov's ideas, he says characteristically: "Never mind! If I will not supply a theory of poetry I will have killed the old ones, killed at one fell stroke all our rhetorics, poetics and aesthetics—and that is not to be sneezed at!" [17]

Clearly, he read both *Eugene Onegin* and *Dead Souls* as indictments of the social system. Neither work, it is true, offered a stirring heroic image nor any sign of positive forces working for a better world, but their liberating destructiveness qualified their *authors* as agents of progress. Although they had performed this heroic task, they themselves were poor candidates for imitation: Pushkin was dead, and the unhappy Gogol drew back in horror from Belinsky's accolade. It was, in fact, a most unheroic moment in Russian history.

Despite this, or perhaps because of it, Belinsky's whole career was a restless hero-quest. The rapid succession in his own life of commitments—each more passionate than the preceding—to the ideas of Fichte, Schelling, Hegel, and, finally, of the left-Hegelians and the Saint-Simonians, illustrates his own sharply felt need for leadership from heroes

[16] Belinsky, *Selected Philosophical Works*, p. 164.   [17] *Ibid.*, p. 152.

of thought. In writing in 1841 of his abandonment of Hegel, against whom he now feels he has "special reason to harbour a grudge . . . for I feel that I have been loyal to him . . . in tolerating Russian reality," [18] he acknowledges his own erraticism: "A year ago my views were diametrically opposite to what they are today, and, really, I cannot say whether it is a fortunate or unfortunate thing that for me to think and feel, to understand and suffer are one and the same thing." [19]

It is interesting that in the same letter to Botkin he sees this kind of shift from one view to its opposite as somehow tragic: "A man himself knows nothing—everything depends upon the spectacles which his disposition, the whim of his nature beyond the control of his will, places on his nose." He then goes on, in what is only apparently a change of subject, to give Botkin the correct text of a passage mutilated by the censor:

If we were to ask Lady Macbeth [he had written] why she had been created so awfully inhuman, she would no doubt answer that she knew as much about it as her questioner and if she followed her nature it was because she had no other. . . . These are questions that are solved only beyond the grave, this is the kingdom of fate, the realm of tragedy! [20]

He adds a note on Richard II which is *not,* as we shall see in later chapters, part of the Belinsky legacy treasured in the USSR:

The king, unworthy so long as he reigned, becomes great when he has lost his kingdom. He becomes conscious of the dignity of his majesty . . . of the legitimacy of his rights—and wise speeches, filled with lofty thought, rush in stormy torrents from his lips, while action reveals a great soul and royal dignity. Insignificant in good fortune, great in misfortune, he is a hero in your eyes. But in order to bring forth the powers of his spirit and

[18] *Ibid.,* p. 149.   [19] *Ibid.,* p. 150.   [20] *Ibid.,* p. 152.

become a hero he had to drain the cup of misery to the dregs
and perish. . . . What a contradiction, and what a rich theme
for tragedy, hence what an inexhaustible source of sublime enjoyment.[21]

Yet, in the same year, he had celebrated a very different kind
of hero, one who "did not believe in the frailties of human
nature," [22] a destroyer who was also a builder, and one far
more sympathetic to the later searchers for positive heroes—
Peter the Great. "Who, throughout our history, can be nearer
both to our heart and spirit?" [23]

Here, discussing Peter, he touches on the vital question of
the aesthetic effect of contemplating virtuous men, which
"rouses us from the drowsiness of humdrum life . . . attunes
the heart to exalted feelings and noble thoughts [and]
strengthens the will to acts of goodness." [24] Peter the Great
or Richard the Second? Belinsky would have it both ways:
he could comprehend both the view of the effective, successful hero whose example leads to positive moral instruction
and that of the hero in defeat who arouses pity, and more
than pity, awe. It remained for later radicals to recast the
image of Peter the Great (stripped of his kingly rank, of
course) as a permanent replacement for the tragic hero.

Toward the end of his career Belinsky dismissed the possibility that large-scale heroic images—whether tragic or not
—might dominate the literature of his time. The downfall
of Shakespeare's kings, whatever it revealed of the greatness
of the human spirit, was to provide no part of Belinsky's
guide to Russian writers, nor was "sublime enjoyment" in
any sense the exclusive goal of literature. Heroes there had
been, in life and in literature, and their influence had been
enormous, but for his contemporaries Belinsky could offer
no similar image. For the new writing had first of all to be

[21] *Ibid.*, p. 153.   [22] *Ibid.*, p. 142.   [23] *Ibid.*, p. 146.   [24] *Ibid.*

"truthful." Heroes were not to be fabricated out of moral abstractions if they could not be found in Russian life. Belinsky had found it Pushkin's great merit "that he disestablished the vogue of monsters of vice and heroes of virtue, depicting instead just ordinary people." [25]

Belinsky also objected to the romantic hero of his own time. The division of the universe into contending factions was reflected in human nature, which was composed, he believed, of more or less equal parts of altruism and "egotism." In the romantic hero "egotism" had full sway. He simply could not be accepted at his own inflated estimate of himself. But when that estimate was deflated by a writer, Belinsky was more hospitable to the choice of such a person as subject. In fact, he wanted the hero's condition to be emphasized if that was "best and most natural." [26] Thus Onegin, stripped of his illusions and seen at a certain remove, inspires pity as a victim of unhealthy social attitudes. Byronism, seen wholly, loses its dangerous fascination. Belinsky took an astringent view of Aduev, the hero of Goncharov's novel *An Ordinary Story*, because he was handled too respectfully by his author. This early version of the superfluous man had a well-developed capacity for self-deception, it was pointed out, and would never be capable of genuine, reciprocal emotion or of effective moral behavior.

Belinsky, before Dobrolyubov, discovered the awful gap between intention and action:

They recognize the lofty and beautiful only in books, and that not always; in life and in reality they recognize neither the one nor the other, and because of this are quickly disillusioned (their pet expression!), grow chilly in the soul, grow old in the flower of their years, stop in mid-journey, and end . . . by becoming reconciled with reality. . . . That is, whatever they do they fall

[25] *Ibid.*, p. 212.   [26] *Ibid.*, p. 469.

straight from the clouds into the mud; or they become mystics, misanthropes, lunatics, or sleepwalkers. Usually they are ludicrous or pitiful . . . but sometimes they are not at all pitiful but dreadful because of their reconciliation with reality.[27]

But if the full cycle of their careers is shown with all the consequences of their imperfect grasp of the world and their final state of degradation (their reconciliation with reality), they are valid subjects to write about. In the reader's pity, laughter, or indignation an educational function will be served; falsehood will be unmasked, and the dialectic of history will receive its forward thrust.

But the question: *toward what?* remains unanswered. Here Belinsky has reached a way-station on the route to something else. The denunciation of false prophets will not forever remain the function of literature. Sooner or later, new prophets, whether destroyers or builders, are bound to announce their presence. Belinsky sensed the impermanence of the period of stagnation he lived in and felt called upon to justify the negative role of his "natural school" as somehow presaging a more positive phase:

The habit of faithfully rendering the negative aspects of life will enable the same men or their followers, when the time comes, faithfully to render the positive aspects of life without placing them on stilts, without exaggerating: in short, without rhetorically idealizing them.[28]

Belinsky felt that periods like his own were not uncommon in human history—periods of stagnation without discernible forward motion and without heroes. But appearances, he suggested, were deceptive: new forces were gathering under the surface and the oppressively motionless world of Nicholas

[27] V. G. Belinsky, *Polnoe sobranie sochinenii* (Moscow, 1955), VI, 672.
[28] Belinsky, *Selected Philosophical Works*, p. 357.

I must inevitably give way to an era of growth, progress, and change:

Progress is not interrupted even during the epoch of decay and death of societies, for this decay is necessary as a means of preparing the soil for the blossoming of a new life, and death itself, in history as well as in nature, is merely the regeneration of a new life.[29]

From time to time Belinsky applied his standard of virtue to the world around him. The samplings were uneven: "A good man in Russia," Belinsky decided at one time, simply has no "terrain" to stand on; whatever virtue he possesses is a simple "gift of nature" retained somehow despite the poisonous social atmosphere he breathes. He will have no opportunity to display his virtue in concrete activity, and the chances are that he will be an imperfectly formed human being, that his moral impulses will be blocked by other flaws. On another occasion, the possibility of enlightened behavior seemed far more encouraging:

It is a fact beyond a shadow of doubt that the number of people who are endeavoring to realize their moral convictions in deeds to the detriment of their private interests and at the risk of their social position has been growing perceptibly with us.[30]

These contradictory observations register Belinsky's changing moods more than they do real shifts in the moral climate. In one sense we may dismiss Belinsky's attitude toward the question of heroes by saying simply that his longing for them was frustrated by their demonstrable absence from Russian life in the 1840s. By combining the qualities he believed the hero should *not* have, however, with a few hints as to the qualities he should possess and that Belinsky, himself, exemplified, it is possible to sketch an outline, at least, of the still undiscovered champion. Incomplete as it is,

[29] *Ibid.*, p. 312.   [30] *Ibid.*, p. 338.

Belinsky's hero figure bears a strong resemblance to the archetype which the radical critics developed in the middle decades of the century and handed down to the Soviet cultural magistrates of the present day.

He will not be a sovereign, a lawgiver, or a conqueror, but a man much closer to his fellows in rank and abilities, distinguished from them only by the firmness of his convictions and the force of his character. He will not be the "brilliant exception," or the man touched by genius, or the man set apart by innate or supernatural qualities. He will be rather the "first among equals," a representative man. His exact social status is not specified, but he will certainly not be a member of the governing class, nor, by all indications, a member of the popular masses. The value attached to the liberating, inspiriting effect of ideas suggests that he will be an educated man. And there is little doubt, finally, that he will be a man in revolt against established values and the social order they justify.

The ultimate sanction for attacking the status quo is the immense suffering caused by the Tsarist regime. The foremost victims, of course, are the peasants and it is in their name, finally, that he acts. What are his relations with the masses; in what sense is he their representative? Belinsky's use of the concept of *narodnost*,[31] the untranslatable term used by all political factions in the nineteenth century to anchor their theories in the aspirations of the peasant mass, gives a partial answer. He includes the peasant-serfs as integral parts of the nation, hence as participants in the forward movement toward national self-awareness. The educated man, then, who is in the forefront of this struggle, is

---

[31] Literally "peopleness" or "nationality"; by extension, the qualities of a people, and, by further extension, identification with the people's interests.

the leader of a vast progressive upsurge toward enlightenment; he is, in the words of a Soviet commentator, the "crest
of the wave." [32]

In the USSR today they welcome this identification of
the active, moral personality with the masses as one of the
most "progressive" discoveries made by Belinsky, and one
that links him closely with the Marxist-Leninist tradition.
Yovchuk, in his introduction to *Selected Philosophical
Works*, says this of Belinsky:

> He found a profound and, in general, correct solution for the
> problem of the role of the individual and of the masses of the
> people in history when he maintained that the masses of the
> people could and would become the decisive force in historical
> development. The masses could be raised to the level of such
> historical activity by the progressive, educated people in society,
> who must be guided by the requirements of society, by the
> spirit of the times, by the interests of the people.[33]

The link is organic, apparently, and the identification of
interests is complete. It is not clear how the hero receives his
appointment to the position of leadership, nor by what
process, exactly, he functions as the representative of the
masses. It is difficult to avoid the impression that he is self-
appointed, and that he represents them on the basis of his
own estimate of their needs. His constituents are a source
of energy and strength. Their plight documents his critique
of the social order and their unarticulated needs are the basis
of his program for the future. But neither the channel of
communications between them nor the pattern of mutual
responsibility is clearly set forth.

Soviet critics have tended to exaggerate Belinsky's contri-

[32] A. Lavretsky, *Belinsky, Chernyshevsky, Dobrolyubov v borbe za
realizm* (Moscow, 1941), p. 65.
[33] Belinsky, *Selected Philosophical Works*, p. xi. Belinsky discussed
the subject in a review of Eugene Sue's *Les Mystères de Paris* in 1844.
(*Ibid.*, pp. 326–27.)

bution to the definition of the new hero. Makedonov maintains that Belinsky devoted his entire intellectual life to the
search for "a democratic man-hero," as opposed to the semi-
divine figures of neoclassic tragedy.[34] Lavretsky says the same
thing in a vast and questionable generalization: "Essentially
the struggle for realism is a struggle for an active human
type, a new man." [35] "Essentially" here acknowledges the
fact that Belinsky never knew that the "new man" was the
goal of all his strenuous endeavors. In an unsigned editorial
in 1936 the matter is put somewhat differently though in
the same vein of exaggeration: "In his teaching about the
new hero, Belinsky posed the question about the kind of man
who is essentially an anticipation, a premonition of the
socialist hero." [36] Again "essentially" marks a stretching of
the truth, but it can be said that Belinsky "posed" questions
that others were to answer, if it is also understood that consciously he taught almost nothing about the hero.

Far more interesting than the official adulation in Zhdanov's "Report," or routine declarations of doctrinal dependence, is the kind of testimony we find in Lebedev-
Polyansky's study of Belinsky, at the point where it lapses
into personal reminiscence. Belinsky's role as a hero for the
early Bolsheviks, both as man and as thinker, is clearly
expressed:

Our generation, born in the eighties of the last century, read
the works of Belinsky with delight, as his contemporaries had
done. And perhaps the great critic's ideas were clearer to us than
they were to his contemporaries; in them we found that content—time had aided us—which was hidden from .Belinsky's
contemporaries: his passion, his moral force, his exceptional

[34] A. Makedonov, "Problema geroya v estetike Belinskogo," *Literaturny kritik*, No. 6 (June, 1936), p. 101.
[35] Lavretsky, *Belinsky, Chernyshevsky, Dobrolyubov*, p. 57.
[36] "Vissarion Grigorievich Belinsky," *Literaturny kritik*, No. 6, (June,
1936), p. 22.

sincerity . . . his idea that literature, while continuing to be
art, must serve the goals of social struggle, must contain precise
ideas, must pass sentence on contemporary life, must be the fore-
teller of the future. . . .

.   .   .   .

In the happy and unhappy accidents of life the youth often
gave each other the works of Belinsky, knowing that in them
one could find moral support and strength. The youth gave each
other the works of Belinsky when, inspired by a great love for
the people, by the idea of struggle, they went out, in Chekhov's
words, "into the unknown distance." [37]

This type of sentimental veneration suggests the force of
Belinsky's personal impact on a culture hungry for heroes.
It is the inspiring image of Belinsky the fighter that was
handed down from generation to generation of Russian
radicals and intellectuals, as part of the Russian revolutionary ethos, and has finally been incorporated in the Soviet
gallery of saints. Men of all persuasions have reacted to the
force of his convictions, his purity, his integrity, and the
furiously righteous style of his behavior. Isaiah Berlin's generous and discriminating appreciation of Belinsky [38] has recently recovered this image as well, perhaps, as it can be
done. He has made allowance for the extremism of Belinsky's
judgments, for his drastic lapses in taste, and for the large
gaps in his education, but he has not properly estimated
those phases of his personality and of his critical practice
that are hostile, in the final analysis, to the free intellect and
imagination.

The ingredients of his moral personality actually are not
so different from those of the Soviet hero-type. He hated
dogma, it is true, and might well have suffocated in the

[37] P. I. Lebedev-Polyansky, V. G. Belinsky, literaturno-kriticheskaya
deyatelnost (Moscow-Leningrad, 1945), pp. 300–301.

[38] Isaiah Berlin, "A Marvellous Decade (III), Belinsky: Moralist and
Prophet," Encounter, V, No. 6 (December, 1955), 22–43.

Soviet intellectual atmosphere, but he was the author of his
own dogmas, which he applied with ferocious assurance to
the world around him. His celebrated sincerity might not
survive in a moral climate of strategic maneuver and deception, but his fanatical attachment to a single system of ideas,
and his intolerance of all others, the rudeness of his manner,
the flat certainty, the right-or-wrong quality of his judgments,
are familiar elements of Soviet behavior and intellectual
practice. These are the qualities of revolutionaries, of wholly
politicalized men. It is not absurd, perhaps, to suggest that
these qualities have survived the metamorphosis of October
which converted revolutionary nonconformists into vigilant
defenders of the revolution's vested interests.

When this personality assumed the office of literary critic,
it is hard to believe that the ultimate interests of literature
were not endangered. Belinsky loved literature, but he
threatened at times to smother it in his embrace. Berlin has
said: "All serious questions to Belinsky were always, in the
end, moral questions." [39] Without quarreling about the kind
of morality, it is enough to recognize that a standard external to literature formed the basis of his literary judgments. The strong partisan certainty of these judgments,
though it is not yet political or programmatic, not yet "party
spirit" as either Matthew Arnold or Lenin meant it, is certainly menacing to a literature of paradox, or ambiguity.
Belinsky believed in "a single knowable truth," as Berlin
says, and "ideas were above all, true or false. If false, then
like evil spirits to be exorcised." [40] It was the critic's job to
bring them to light (to "unmask" them, Soviet Marxists
were to say), and "all books embody ideas even when least
appearing to do so." [41] The moral validity of the uncovered
idea, then, forms the basis of the critic's judgment.

[39] *Ibid.*, p. 26.   [40] *Ibid.*   [41] *Ibid.*

This kind of standard becomes possible because Belinsky did not honor certain important distinctions between life and art. The idea he sought (which also is an "attitude" or a revelation of preferences) "requires to be judged," Berlin says, "as it would be in life; in the first place for its degree of genuineness, its adequacy to its subject matter, its depth, its truthfulness, its ultimate motives." [42] This kind of *moral* judgment of art contains the seeds of all the brands of prescriptive criticism which accompanied the development of the Russian revolutionary movement. The work of art acts upon life and is judged in the end for the effect it has on the moral condition of its readers. The critic is the custodian of the meanings of "genuineness," "depth," and "ultimate motives," and the guardian of the truth of history as well. Thus a writer who fails is not only a poor craftsman, he is also a liar, or a hypocrite, or an obscurantist.

Unknown to himself, and despite his admirable devotion to truth, beauty, and justice, Belinsky is the author of an image of man (in his own person) steeped in hatred, which had only to be simplified, hardened, and shorn of senti-mental scruple to become the revolutionary monolith of later generations. He is the author too of that strange Russian hybrid, the critic-revolutionary, who transformed the char-acter traits of the political revolutionary into criteria of literary judgment. Belinsky was neither utilitarian nor totali-tarian, Berlin insists, but he was the indispensable predeces-sor of both.

IV

Where Belinsky appears inadequate to Soviet critics the assumption is that he *would have* reached these conclusions if conditions had been different. Perhaps. But it is a fruitless

[42] *Ibid.*

speculation which rests on the questionable view that literary theory evolves in a single, determined line of development from lower to higher stages.

Belinsky's real contribution is a set of ideas that has remained operative to the present day, even though it has been amended, embellished, upended, and given, with the ascendancy of Marxism, a new metaphysical foundation:

Optimism. Soviet commentators have welcomed every sign in Belinsky of the singularly cheerless optimism that has characterized the Russian revolutionary ethos. History unfolds in a necessary evolutionary order; the direction is forward and upward, toward the coming emancipation of men from the slavery of want and material contingency; and works of art created in awareness of the world in motion cannot fail to reflect the promise of the dialectic.

Under the influence of these assurances, literature will become less exclusively concerned with exploring the past and explaining the present. Conceived as dissent, and tied to the present and to life as it is, the new literature will go further and try to argue the likelihood and the desirability of moving from the imperfect present to a better future.[43] In the shift from present to future tense realistic literature will undergo basic changes in its traditional functions: from descriptive analysis to prophecy, from reminiscence to inspiration. It should be pointed out that the optimism of the dialectic is not based on glib promises or easy solutions. Allowance is made for the presence of pain, suffering, and partial or temporary defeats, but the total defeat of both

[43] Compare Belinsky's remark that literature is the record "of treasured thoughts of the whole of society, of its . . . still indiscernible aspiration" (*Selected Philosophical Works,* p. 426), with Timofeev's injunctions that "the artist sees today in the light of tomorrow" (L. I. Timofeev, *Teoriya literatury* [Moscow, 1938], p. 327), and that art must represent "the new, the growing, that which is not typical today but will surely be so tomorrow" (p. 302).

the hero and the values he represents, in a downfall so complete that it counsels reconciliation or quietism, is impermissible in the new writing that is to grow from Belinsky's premises. In this emphasis, the crucial quarrel with tragedy and with the tragic view of life is prefigured in Belinsky's thought, although he himself never took a positive stand on the question of "the happy ending."

Service. Zhdanov said in his "Report":

From Belinsky onward, all the best representatives of the revolutionary democratic Russian intellectuals have denounced "pure art" and "art for art's sake" and have been the spokesmen of art for the people, demanding that art should have a worthy educational and social significance.[44]

In "A View of Russian Literature in 1847," Belinsky wrote of the new trends which replaced the former interest in "pure art":

Artistic interest . . . could not but yield to other more important human interests and art nobly undertook to serve these interests as their spokesman. Art has not ceased thereby to be art, but has merely acquired a new character. To deny art the right of serving public interests means debasing it, not raising it, for that would mean depriving it of its most vital force, i.e., idea, making it an object of sybaritic pleasure, the plaything of lazy idlers.[45]

Soviet theorists have adapted this notion by interposing the intermediary of the Party and state through which the service to human welfare is rendered. In this tradition, art serves the people by educating them in principles that will lead to their own betterment. The issue is not merely a matter of reestablishing, as Zhdanov would have us believe, the principle that art must serve more than its own ends,

[44] A. A. Zhdanov, "Doklad o zhurnalakh *Zvezda* i *Leningrad*," *Literaturnaya gazeta*, No. 39 (September 21, 1946), p. 3.
[45] Belinsky, *Selected Philosophical Works*, p. 431.

but of harnessing it to increasingly detailed notions of what men should learn and of how and why their minds should be changed.

Typicality. The emphasis in the radical tradition on art's generalizing capacities really stems from the radicals' interest in controlling the content of the generalization. It is one thing to proclaim that art deals with the typical, quite another to prescribe what *is* typical, and what, therefore, is the legitimate concern of art at any given time. This prescriptive control over the choice of subject matter, which also operates as a principle for excluding undesirable (i.e., untypical) material, is central to the utilitarian approach.

The critic is free to challenge (and the editor to reject) the very conception of a novel, ignoring the writer's fulfillment of his intention, if the intention itself is "incorrect" or "harmful." The concepts of the "true," the "typical," and the "significant" are general descriptive terms about the nature of literature, until they are given exclusive, doctrinal definitions. Then they become tools for governing the very substance and significance of the work of art.

Belinsky's theory of realism offers with one hand what, in effect, it withholds with the other. The writer is *not* free after all to wander at will through Russian experience, nor will his decision about what is valid material for investigation be respected as the exercise of the artist's inalienable prerogative. Belinsky stopped short of exercising the censorious potential implicit in his theory. It requires a fair measure of hindsight to isolate it in his writing and we cannot know how he would have felt about the subsequent use made of it. The increasingly political nature of literature in the years to come might have coincided with his own revolutionary aspirations, but it seems certain that he would not have accepted the conclusions his successors drew from his premises without a genuine sense of loss, a sense of the death of the "magic" of art, which he continued to value even as he undermined it.

Belinsky, in effect, issued a challenge to his successors: although he did not hope to find them in his own time, sooner or later heroes must exist: "society's tyranny demands heroes to combat it." [46] The radical critics of the fifties and sixties, armed with Belinsky's precepts and fired by his example, made the search for the new hero the focal point of their literary and—behind this necessary disguise—of their urgent political concerns as well.

[46] *Ibid.*, p. 240.

4

DOBROLYUBOV
Beyond the Superfluous Man

N. A. Dobrolyubov (1836–61) is the eternal, perhaps one should say the professional, youth of the Russian revolutionary movement. His brief career, brought to an end by consumption at the age of twenty-five, summarizes all the virtues and vices of the youthful radical. For his partisans, then and now, he expressed the energy, the optimism, the critical brilliance, and the refreshing anger against injustice that characterize the best of the radical ethos. To his enemies, his brilliance was arrogant precocity, his optimism callow, and his anger and energy were expressed in a blind urge to destroy. In all the senses that radicalism is youthful, Dobrolyubov comes down to us a classic example. In this role he was a compelling figure in his own time. He was a constant topic of discussion in public and in private and he was thought to be the model for a number of studies of the new man, including such "unfavorable" versions as Bazarov, the hero of Turgenev's *Fathers and Sons*. Turgenev denied it, but Bazarov's cocksureness, impatience, and scorn are certainly duplicated in the quality of Dobrolyubov's thought as expressed in his critical articles.

There had been changes in the intellectual climate since Belinsky's death in 1848. Less than a decade later, the atmosphere of intellectual and moral stagnation which had compelled Belinsky to qualify his faith in progress had been dissipated by new and parallel currents of imaginative vitality and social protest. Turgenev, Goncharov, Ostrovsky, and the promising young writers, Tolstoy and Dostoevsky, had been heard from, and the new generation of radical critics, with whom some of the new writers were now in fruitful, if short-lived, alliance, had sharpened the radical challenge to the status quo after its momentary eclipse in the post-1848 repression. In this quickened climate Dobrolyubov led the attack on the social system in the pages of the influential journal *Sovremennik* (Contemporary), using the detour through literary criticism Belinsky had already charted.

Dobrolyubov's indebtedness to Belinsky is direct, heavy, and explicit. He felt a strong spiritual kinship with his predecessor, that "pride, glory and adornment" of Russian literature, and his intellectual dependence on Belinsky is evident in everything Dobrolyubov has to say about the nature of art and society. Frequently he gave sharp, dogmatic utterance to ideas which had been half-understood or unexplored premises for Belinsky. Dobrolyubov presents restatements of Belinsky's three key premises, optimism, typicality, and service, indicating that they are central in his own thought. We find him, for example, defining the problem of dialectical optimism with an assurance which Belinsky had lacked a decade before:

Recognizing the immutable laws of historical development, the men of the present generation do not place unreal hopes upon themselves, do not think they can alter history at their own will, do not think they are immune to the influence of circumstances. . . . But at the same time they do not in the least sink into apathy and indifference, for they are also aware of their own worth. They look upon themselves as one of the wheels of a machine, as one of the circumstances which govern the course of world events. As all world circumstances are interconnected and to some extent subordinated to each other, they,

too, are subordinated to necessity, to the force of things; but
beyond this subordination they do not bow to any idols whatso-
ever, they uphold the independence and sovereignty of all their
actions against all casually arising claims.[1]

Dobrolyubov's formula for the individual's release from the
power of circumstance resembles Engels's definition of "freedom" as the "recognition of necessity." The strong note of
emotion on which it ends establishes a connection between
true awareness of the world and the kind of independent,
defiant, and self-contained personality which can operate
most successfully in it. The ingredients of heroic behavior
are, it is suggested here, implicit in the very nature of the
historical process.

If Dobrolyubov sharpened some of Belinsky's ideas, he also
reduced the range of his interests and eliminated the contradictions, always in favor of the prescriptive element, always to the detriment of literature's independence. There is
no doubt that the narrow, systematized version of Belinsky
used by Soviet critics had its beginnings here. That literature
performs a kind of secondary service in the intellectual
activities of the day is stated far more uncompromisingly by
Dobrolyubov than by Belinsky:

Thus, speaking generally, literature is an auxiliary force (the
importance of which lies in propaganda, and the merit of which
is determined by what it propagates, and how it propagates it).[2]

[1] N. A. Dobrolyubov, *Polnoe sobranie sochinenii* (Moscow, 1937),
IV, 62.

[2] N. A. Dobrolyubov, *Selected Philosophical Essays*, ed. M. T. Yovchuk (Moscow, 1948), p. 565. Parentheses in the quotations indicate
censored material throughout this chapter. There have been writers in
the past who have raised literature above this auxiliary function, Shakespeare, for example, who, "like great scientists and political leaders, have
extended the broad frontiers of human awareness," but there are none
among Dobrolyubov's contemporaries who have earned this exemption
from service.

The writer is given no leeway to distort or falsify; nor, though he works under the guidance of an idea, is he permitted to inject this idea as learned from a philosopher into his work. It must be verifiable against an objective norm, usually described simply as "real life." [3] Literature, then, is accountable to experience, but the principal reason for this restriction is that its propagandist function is impaired by falsification:

Thus we think that the principal function of literature is to explain the phenomena of life, and that is why we demand that it should possess a quality without which it can have no merit whatever. This quality is *truth*. The facts from which the author proceeds, and which he presents to us, must be presented truthfully. If he fails to do that, his literary production loses all significance; in fact, it becomes harmful, because it serves not to enlighten the human mind, but, on the contrary, still further to obscure it.[4]

Though the writer may end by agreeing with the philosopher, he must proceed to his conclusion by a different route. In comprehending social discontent, for example, the philosopher will analyze facts and then proceed to formulate general principles which will aid in the removal of the unrest. But "the author-poet . . . noticing the same discontent, paints such a vivid picture of it that it attracts universal attention, and of itself suggests to people what it is they need." [5]

Both aspects of the truth have the same final purpose: the abolition of the unacceptable present and its replacement by a better future. Literature performs its "special services" by "awakening . . . the consciousness of the masses to what the advanced leaders of mankind have discovered," and by revealing to them "what, as yet, lives in them vaguely and indefinitely." [6] It is clear that another part of the truth

[3] *Ibid.*, p. 566.   [4] *Ibid.*   [5] *Ibid.*   [6] *Ibid.*, p. 565.

contains a prediction about what will happen soon. The writer becomes a kind of prophet, and even when his expectations turned out to be premature, they still were to be considered "true" at the moment they were expressed. In their own time the radicals felt sure that history's promises had not been proved false, though they were sometimes forced to conclude that their estimated time of fruition had been badly miscalculated.

Actually, description is a small part of the literary "truth." Literature is a technique for understanding experience in a very special way and the writer must be quite clear about the standards he uses to interpret and evaluate what he has seen. This is a far more calculated procedure than Belinsky's view that the writer worked under the hypnotic influence of an idea he might not fully or rationally comprehend. The writer consciously selects, sifts, evaluates, and pronounces judgment on the material he incorporates in his work, and, according to Dobrolyubov, must possess a trained clairvoyant sense to enable him to detect major trends in their incipient phase.

A view of man more firmly in the grip of history's laws, yet freer because he understands them better; a much narrower definition of literature's obligation to serve social change; and a heightened emphasis on the tendentious uses the writer was to make of "the truth"—these changes betray the drift within the premises of the radical theory.

There had, of course, been major changes in the intellectual climate of Russia since 1848 which seemed to forecast even greater changes in the social structure. Dobrolyubov was stimulated by widespread restlessness and by the rising note of agitation which preceded the Emancipation Act of 1861. He found evidence in life and in literature to justify his optimism and to validate his philosophy of social action.

In addition to the belligerence among the leftist intellectuals, there were strong "murmurings" from the people. And nothing seemed to offer a stronger guarantee that one era was about to give way to another than the discovery that a revolution was taking place in the personalities of Russia's men of conscience:

No matter where you look, everywhere you will find an awakening of personality (a claim for its legitimate rights), a protest against violence and tyranny (in most cases still timid, indefinite, ready to hide, but for all that) already making its existence felt.[7]

This new kind of person was a symptom of impending change as well as the agent who was to carry it out. Also, by all the tenets of Dobrolyubov's creed, he was an obvious candidate for the role of the literary hero. The quest for the hero gives a focus to all Dobrolyubov's moral, social, political, and literary concerns, and to his brief, hectic career as well.

II

Dobrolyubov's controversial manifesto, "What Is Oblomovism?" was intended to proclaim the ceremonial burial of the superfluous man. Looking back over thirty years of the new Russian realism, Dobrolyubov claimed to have made a striking discovery about Russian literary heroes. Using Goncharov's *Oblomov* as his point of departure, he generalized angrily about the unvarying pattern of weakness, egotism, and inactivity these heroes describe. A generalization which links Lermontov's Byronic bully, Pechorin, with Goncharov's amiable sloven, Oblomov, may seem too careless of distinctions to possess much meaning. But if we recall basic

[7] *Ibid.*, p. 575.

assumptions of the radical school the important likenesses shared by Onegin, Pechorin, and Turgenev's Rudin become clear. Literary event and literary character are seen and judged exclusively against the world they are taken from. These imagined figures are treated as *descriptions* of types in the real world and their common crime is their failure to act morally and effectively in the fictional semblance of the real world. Dobrolyubov is perfectly clear about this: Oblomovism is a moral and social disease widespread in Russian life itself. Literature has done its job well in exposing and diagnosing the illness. But life has moved on and literature must bestir itself to catch up.

Many reasons were advanced for the fatal self-absorption and the paralysis of will which afflicted these unhappy men. The crucial determinants, in Dobrolyubov's view, were the multiple pressures arising from the feudal environment. In the atmosphere of tyranny and stagnation, a number of people, it is true, had been able to achieve a certain independence from dominant values. But even when they had reached the point of formulating their code of dissent, exhaustion or cowardice or self-deception prevented them from acting. Their intentions often remained uncorrupted, but they were never tested by use. Serfdom, however, was in its death agony, and the superfluous men, who had filled a genuine need by questioning or standing aloof or preaching, were now felt to be inadequate to the task of moving society forward to the new order. With the further decay of the social order would come a lessening of its poisonous effects on moral character, a trend which would make it easier for men to liberate themselves and assert their "natural" virtue. Convictions held in idleness could no longer be considered a praiseworthy achievement, or a sufficiently spirited response to the hateful milieu. "We need men of action and not of abstract . . . argument," [8] Dobrolyubov wrote in his review of Turgenev's *On the Eve*, which bears the characteristically impatient title, "When Will the Day Come?" Correct principles have become common property, and now await the kind of men who will put them into practice.

The successor to the superfluous man had a name and a set of characteristics before he had been reliably reported to exist: he was called "the new man." As first conceived, he was in one sense a development beyond his predecessors, and in another sense—notably in his thirst for action—a direct antithesis to them. Writers were obliged to search for the new active man in fulfillment of their public responsibilities. The writer who continued to reproduce the images of alienated men and the aura of defeatism that surrounded them made a bad work of art because he had made an "incorrect" selection of subject matter. Dobrolyubov is clear about the possibilities of error on this score:

If . . . he [the writer] has tried to raise one of his personages to the level of a universal type and the critic proves that the importance of the character is extremely limited and small, it will follow clearly that the author has spoilt his production by his false views concerning the hero.[9]

But Dobrolyubov's tireless scrutiny of literature indicated that the image of the positive hero was disappointingly elusive. He suspected at times that the new type existed only in his own expectations. At other times, he indicated that

[8] *Ibid.*, p. 396.
[9] *Ibid.* Here the critic appears as the custodian of the truth. Later, Dobrolyubov insisted that the new man must occupy a central position in literature because the public demanded it: "Russian life has at last reached the stage where virtuous and esteemed, but weak and spineless, individuals no longer satisfy the public conscience and are regarded as totally useless. An urgent need is felt for men who, if less beautiful in character, are more active and energetic" (*ibid.*, p. 594).

he was very close to finding him, or that the hero had been discovered in some incomplete form, or that a careless author simply had not known a hero when he saw him. Then again, Dobrolyubov seemed ready to conclude that the circumstances of Russian life were still exercising their harsh sovereignty over the growth of the new moral personality, and, though the public expected him and the movement of history guaranteed that he would come, he had not yet reached maturity. But Dobrolyubov persisted in the certainty that the new moral type must ultimately come to exist.

III

According to Dobrolyubov's optimal expectations, the new man, freed of the curse of inertia when he became aware of his condition, would know his own strength, who his enemies were, and how to attack them. Factual knowledge of his environment, which had become widespread by this time, was not the only resource available to the man who thirsted to act. He was blessed with a generous endowment of "natural" goodness and strength, and a vivid emotional awareness of his "natural" rights. These resources, if they managed to survive the gauntlet of the Russian environment, including the adverse effects of a false educational system, would supply him with the energy and courage to put his principles into practice, and to make use of his knowledge.

These natural attributes of character which are the birthright of all men are described variously by Dobrolyubov at various points in his work, but they have one common denominator: they are the virtues that overcome inertia and lead to fearless, direct action. Dobrolyubov drew a sharp contrast between the moral characteristics of the people and of the gentry. The primary virtues retained by the people (and lost by the gentry) are not those the Slavophiles claim to find—passivity, endurance, resignation—nor are the common people without serious faults. But the burden of the destructive environment, contrary to belief, has weighed more heavily on the upper classes and caused a much greater disfigurement of moral character than it has among the working people. The idleness and artificiality of the landowners' lives create a personality without purpose or resolution or the ability or inclination to act for moral ends:

General debility, morbidness, incapacity for concentrated and profound passions, characterize, if not all, then at all events the majority of our "civilized" brothers. That is why they are continuously darting hither and thither, themselves not knowing what they need and what it is they are sorry for. Their desire is so strong that they cannot live without gratifying it, and yet they do nothing to gratify it; their sufferings are so great that death is preferable—but they go on living just the same, except that they assume a melancholy air.[10]

Despite the effects of social inferiority and economic oppression, the people have kept intact much more of their inherited legacy of natural virtues: a natural acceptance of work, hatred of tyranny and exploitation, and a strong sense of the inviolable dignity of the human person. In the pursuit of a desired object, their behavior reflects these simple virtues:

Either he [the common man] ignores, pays no attention to an object, and certainly does not talk about his desires; or, if he becomes attached to anything, if he makes a decision, he does so vigorously, with concentration, and pursues his object relentlessly. His passion is deep and persevering and no obstacles daunt him when it is necessary to surmount them in order to achieve what he passionately desires and has deeply planned. If the object cannot be achieved, the common man will not stand by with folded arms; he will change his situation, his whole way of life; he will run away, join the army, enter a monastery; often

[10] *Ibid.*, p. 511.

he simply does not survive failure to achieve an object which
has permeated his whole being and has become essential to his
existence . . . he does not hesitate to commit suicide. This,
too, serves to prove to us that for the common, healthy man,
once he has become conscious of his personality (and of its
rights), the barren, useless life of an automaton (without principles and strivings) without meaning and truth . . . becomes
unbearable.[11]

Presumably, suicide registers in an ultimate way an individual's determination and capacity to act. It did not seem
absurd, apparently, to the angry young revolutionary to consider suicide or martyrdom as "healthy" acts of rebellion.
Although he never said it in so many words, he seems at
times to be making the even more absurd proposal that
suicide is a kind of program for social action. Dostoevsky
may well have found his cue here when he created Kirillov,
the brilliantly absurd philosopher of self-destruction in *The
Possessed,* who hoped to liberate men from their fear of
death and of God by his own exemplary suicide. Dobrolyubov
had no such grandiose intentions but the gesture of angry
defiance is the same in each case, and it seems plausible to
read Kirillov as a grotesque extension of Dobrolyubov's light-
minded views on self-destruction. As a plain tactical matter
it would seem that Dobrolyubov's heroes are a little too ready
to die to do the cause much good.

Suicide, in Dobrolyubov's uncomplicated understanding of
it, signifies a simple kind of virtuous strength, which is found
in abundance among the common people. Dobrolyubov is
not suggesting that the new hero will be from the lower

[11] *Ibid.,* p. 512. These contrasting evaluations are taken from the
article "Features of the Russian Common People," in which Dobrolyubov develops his theory of human nature. The central problem is to
harmonize personal with social interests, a synthesis denied the "civilized"
man because "lack of self-confidence" has corroded his sense of his own
rights and caused him to doubt the workings of his mind.

orders. He is saying, rather, that the new man in his search
for moral strength should learn from the people in whose
name he finds the ultimate justifications for his acts. It is the
grievances of the common people that dignify his efforts, it
is their terrible anger that he must arouse, and their strength
that he must direct. They may provide, too, in the example
of their lives, the answer to the fatal breakdown of character
which paralyzed the potential leaders of preceding generations.

With this blueprint in hand, Dobrolyubov set out in search
of the hero of his time among current literary portraits. A
number of examples are rejected out of hand. Any suggestion
of the superfluous man's faint heart is unacceptable because
history has rendered it obsolete. Also invalid are all efforts by
writers to inject their own abstract notions of Russian valor
into an imagined protagonist. The character must have
genuine moral stature, must be capable of action, and must
be presented in compelling and verifiable detail.

Anany, the peasant hero of Pisemsky's *A Bitter Fate*, is
dismissed as absurd.[12] Driven to physical violence by the
landowners' dalliance with his wife, he undermines the moral
value of his position, thereby, and exhibits in his behavior
nothing more than brute strength. Goncharov's Stolz (in
Oblomov), one of the most deliberate efforts to create a
wholly positive, emblematically good man, is dismissed on
two counts: the limited, mundane quality of his morality,
and the abstractness of his literary portrait. The self-disciplined, practical businessman represents an advance, in some
ways, over earlier types, but the practicality of his concerns
denies him participation in loftier matters of social principle.
Of this new bourgeois type, Dobrolyubov says:

[12] *Ibid.*, p. 595.

The best that we can hope for as regards these practical men is that they should resemble Stolz, that is to say, be able to make a clean job of all their affairs without sinking to roguery; they cannot, however, become virile (public) leaders.[13]

"No greater hopes" can be placed in this individual than in the "man of pathos" as "representatives of the public movement" that has come alive in Russia.[14] This is enough to disqualify them as heroes in Russian life, hence, according to the view that recognizes no important differences between life and art, in works of the imagination as well. But Goncharov's failure to create Stolz with the wealth of detail that he lavished on Oblomov is further justification for rejecting him. He moves "in a mist," without effective motivation, without an inner life that explains his self-confident behavior.

Turgenev's *On the Eve* was carefully scrutinized for traces of the new Russian heroism. Insarov, the central male figure, is disqualified on technical grounds—he is a Bulgarian, not a Russian! In addition, he suffers from the blurred delineation that mars the image of Stolz. "As a living image, as a real personality, Insarov is extremely remote from us," Dobrolyubov said, and "is depicted for us only in pale and general outline." [15] Because of his "indomitable loyalty to an idea," he is a challenging figure, nevertheless, to find in a Russian novel. He displays, in the unity of his private and public emotions, and in his total dedication to the liberation of his country, an integration of mind, body, conscience, and heart in the service of a cause that Dobrolyubov was never to find realized in a Russian character. His abstract "outline," vague and unsatisfactory as it is, stands as a master design for the dedicated revolutionary, as relevant in some ways to the Communist present as it was to the generation of the fifties and sixties. The points of similarity are the total mo-

[13] *Ibid.*, p. 598.   [14] *Ibid.*, p. 599.   [15] *Ibid.*, p. 419.

bilization of personal resources in the fulfillment of a single
purpose, always a public one, the unquestioned rejection of
the private pursuits of ordinary man, and a willingness to
endure any sacrifice. He has no doubts: "The happiness of
his whole life is vitally engaged in the single project; he has
no personal ambitions at stake, and no disposition, for example, to quarrel over the leadership of his movement." [16]
"Insarov's love for the freedom of his country lies not alone
in his mind, or in his heart or in his imagination: it permeates his whole being, and whatever else penetrates his
being is transformed by the power of this feeling, submits
to it, and merges with it." [17] Dobrolyubov invokes his favorite
measure to show the effects of frustration on Insarov if
circumstances were to deny him the chance to perform his
duty: "He would die." [18]

Eliminated from the Russian hero competition on a tech-
nicality, Insarov is nevertheless useful to Dobrolyubov as a
yardstick against which to measure the Russians in the same
novel. They are more brilliant and more complex than
Insarov, and men of equally lofty moral aims. Yet they do
not act. They still measure their private interests against the
interests of society—a meaningless dichotomy for Insarov—
and keep their highly developed sense of principle intact by
never risking it in action. The Russians are not members of
an inferior order of humanity. But they are deprived of a
tangible enemy, and cannot play the relatively simple role
of "hero-liberator" against a foreign occupier:

An external enemy, a privileged oppressor, can be attacked
and vanquished far more easily than an internal enemy, whose
forces are spread everywhere in a thousand different shapes, elusive and invulnerable, harassing us on all sides, poisoning our
lives, giving us no rest. . . . This internal enemy cannot be

[16] *Ibid.*, p. 410.   [17] *Ibid.*   [18] *Ibid.*

combated with ordinary weapons; we can liberate ourselves from him only by dispelling the raw, foggy atmosphere of our lives in which he was born, grew up and gained strength, and by surrounding ourselves with an atmosphere in which he will be unable to breathe.[19]

Dobrolyubov's conclusions are gloomy. There is no arena in Russia for Insarov's kind of heroism. In addition, the hostile environment has begun to disfigure the moral character of potential heroes from the earliest days of their education. Only a clear-cut, unambiguous cause could provide the scope for action which would release the latent energies of the men of good will. Dobrolyubov veers close to despair:

(How can you expect heroism here? And if a hero is born, where is he to obtain the light and wisdom to enable him to expend his strength in the service of virtue and truth instead of wasting it? And even if he at last acquires this light and wisdom, how can he, weary and broken, display heroism? How can a toothless squirrel nibble nuts?) [20]

The individual's struggle to reach the threshold of heroic public service is itself a work of heroism, but he has so often suffered serious moral injury in this preliminary battle that the absence of a goal when he finally arrives causes him to succumb to his wounds or waste his remaining energies in trivial activities, "playing the Don Quixote."

IV

Is there any way to break out of the smothering environment without being destroyed in the effort? Are there any more trustworthy signs that the new personality, capable of rising above the world that created him, is likely to make an early appearance? There are, in fact, a number, and through

[19] *Ibid.*, p. 437.   [20] *Ibid.*, p. 433.

a knowledge of them, sketchy and premonitory though they
are, we shall arrive at Dobrolyubov's clearest definition of
the nature of the new hero and of his arenas of action.

Not all the Russian characters in *On the Eve* are "toothless squirrels." There is one person who has moved beyond
the stage of indoctrinated paralysis that afflicts the Russian
men in the novel. This individual, together with two others,
the creations of Goncharov and Ostrovsky, the dramatist,
form, in composite, the most complete profile of the new
man Dobrolyubov was able to find. Curiously, it is a woman's
face that emerges. Dobrolyubov arranges three literary hero-
ines, typical of the impulsive, straightforward feminine figures in Russian literature since Pushkin's Tatyana, in an
ascending order of virtue and effectiveness. Beginning with
Olga in *Oblomov*, proceeding to Elena in Turgenev's *On the
Eve*, and ending with Katerina in Ostrovsky's *Storm*, he
thought he had discovered the basic trend toward stronger,
more resilient characters. Though not yet fully developed,
they were the first authentic images of the new type.

Olga is much preferred by Dobrolyubov to Stolz, the busy
entrepreneur, more German than Russian, whose motivation
is never made clear, whose goals lack public significance. It
is true, the scope of her activity is scarcely of heroic dimensions. But in her hopeless effort to win Oblomov's love
and reclaim him from sloth, she displays genuine moral
strength; she is determined, ready to defy convention, and
the picture of a vital "natural" woman in love. Though the
rehabilitation of a good-natured sluggard is ludicrous as a
social project and is doomed, morever, to failure, she has
acted throughout with understanding and decision. She has,
in addition, recognized one face of the ubiquitous internal
enemy in the pitiable and, "repulsive" figure of Oblomov and
has fought strenuously against it. Finally, Dobrolyubov

praises her because her defeat has not seriously discouraged her. A single hint in a conversation with Stolz that she is readier than he to fight against encroaching "troubles" is taken as final proof of her dignity and promise.[21]

Turgenev's Elena is the same kind of person, endowed in addition with the special radiance of all his feminine characters. Her sensitivity to the suffering of others and a habit of questioning dominant values have prepared her for purposeful activity. But, again, the arena of action open to her is severely restricted. She operates on a trivial scale, giving alms to the poor and rescuing stray kittens. Her one major act, however, her marriage to the Bulgarian activist, Insarov, is carried out with exemplary courage and directness, and in open defiance of social convention. Unfortunately for the novel's topical usefulness, her act removes her from Russia and serves only as a final preparation for a career of active service outside the framework of the novel. But the example of her virtuous behavior in these personal matters indicates the trend toward more and more effective people, specifically, toward a Russian Insarov.[22]

Ostrovsky's Katerina, the heroine of *Storm*, trapped in the suffocating tyranny of her husband's merchant family, is in a more desperate situation. She is bullied by her mother-in-law, is, in effect, deserted by her husband, and finally compromises herself in a hopeless effort to find love outside marriage. Consequently, she acts more drastically to free herself—by committing suicide. Dobrolyubov sees this as an act of defiance, not of despair, the only unblocked path to her liberation. Her refusal to submit to a way of life which smothers all her "natural" strivings is interpreted as the moral equivalent of an act of political rebellion. In the patriarchal household of one merchant family, Dobrolyubov found in

[21] *Ibid.*, p. 216.   [22] *Ibid.*, p. 436.

microcosm the worst of Russia, "the kingdom of darkness."
The rebel against it, then, represents in her single person
vast legions in the outside world.

Katerina's character is analyzed at length to uncover the
source of her strength. The central virtue she possesses is one
which is lacking in the noblest and most brilliant of her
superfluous predecessors. With a mind uncluttered by abstractions, she is motivated solely by the "instinctive consciousness of her inalienable right to life, happiness, and
love." [23] Her awareness of her rights is so urgent that she
meets and passes the supreme test of her courage, the willingness *to risk* death. Convinced that her death symbolizes
an ultimate challenge to the existing order, Dobrolyubov insists that it is a "joyous" and "inspiring thing," serving notice
to tyranny that "it is impossible to live any longer with its
violent and deadening principles." [24] Contrasted with her
husband, a "living corpse," who is afraid to die, Katerina's
death reminds us of her life: ("What joyous, fresh life
breathes to us from the healthy personality which finds the
resolution to put an end to this decaying life at all costs.")[25]
Her death is an inspiration.

V

The problem of the hero's need to break through the en-
circling environment comes into focus in recapitulation.
Knowledge, both factual and theoretical, is a first require-
ment for the new man. But this need has long been met.
First principles have been enunciated; facts to buttress them
have been gathered and analyzed; and the hard-won legacy
of Belinsky's generation is by now common property. Enough
people have survived the Russian environment intact, and
have reached an understanding of the need for radical

[23] *Ibid.,* p. 614.   [24] *Ibid.,* p. 626.   [25] *Ibid.*

change. Now the formula for social consciousness has been brought to the verge of completion as Dobrolyubov conceived it: from fact to idea to intention to longing and finally to action. The last was the most difficult step of all, the insuperable barrier for all the superfluous men. Since Dobrolyubov was sure that knowledge of the laws of history must lead to action, it is clear that an essential ingredient is still missing. It is, we are told, the inner moral strength of individuals which will finally set the mechanism of change in motion. "One must have," it is true, "the mind of a genius," but one must possess as well "the pure heart of an infant and a will of titanic power to dare to enter into a real and effective struggle against the environment." [26] Despite the relative triviality of their feats, and the modesty of their intellectual equipment, Olga, Elena, and Katerina redress a most important imbalance. The superfluous ones had been men whose minds had been overdeveloped at the expense of their hearts. Now Russians had been shown vivid human images who incorporated a finished design for a harmonious relationship between intellect and emotion. This kind of harmony is the final desideratum in the prescription.

Action is generated in the individual's awareness of the discrepancy between the "natural strivings" of his heart and the repeated, senseless violations of human dignity in Russian life. The "natural" man, the vital, wholehearted person who has preserved his total human birthright, confronted with intolerable conditions, will simply refuse to submit to them. This new "strong Russian character," the prospective agent of social change, "is guided not by abstract principles but by practical considerations, and not by fleeting pathos but simply by its nature, by its whole being." [27] Dobrolyubov continues: "The integrity and harmony of this

[26] *Ibid.*, p. 287.   [27] *Ibid.*, p. 597.

character constitute its strength." He is "concentrated and resolute, undeviatingly loyal to the sense of (natural) truth, imbued with faith (in new ideals) and is self-sacrificing (in the sense that he prefers death to life under a system which he detests)." [28]

The hero's moral personality contains the program and the means for action, as well as the guarantee of its success. The hero, in a sense, *is* the revolution. Discussion of doctrine and of action groups—parties, cells, circles, unions—was proscribed in the press. But the impatient Dobrolyubov suggests that as soon as the new hero has appeared in sufficient numbers, the process of change will be launched without the need for further preparations. This man, in whom such extravagant hopes were invested, would not be alone—any number could join his ranks; the virtues and the ideas that would motivate him were available to all, even the illiterate; and he would have willing followers among all oppressed sections of the population.

From his criticism of Goncharov, Turgenev, Saltykov, Pleshcheev, and others, it seems clear that if a literary protagonist acted with moral courage in virtually any personal relationship—a love affair or a family situation, for example—Dobrolyubov was ready to accept his conduct as proof of his capacity to act positively and humanely in other arenas. It was a commonplace of Russian criticism to view a novel's intimate personal settings—Turgenev's drawing rooms and rose arbors, for example—as testing grounds of behavior in more dangerous, frequently unmentionable, arenas of action. With this reduction of scale, it is easier to identify the enemy. Since the crushing of human personality by any means is the ultimate measure of society's evil, artificial conventions, or tyrannical parents, or the compound injustice

[28] *Ibid.*

of woman's status are seen as *causes* of human suffering and acceptable targets for those not yet able to attack the social system *in toto*. A strong, active, flexible person will meet these hostile forces head-on by acting morally as father, husband, lover, employer, or friend.

The enemy, once the "raw, foggy atmosphere" has been dispelled, can be found, and every blow struck against him is valuable. There are only preliminary engagements, it is true, but they lead directly into the final, decisive conflict. Dobrolyubov's essays are full of cryptic references to the approaching moment of explosion.[29] This note, which sounds just below the surface of his writings, promises a no-quarter, physical struggle, which, until now, had been waged only in the indirect discourse of literary criticism. In one of the analogies favored by these critics, as necessary circumlocution, Dobrolyubov compares progress to a road reaching into the future. The road is blocked by an "obstacle" which has thwarted the effort of previous generations, forcing them on hopeless searches for detours, or destroying their characters by its immovability. Dobrolyubov's prescription was simple, and of course unprintable—("blow it up!").[30] Literature stands fully revealed now as a camouflage for more urgent purposes. We may conclude that when Dobrolyubov's hero reaches the height of his moral and intellectual power he will be a disciplined, dedicated, one-man revolutionary movement, incapable of compromise and indifferent to personal defeat. And his literary representation will have been no more than a means to bring him into being.

Dobrolyubov's theory of human nature and his view of the sources of social consciousness have been criticized by some Soviet commentators who felt that he was too inclined

[29] Their dangerous import is confirmed by the censor's deletions.
[30] Dobrolyubov, *Selected Philosophical Essays*, p. 452.

to fix the locus of the conflict between old and new in the
realm of ideas, in the mind, and within the individual's
power to arbitrate. But the profound shift of emphasis since
1930 in the Soviet theory of human behavior has brought
Soviet critics to a more sympathetic consideration of Dobrolyubov's view of freedom.[31] His hero and the new Soviet
man are conscious, disciplined, morally responsible individuals, made free by their knowledge, yet entirely dominated
by their sense of responsibility to history and to the public
welfare. All their choices are preceded by an act of basic
commitment to the cause which may be likened to a one-
party election, that is to say, it is a one-choice decision. But
the theorists of both views place heavy emphasis on will,
initiative, and consciousness within the limits of the code
of loyalty.

It is well to remember that Dobrolyubov frankly disquali-
fies himself from the traditional offices of literary criticism.
"The main task of the literary critic," he wrote, "is to explain
the phenomenon of reality which called a given artistic production into being." [32] This explains the fact that he ignored
the problem of incorporating the new affirmative hero in
conventional literary forms. He assumed, apparently, that the
new hero would succeed the tragic-pathetic figures of the
superfluous era without difficulty on the formal level. The
new literature would be better simply because it reflected a
more advanced social morality. The writer, expected to produce a condensed record of Russian life, had only to worry
about the accuracy of his eye and the soundness of his judgment in discerning the true, the typical, and the significant.
Dobrolyubov never dwelt at length on problems of conflict

[31] This is confirmed in a recent study by V. S. Kruzhkov (*Mirovozzrenie N. A. Dobrolyubova* [Moscow, 1952]).

[32] Dobrolyubov, *Selected Philosophical Essays*, p. 391. Elsewhere he
describes his work as "factual criticism."

or suspense, or of dramatic resolution, whether tragic, comic, affirmative, or inspirational. The degree of his indifference is made clear in his misreading of Ostrovsky's *Storm*. He simply overlooks the fact that Katerina kills herself in a mood of despair, not of defiance. By this ingenious misinterpretation in which he is encouraged by his peculiar view of suicide, he reads his own topical concerns into the play and converts it from a conventional tragic drama into an inspirational document with a kind of happy ending. Dobrolyubov simply felt that an heroic death moved people to admiration. In one of his first prescriptions for the new man he pointed out that he must be unafraid of death, but that if he does die (whether or not by his own hand) the example of his defiant courage, as recorded in some sort of literary communiqué, will surely summon others to fill the gap he has left.

5

CHERNYSHEVSKY
"The Salt of the Salt of the Earth"

Nikolai Chernyshevsky (1828–89) was the encyclopedist of the radical democratic movement. He worked in many disciplines—philosophy, political economy, history, philology, and literary criticism—to provide an intellectual foundation for the movement of political protest he headed. Among many accomplishments, he gave consistency and unity to the doctrine of the literature of social service. In his celebrated dissertation, *The Aesthetic Relations of Art to Reality*, he formulated the critical ideas of his school in the terms of formal philosophical discourse. When no one else could meet his literary standards he wrote a novel, the celebrated *What Is to Be Done?* By his work at these opposite ends of literature, and by the sheer weight of his influence, he established himself as the central figure in the radical literary tradition. He performed the principal work of interpreting (and reducing) Belinsky; he supplied Dobrolyubov with the philosophical assumptions of his journalistic criticism; and his novel is the chief literary souvenir of this phase of the utilitarian movement. The full extent of his influence on Soviet thinking is yet to be assessed. It has become apparent, for example, that he was an enormously important figure in Lenin's life,[1] and must be considered one of the principal authors of the native strain in Soviet Marxian ideology.

[1] See below, pp. 105–6.

In his dissertation Chernyshevsky attempted to fix his view of literature with respect to some of the permanent problems of art—the nature of the beautiful and of artistic invention, and the quality of art's relations with nature and society. His enforced adherence to canons of academic respectability and to the idiom of abstract argument kept his topical concerns in the background, though there is evidence that they were obscure to no one: his followers welcomed the dissertation as a powerful new weapon in their armory; Turgenev reacted as though stung; and the academicians expressed their doubts about its disinterestedness by piously delaying their approval.[2] No doubt, his ultimate point of reference in this essay, as in all else he wrote or did, was the unhealthy condition of Russian society. He wrote a number of popular articles— one an unsigned "self-review" of his published dissertation— to give his ideas a cutting edge for use in the literary battles of the time. With the help of this comment and interpretation by the author we are able to move from a level of abstraction, to the level of polemical comment inhabited by Dobrolyubov, and, finally, to the act of literary creation itself. The novel *What Is to Be Done?*, with its gallery of radiantly virtuous new men, appears as the logical end product of the theory, a kind of pilot-model, designed to illustrate his new aesthetic principles. As a result of this link between theory and practice, Chernyshevsky's work transcends its local origins in Russian intellectual history and presents the essence of the radical utilitarian literary position.

The tenor of Chernyshevsky's approach is suggested by his approval of Plato's scornful estimate of art's value to a well-ordered society. The Russian critic felt that Plato's "sar-

[2] N. G. Chernyshevsky, *Estetika*, ed. N. G. Bogoslovsky (Moscow-Leningrad, 1939). See Bogoslovsky's introductory article for a summary of these reactions.

casms" were perhaps too cruel and "one-sided" for modern times.[3] But his sympathy with the underlying trend of Plato's thought is evident, and there is an ironic forecast, too, of the relations between poet and magistrate—and of the arguments used to justify them—in the Soviet Union:

First of all Plato thought that man must be the citizen of a state, must not dream about things not needed by the state, and must live nobly and actively, promoting the material and moral welfare of his fellow citizens. . . . He looked on science and art, as he looked on everything, not from the scholarly or artistic but from the social and moral point of view. Man does not live to be a scholar or an artist (as many great philosophers have thought, among them Aristotle) but science and art must serve man's welfare.[4]

Chernyshevsky was not concerned, of course, with protecting the stability of a future social order from art's subversion. In his view a frivolous, irresponsible, or self-serving art was simply a pernicious waste of time. Therefore, though he agreed with Plato in demeaning all views of art as "play," or as an object of pleasure, his attitude was one of suspicious impatience with art, rather than of fear of its effects. His tone is drastic, nevertheless, and his denunciations are sweeping.

Chernyshevsky begins with one basic proposition: that art

[3] See Chernyshevsky's review of a contemporary translation of Aristotle's *Poetics*, "O Poezii, sochinenie Aristotelya," in *Estetika*, pp. 224–28.

[4] *Ibid.*, p. 226. Chernyshevsky's views differ considerably from Soviet attitudes toward Plato and Aristotle. Despite resemblances between the authoritarian elements in Plato's prescription for the model society and certain aspects of Soviet reality, his overall position is rejected as "idealist" and reactionary. Aristotle, on the other hand, is celebrated as the first materialist aesthetician, the first "predecessor," therefore, of the Marxist aesthetic (see L. I. Timofeev, *Teoriya literatury* [Moscow, 1938], p. 42). Aristotle is a figure of special importance in this study because his theory of tragedy is the most enduring obstacle in the way of the literature of positive heroes.

is in all ways subordinate to life, that it is dependent on the external world for its substance, its form, its energy, its relevance to human affairs, and, inasmuch as it is a concern of art at all, for its appeal to man's sense of beauty.[5]

The severity of his attack on all inflated estimates of art's mission is prompted in part by the extreme position of his hand-picked opponent, the German idealist, Vischer.[6] But in his denunciation of Vischer he challenged positions much closer to home, notably Turgenev's. He quarrels with all views which assert that art improves on reality, or completes or gives permanence to it, or has the right to impose on it a design of its own. Art dare pretend to no such preeminence over the world it depends on and rather imperfectly reflects. And when Vischer maintained that art was a search for absolute truth, above the imperfections and the impermanence of natural phenomena, and that fantasy, which departs entirely from reality and bases its perceptions on dreams, was the highest form of art, Chernyshevsky felt that an ultimate absurdity had been reached. In rebuttal, he asserted flatly that the material of art is always and unavoidably drawn from life, and that art may record experience well or badly, but it may never claim to transcend its model, which is the source of all significance and beauty. Art is essentially a medium for discovering the meaningful facts in the real world, and for transmitting this information directly to the reader. Its value depends on the accuracy with which this relatively humble act of reporting is carried out; and any effort by the artist to interfere in this process by embellishing the original, or by imposing "artificial" formal patterns on it, can only result in falsification.

[5] *Estetika*, pp. 12–13 and pp. 50–55.
[6] Friedrich Theodor Vischer, whose six-volume *Aesthetik oder Wissenschaft des Schoenen* (Leipzig, 1846–58) is the single source he cites in his dissertation.

The imaginative faculty itself comes under attack in this connection. It is first of all weak:

The power of our imagination is extremely limited and its creations are very pale and feeble compared with reality. The most vivid imagination is overwhelmed by the thought of the millions of miles that separate the earth from the sun.[7]

Careful observation of everyday life indicates that the most intensely imagined hero or villain can always be eclipsed by instances from life, and that art deals only with "copies of what is provided by the phenomenon of reality."[8] Elsewhere he suggests that the imagination is associated with self-serving daydreams and the fantasies of self-indulgence. Here he collides head-on with Turgenev and others who felt that the artist's vocation was a kind of priestcraft, that the truth of art was a special kind of personal vision, and that the imaginative ordering of experience was the indispensable means to its unique discoveries.

Chernyshevsky's definition of what art is not and cannot do rests on his view of the aesthetic process itself. The beautiful, as we have seen, is a property of nature and is not "created" by the artist. Even in its original state the beautiful is a by-product of natural processes, incidental to their purposes, and irrelevant for the most part to human life. The enjoyment of beauty is a secondary aspect of the emotion communicated by art, but is one of the many services, nevertheless, that art provides. To maintain that pleasure in the beautiful is the end of art is to debase it, Chernyshevsky insisted, to reduce it to the level of a good dinner or a comfortable apartment.[9]

Art's purposes are far more solemn and more profoundly

[7] From the seventh of the "Essays on the Gogol Period of Russian Literature" (N. G. Chernyshevsky, *Selected Philosophical Essays* [Moscow, 1953], p. 489).
[8] *Ibid.*   [9] See *Estetika*, pp. 229–30.

concerned with vital problems of human existence: "The source and aims of art are the needs of man," Chernyshevsky wrote in his "self-review," [10] and the legitimate province of art, as a consequence, is simply "everything that interests man." [11] Freed from arbitrary limitations on its subject matter and endowed with a purpose much greater than pleasurable gratification, art is prepared for the career of service which alone entitles it to man's highest respect.

Having arrived at Belinsky's definition of literature's basic moral purposes, though by a different route, Chernyshevsky twice (and rather casually) connects the idea of the beautiful with these purposes. The search for beauty must not become the artist's primary activity, but, since it is a legitimate end, let the artist know where to look for it. Beauty is found in life and in nature but there are differences of degree in its intensity. No landscape painting or nature lyric can bear comparison with the representation of man, himself, in art. Since man is nature's "highest" product he is, therefore, its most beautiful object:

In the entire sensuous world man is the highest being, therefore, the human personality is the highest being in the world which is accessible to our feelings, and all other aspects of existence partake of the beautiful only to the degree that they allude to or remind us of man. . . . The highest sphere of the beautiful is human society.[12]

Since a moral and social ideal of man is at the very heart of the concept of the beautiful, the artist who represents virtuous men in their social role is assured that he is at the same time "copying" nature and conveying beauty to his readers.

In another connection Chernyshevsky identifies the beau-

[10] *Ibid.*, p. 206. [11] *Ibid.*, p. 88.
[12] Quoted in Timofeev, *Teoriya literatury*, pp. 45–46.

tiful with the morally and socially desirable. Summoning
Aristotle to his support, Chernyshevsky includes both elements of the famous distinction between life "as it is" and
life "as it should be" as essential ingredients of his realism.
In his dissertation he offers this definition: "The beautiful
is the essence in which we see life as it should be according
to our concepts." [13] There can be no doubt that however
"should be" is defined—as the necessary, the probable, the
desirable, or the hoped for—it introduces an alien element
which may challenge realism's canon of verisimilitude. Elsewhere he puts it this way: "The beautiful is that in which
we see life as we understand it and wish it." [14] Chernyshevsky did not insist too much on this point—it is even possible
that he did not sense the difficulty—but, as we shall see, by
injecting his expectations into the fabric of his own novel,
without distinguishing them from "actual" events, he dam-
aged his novel so badly that he subverted his own purposes.

On this abstract level Chernyshevsky's thought pursues a
course already observed in Belinsky: from a broad attack on
conventional restrictions, he goes on to impose a new pattern
of limitations on the artist. In this pattern we discover the
actual conditions of art's subordination to "life," to "nature,"
and to "human needs." Art occupies a secondary position,
for example, with respect to the social and natural sciences:

Poetry distributes an enormous amount of information among
the mass of readers, and, what is more important, a familiarity
with concepts developed by science—this is poetry's great significance for life.[15]

Art will convey this data in its own idiom but its value to
mankind will depend on the performance of this task, not
the grace or skill with which it is done. The transmission

---

[13] Chernyshevsky, *Estetika*, p. 8.   [14] *Ibid.*, p. 20.
[15] *Ibid.*, p. 231.

of this kind of data is a logical consequence of literature's obligation to serve human needs and to deal with whatever "interests men." When we realize what "interested" Chernyshevsky and what he assumed "interested" the reading public, it becomes clear that under the pretense of broadening literature's horizons he has only shifted its focus to material as marginal to the concerns of realism as the "fantasies" of Vischer. By converting art into an educational medium, or a means of publicizing the findings of other disciplines, he renders more explicit his desire to make art's local utility the first standard for judging it. The desire to communicate data and ideas about social and economic problems—the status of women, the advantages of producer cooperatives, his ethic of social service—was Chernyshevsky's primary motive in writing his own novel.

His general insistence that art subordinate itself to "life" or even to human needs need not, in itself, have offended leading writers. The view that art existed for its own or for the artist's sake had no great currency during the fruitful years of the classical tradition. But Chernyshevsky's further restrictive definition of these terms betrays the real narrowness of intention, which was decisive in alienating the great writers from his views. Turgenev reacted violently to Chernyshevsky's celebrated description of art as life's "surrogate," [16] or "textbook," and raised important objections to the whole radical aesthetic:

Concerning Chernyshevsky's book—here is my chief objection to it: in his eyes, art, as he himself expresses it, is only the surrogate for reality, for life—and in essence is suited only for immature people. Whichever way he turns, this idea of his lies as the basis of everything. And this in my opinion is nonsense. In the real world there is no Shakespearean Hamlet—or perhaps he exists—but Shakespeare discovered him and made him public

[16] *Ibid.*, p. 83.

property. Chernyshevsky takes a great deal on himself if he imagines he can always go to the heart of life. . . . No, brother, his book is false and harmful.[17]

Art is only a substitute for firsthand experience, or, as Chernyshevsky sometimes puts it, it "reminds" (the word suggests vacation snapshots or family portraits on the wall) the reader of what he has already experienced. He could, of course, simply assert that this was so. But to establish his point he had finally to come to terms with literature's traditional modes of expression: the comic, the sublime, and—a major obstacle for the advocate of an optimistic literature— the tragic.

The persistence of tragic forms through history, and their repeated success in organizing experience into meaningful moral patterns, presented Chernyshevsky with a primary challenge. His response was to discredit the entire tragic mechanism by demonstrating its rigidity and falsity when set against the variety, the accidents, and the consequent unpredictability of experience. The source of tragedy's inflexibility he traced back to Aristotle, who taught, he said, "the writing of tragedy . . . according to recipe":

From this it is evident that Aristotle as an aesthetician belongs to the times of the decline of art: instead of a living spirit there is the teaching of rules, a cold formalism.[18]

The tragic "rules" are harmful because they offer only a single mold into which a countless number of human situa-

---

[17] Letter to V. P. Botkin (July 25, 1885), *Sobranie sochinenii*, XI (Moscow, 1949), 130. We simply note here the vehemence of his feelings and the quality of his objections. In the flurry of letters he wrote after he read the dissertation his language is sometimes even stronger— words like "filth," "vermin," "outrage," are close to the limits of the well-mannered Turgenev's vocabulary.

[18] Chernyshevsky, "O Poezii, sochinenie Aristotelya," in *Estetika*, p. 228. The attack on tragedy is developed at much greater length in the dissertation itself.

tions must be forced, and they offer only one kind of response for the spectator, catharsis through pity and terror. The tyranny of this single pattern rests on the unchallenged supremacy of formal devices and the uncritical acceptance of primitive superstitions. The concept of fate, for example, is an outworn legacy from the primitive Greeks without basis in scientific fact. Nature is not the capricious, vengeful force the Greeks called fate, but is, as modern science has shown, supremely indifferent to the just or unjust punishment of individual men. A formula which rendered the tragedies of accident bearable for a primitive people has no relevance for modern man. And with fate must be discarded the ancient notion of tragic guilt blindly incurred and inexorably punished. Even in the higher tragic forms of modern times, in which the conflict is between two individuals, or between the conflicting desires of a single individual, the effort to resolve the dramatic situation through the intervention of moral law merely repeats the error of the Greeks in a new form. A glance at history is enough to demonstrate that the evil deeds of great public men are more often than not exempt from external correction by moral law or by the public conscience. Test the artificial symmetry of Macbeth's rise and fall against the life of Gustavus Adolphus, who died by accident at the height of his conquests, whose death, therefore, can in no way be construed as a punishment for his crimes. The history of the Swedish king is closer to the rule than the exception and we must, therefore, regard the enforced tragic destiny of literary heroes simply as adherence to a literary convention, not as a description of experience itself.[19] This is not to say, of course, that human experience is not at times tragic. But art's treat-

[19] The question of fate and accident are discussed at greatest length in the dissertation itself. See *Estetika*, pp. 21–30.

ment of suffering should correspond to its occurence in life both as to incidence and as to cause. Thus viewed, the tragic takes its place with many other kinds of experiences as simply "the terrible" in human life. Tragedy is not banished from art, but its monopoly must be ended.

The tight pattern of inevitability in tragic dramas in which denouement flows inescapably from the previous action is also brought into question by Chernyshevsky, and again the diversity of experience is invoked to lift its restrictions from the artist. The kingpin of *tragic* inevitability is the concept of fate. But once it is removed the result is not necessarily the reign of accident in art. Rather the true design and coherence of the necessary in actual experience takes its place.[20] Thus a genuine inevitability supplied by life replaces the false inevitability of form which shapes life to its own monotonous ends. Chernyshevsky enjoins the artist to

choose the coherent and lifelike event and tell it as it was in actuality: if your choice is not bad (and this is so easy!) then your story, not recast from reality, will be better than any story remade according to the "demands of art," that is, according to the requirements of literary display.[21]

Here Chernyshevsky denies the writer the right to manipulate experience at all. He attempts to anticipate objections: "But what then will manifest creativity? In that you [the artist] will know how to separate the necessary from the unnecessary, what belongs to the essence of the event from the extraneous." [22] For the artist as Turgenev conceived him, this completely denies his creative function, placing the emphasis exclusively on acuteness of observation.

[20] Chernyshevsky's extreme position is not shared by many members of his school. Timofeev favors a tight dramatic structure for all prose narrative. In his prescription he actually uses the Aristotelian concepts of "tying" and "untying" (Russian *zavyazka* and *razvyazka*) as the basic moments in the organization of the action.
[21] *Estetika*, p. 240.   [22] *Ibid.*, p. 241.

Chernyshevsky turns at last to the conventional tragic hero. His challenge to this traditional literary type is issued casually and is directed only against falsified historical novels, but it brings us close, we may feel sure, to the heart of his intention:

What purpose is served by these invented heroes who stand in the way of real heroes, who are introduced only to "provide," with their fabricated adventures, "a poetic unity" to the representation of the epoch, as if it were impossible to find truly poetic events in the life of our current heroes.[23]

With the apparatus of tragedy lying in ruins at his feet— fate, guilt, inevitability all destroyed by exposure to "real life"—the way is cleared for the entrance into literature of other kinds of heroes to whom an infinite variety of destinies will be permitted. One of these, of course, will be the courageous, virtuous man who instructs by his example and whose victory over hostile circumstance is expected to stimulate others to imitate him. This remains implicit in Chernyshevsky's formal writings on aesthetics, but it is made perfectly clear in his critical articles. He issued the first call for new heroes in 1856, in a review of Ogarev's poetry, which noted the passing of the superfluous men, in terms already made familiar to us by Dobrolyubov, and went on to describe the type that would replace them, and, presumably, the long line of tragic heroes extending back to the Greeks:

We are still waiting for this successor, who, having accustomed himself to the truth from childhood, regards it not with tremendous ecstasy but with joyous love; we are awaiting such a man and his speech, a very cheerful . . . calm . . . decisive speech, in which would sound not theory's timidity before life, but proof that reason can achieve mastery over life and that man can harmonize his life with his convictions.[24]

[23] *Ibid.*
[24] N. G. Chernyshevsky, *Estetika i literaturnaya kritika,* ed. B. I. Bursov (Moscow-Leningrad, 1951), p. 409. The article in question,

Here certainly is a design for a literary hero who, granted lasting "mastery over life," is as antithetical to Oedipus and Hamlet as he is to Oblomov and Rudin. It is clear from this and from other sources that the Russian advocates of a "civic" literature hoped, by reversing a local trend, to effect a major change in the direction of world literature. The extent of their expectations is suggested by Chernyshevsky's testy dismissal of Shakespeare as a model for modern writers: "Now . . . when the reasons for objecting to the too passionate imitation of French writers have passed, it would perhaps be as unnatural to give Shakespeare uncontrolled dominion over our aesthetic convictions . . . to introduce his tragedies as examples of everything that is beautiful." [25]

It is not surprising that a spokesman for radical social change would distrust those aspects of tragedy which counseled reconciliation with the status quo, and would dismiss the intervention of restraining forces, in whatever guise, as manifestations of the vested interests of inertia. But his willingness to invade the inner frontiers of the literary craft —in what doubtless appeared to him as a gesture of liberation—promised such wholesale destruction that it seemed to invite formal anarchy. Under the pretext of removing one ancient formula, he seems to have deprived art of the right and of the means to organize experience at all. His repeated references to the role of chance in life threaten to reduce literature to a purposeless description of the accidental. We may justly ask what traditional prerogatives of the artist he proposes to keep, what he proposes to substitute for the aspects he discards, and how, if at all, the artist's functions will differ from those of mere copyist and moralizer?

"The Poetry of Ogarev," appeared three years before "What Is Oblomovism?"

[25] *Estetika*, p. 243.

As we have seen, the essence of creativity lies in the writer's ability to separate the necessary from the extraneous. The artist must be a superb observer. But he is also an observer with *a priori* notions that direct his eye and help him to discern the necessary, the general, the probable, and the significant in the chaos of experience. The principle of selectivity, first invoked by Belinsky, is the only substitute Chernyshevsky offers for invention, manipulation, and all formal organizing techniques, which are suspect in his eyes because they embellish, rigidify, or otherwise falsify life. An art based on selectivity alone must find its design in life and must therefore seem at first glance to be totally dependent on observation. But the second aspect of selection, the principles that lie behind the observing eye, introduces value judgments to an almost unlimited extent, and tends to reverse the order of priorities in the creative process. Whereas formal structure at first seemed to be conferred by life, the reverse often turns out to be the case: design is stamped upon the work by the defining principles, life becomes a source of documentation for them, and the artist finds himself merely an illustrator of principles derived from extraliterary sources. By demeaning formal discipline, Chernyshevsky has opened literature to alien material, and at the same time diminished literature's ability to digest it.

In his bout with the tragic, Chernyshevsky has failed to replace other elements he can ill afford to ignore. Nothing is said of the psychological process by which aesthetic emotion is transmitted. Tragedy weakens the will of the spectator by summoning superhuman antagonists to crush the hero with whom he is identified. Viewed thus, without allowance for the disengagement permitted the spectator through catharsis, or for the possibility of affirmation achieved despite defeat, tragic literature is simply "pessimistic." Chernyshevsky is obliged, one would think, to replace the traditional effects of "pity and terror" with an equivalent combination—"respect and inspiration," for example—more suitable to his "optimistic" purposes. But no such effort is made. The nature of the aesthetic transaction is largely ignored by him, as it is, for the most part, by his successors. Though it is never made explicit, a theory of direct identification between the reader and the hero, with emulation in thought and *in action* as the end, underlies the whole of his theory.

When we add the obligation to choose (and, of course, to exclude) material to all the other roles that are assigned to literature—the conveying of "scientific" ideas, the representation of beauty as aspiration, the stimulation to action as an aesthetic aim, the portraiture of men who have gained "mastery over life"—it becomes evident that the artist operates with a set of blinders at least as restrictive of his freedom as the formal demands of tragedy, and far less congenial to the possibilities of his medium. When we consider, further, that each of the charges laid on literature is subject to specific interpretation—the ideas to be propagated, the aspirations to be fostered, the action to be encouraged, and the masterful type to be shown—we comprehend the distance Chernyshevsky has traveled from his initial insistence on art's subordination to life to his final assertion that art rises above life not only "to explain it" but "to pass judgment" on it. He has reassigned the artist to the position of superior vantage from which great works of art issue, but under such a burden of injunctions and inhibitions that we may predict the kind of directed verdict the artist must render under such conditions.

II

One of the critics' aims was to validate their credentials as guardians and supervisors of the literary product. It was

the intemperate pressing of this claim that alienated so many
of the important writers, and drove them into opposition.
In the case of Chernyshevsky's *What Is to Be Done?* [26] the
friction between critic and writer is happily eliminated since
the critic himself has turned novelist and undertaken to fulfill his own importunate demands. For this reason we may
consider this work with the certainty that it stands as a perfect point-by-point illustration of the radical democrats' blueprint for fiction.

Allowance has to be made for Chernyshevsky's inexperience with the craft, and the inhibiting conditions under
which it was written: he was a prisoner in the Peter and
Paul Fortress en route to years of exile. These circumstances
may be advanced to forgive flaws in the execution but they
do not excuse the eccentricities of its conception. In point of
fact, the imperfections on the novel's surface point to faults
in the novel's design, and to the principal difficulties inherent
in this kind of writing.

In the tension already noted in Chernyshevsky's thought
between description and aspiration, between "is" and
"should be," he has yielded in practice almost entirely to
the second. The desired and the hoped-for dominate not
only the selection of characters—the novel's subtitle, "From
Stories about the New Men," tells us that we have at last
caught up with Dobrolyubov's quarry—but determine their
every action and utterance. With the initial decision to
write a *roman à thèse*, picturing the future, and personifying
worthy moral qualities, Chernyshevsky might have made the
clean break with reality that distinguishes certain kinds of
Utopian fiction. Though the "is" in his novel is hidden
under a heavy gloss of "should be," he nevertheless insists on

[26] The novel first appeared in the March, April, and May issues of
Sovremennik in 1863. It was an immediate success with the revolutionary
youth because of its partisan views, and failed for the same reason with
other factions.

grounding his novel in the illusion of the contemporary and the everyday. The only deliberate use of literary artifice is an attempt to create suspense through the melodrama of a faked suicide. On this flimsy device is heaped the heavy load of instruction—by example, by exposition, and by exhortation— that forms the substance of the novel. Every motive of the characters is contained in a creed. An ethical theory under- lies the entire work and guides the behavior of the principals at every step in the story of a model marriage between two representatives of the new men, a subsequent triangle in- volving a third new man, and a miraculously rational resolu- tion.[27] The novel illustrates Chernyshevsky's formula for marital relations, with its ludicrously elaborate code for as- suring the rights of each partner, which is, at the same time, a manifesto calling for the liberation of women. The charac- ters' control over their emotions rests on the moral formula, "enlightened self-interest," borrowed without alteration from the British Utilitarians, which is commended to the reader's attention for his instruction. These marriages are made com- plete—in this arid atmosphere we might almost say consum- mated—by a program of shared activity in the service of others, as scientists, doctors, educators, and directors of coop- eratives. At the basis of these doctrinal tags which direct

[27] The resolution is connected with the "suicide," which is arranged to ease Vera's transfer of affections from Lopukhov to Kirsanov and is explained to her when she has completed the switch, bringing the story to a happy conclusion. Lopukhov by this time has found himself another "new person" and they all settle down in a very proper *ménage à quatre*. The poverty of invention reflects Chernyshevsky's indifference to formal problems. His own plan for the novel is instructive: he conceived it as a kind of illustrated manual for his *Encyclopedia of Knowledge and Life*. He wrote to his wife from prison: "I am rework- ing this book in the lightest, most popular spirit, almost in the form of a novel, with anecdotes, scenes . . . so that it will be read by people who read almost nothing but novels." (Quoted by N. Vodovozov in a postscript to a recent Soviet edition of the novel, N. G. Cherny- shevsky, *Chto Delat?* [Moscow, 1947], p. 465.)

their lives and which their lives, in turn, illustrate stands the public emotion "Love of Mankind." No action of the characters occurs—or can conceivably occur without forfeiting their standing as "new men"—which violates this all-embracing commitment.

One character stands apart from all the others, a truly "uncommon man" among uncommon men. Though he plays a minor role in the central intrigue—intervening at one crucial point to set everything right with his superior wisdom —the entire novel, in a sense, is his vehicle. He is Rakhmetov, the "rigorist," and, though Chernyshevsky can never say so, a dedicated professional revolutionary. Having chosen his career consciously and deliberately, he embarks on a fantastic training program designed to broaden his mind, toughen his body, and harden his will. His regime of gymnastics, hard physical labor, raw beefsteak diet, voracious though selective reading, and sexual continence reaches an absurd climax when he arises one morning soaked in blood from head to foot after a night spent on a bed of nails. Once trained, every resource of his heart and mind is submitted to a self-defined concept of duty. He is impersonal, abrupt, and businesslike in all his relations with others.[28] Though he is once tempted by a beautiful young widow, he is "not free" to love or to marry. In all his character traits he is a nearly perfect early model of the Bolshevik. He does not have the apparatus of the Party to discipline and direct his energies and Chernyshevsky cannot tell us much about his specific political activity, but in his *mystique* of dedication and, above all, in his reliance on a will of steel, Rakhmetov prefigures the personal moral code of the "leather men in leather jackets." He is, like them, a member of a tiny elite which aspires to change the world. "They are few in number," Chernyshevsky wrote,

[28] For Rakhmetov's biography, see *Chto Delat?* pp. 258–78.

"but through them the life of all mankind expands." He is "marked" for leadership, but not by birth or intrinsically superior qualities. He is a self-made superman who has shaped himself into a revolutionary instrument out of the natural resources that are given to all men. Men like him are, at the height of their powers, "the flower of the best people, the movers of movers, they are the salt of the salt of the earth." [29]

It is the mood of superlatives, of course, that robs him of literary credibility, and it is the power of his will, the most important ingredient of his character, that makes him aesthetically impossible. (It is clear that the political saint is no easier to present in a novel than any other kind.) A great deal of the difficulty has to do with the fact that the characters' primary motivations are doctrinal. Yet this is an indispensable attribute of political men—only by subordinating themselves to these guiding concepts did the new men achieve the mastery over events and over themselves that gave them the freedom and the courage to act. The new man enters this state of grace not by study alone (Dobrolyubov has already suggested that too much intellection might blur the need to act), nor by responding consciously or unconsciously to one's experience as a member of an economic class. The awareness comes through a simple revelation, by opening one's eyes and stepping from the "cellars" of prejudice and regressive values into the sunlight of natural truth.[30] The discovery of "natural truth," which is most often achieved with the help of an earlier convert, is then followed by a deliberate decision to act forever after in the light of its dictates:

Consciously and firmly he decided to renounce all the advantages and honors which he might have demanded of life in

[29] *Ibid.*, p. 278.   [30] *Ibid.*, p. 102.

order to work for the benefit of others, finding his own greatest interest in the pleasure from that kind of work.[31]

The life that follows is rigorous, dedicated, and self-disciplined, we are told, but quite lacking in hesitation, anguish, or doubt. When the new man has reached his full stature, he is a model of modest, virtuous behavior. He has overcome "inertia," "ennui," "exaltation," "romanticism," "whimsicality," all the vices of his superfluous predecessors, and has learned "tact, coolness, activity . . . the realization of common sense in action." He is "bold," "resolute," and of "irreproachable honesty." [32] His private moral behavior is inseparable from his public activity, since the publicizing of every phase of his existence is one of the *social* functions of the novel. He emerges finally as the monolithic personality Dobrolyubov sought in his criticism, with hardly an identifying mark of his humanity, or a single flaw to involve him in interesting, tension-producing situations. He makes difficult decisions, but the process itself is so calmly rational, and the outcome so foregone, that no sense of loss or sacrifice is communicated. Every source of the novel's unreality can be traced back finally to the qualities of the new men—their total self-assurance (as smug as it is arrogant), their absolute incorruptibility, their unquestioned expectations, and their apparent inability to hesitate, stumble, or fail.[33]

The falseness of the hero guarantees the failure of the work of art in this kind of writing. Much may be attributed to Chernyshevsky's inexperience as a writer or to his indiffer-

---

[31] *Ibid.*, p. 92.　　　　　[32] *Ibid.*, p. 190.

[33] Chernyshevsky anticipated this problem: "Kirsanov and Lopukhov appeared to the majority of the public as heroes, as people of the loftiest kind, perhaps even as idealized figures, perhaps even as people who could not exist in reality because of this too lofty nobility. No, my friends, they do not stand too high, you stand too low" (*Chto Delat?* p. 302). This hardly solves the problem: the *relative* moral positions of the literary heroes and the readers are unchanged.

ence to the canons of the developing literary tradition that
surrounded him. But the novel's sins are more significant as
errors of commission than of omission, errors which arise
from the deepest operating assumptions of the radical literary doctrine as formulated then and still practiced today.

This kind of novel begins, as we have already suggested,
from a tiny patch of reality which is subjected to specific
ideological tests to determine its significance, its typicality,
and its potentialities for development.[34] Then, through all
the openings Chernyshevsky permitted himself, the certified
area is saturated with the writer's interpretations and expectations, and it is at this point that the question of "isness"
and "oughtness" (as Harold Laski put it) comes to the fore.

The Russian radicals misused the idea as it was conceived
by Aristotle and other formulators of the tragic discipline.
In tragedy, "life as it should be" exists largely as a negative
inference to be drawn from the drama's presentation of life
as it *is* and should *not* be. The Russian radicals on the other
hand incorporated their vision of life as it should be into
the literary work itself and presented it as the inevitable
and desirable extension of life as it is. This involves a second,
related distinction. Tragedy rests in part on the premise of
an unchanging universe. Faced with the same set of conditions that confront the hero of tragedy, let the reader not be
tempted to emulate him. The didactic aim, in broad terms,
is stasis, reconciliation, and harmony. But in the dialectical
view of the universe, not only are the same set of conditions
never repeated, but change toward the better is in the nature

[34] No one can say, of course, that the new men did not exist in the
Russia of the sixties. Though he pointedly denied it, Chernyshevsky
might well have been writing about himself or his friends. If he had
been immodest enough to make himself the hero of a novel, the long,
bitter struggle between the forces of tsarism and his own revolutionary
toughness would certainly have produced a better story than the moraliz-
ing do-gooders he chose to represent.

of things and is to be sought and encouraged. A strong quotient of "shall be," therefore, is added to "should be," and it is not difficult to anticipate the moment when "should be" is translated into the "must be" of the five-year plan and other policies of the Soviet government. The writer, in other words, invites the reader to view the future through the prism of an ethical imperative that is soon to be enacted. The juxtaposition of "is" and "should be" gives rise, in this case, not to reconciliation but to discontent, which is balanced with the assurance that the better future is within man's grasp, provided he accepts the obligation to bring it into being. Thus, tragedy, in any form, is challenged at its very foundation by the optimism of the dialectic.

Entanglement with the future involves the writer in a number of difficulties. It confronts him first of all with the general problem, perhaps insoluble in the nature of things for the realist, of "describing" what has not yet taken place. He runs the serious risk of setting forth his optimistic prediction of the course of events, reflecting his own aspirations, while the world, containing a far more complex and much less hopeful "emergent reality," stands by, as it were, to correct his predictions. Hindsight suggests the hollowness of Chernyshevsky's optimism: the belief that Russia's future well-being lay in the spread of a new sexual morality, in the steady multiplication of the number of morally motivated people (the new men), in the gradual spread of Fourierist producer cooperatives—all this now seems like the "fantasy" which Chernyshevsky himself attacked so strenuously in his dissertation.

In the shorter view the risk is even graver. The novel's immediate function, as Chernyshevsky saw it, was to hasten progressive social forces by giving them attractive publicity, and by enlisting the efforts of larger and larger numbers of men in their service. The new man, Chernyshevsky said, represented one man in ten in Russian life at the time the novel was written.[35] The number was growing irresistibly, would soon constitute a majority, and, by this simple arithmetic progression, Russia might in a very short time enter a new era.[36] *What Is to Be Done?* is a primary document in the recruiting campaign, and exerts in this way its own pressure toward social change. In this short-run view the writer's commitment to the future is concerned with that hairline between the present and the immediate sequence of moments that follow it. He stirs men's emotions, in the hope of pushing them over the borderline between conviction and action, and assures them that their concerted actions will bring what all virtuous men want, and relatively painlessly at that. The serenity and assurance of his heroes, then, involves him in the deceptive promises of the propagandist, and their portrait is as false, for what it omits, as recruiting posters in the post office.

The picture of the whole truth, we must conclude, would have endangered the novel's extraliterary purposes. The writer who predicted the mangling or destruction of such a person in his unequal struggle with Russian reality, or showed him wearied by the passage of time and the endless series of obstacles stretching into the future, or discovered a dangerous flaw in his character or in his view of the world —who, in short, suggested the bitter conflict or the frustrations or the suffering he faced—would have contributed,

[35] Apparently there are two categories of new men, the leaders and the rank-and-filers. The first group remains small and select, while the second group is capable of infinite numerical expansion. There is a contradiction between the kinds of political action each is to engage in. It is possible they represent alternative paths to social change: the rank-and-filers proceed there by peaceful, evolutionary means; the leaders are to direct this movement, or, if it becomes necessary, to undertake acts of violence.

[36] See *Chto Delat?* pp. 12, 55–56, and 191.

however unwittingly, to the mood of futility which arose from the literature of alienation. This, at least, is the radical position and, stated thus, it serves to illustrate the central dilemma of their tradition. We need not wonder at the uproar on the left that greeted Turgenev's portrait of the new man in *Fathers and Sons*. Bazarov is not simply a revolutionary who is defeated through his own fallibility; what was more offensive to the practicing revolutionaries of the time, his downfall is brought about through a fatal split along the crucial and vulnerable line where personal emotions are fused, according to the radical critics, with social convictions. On this point and on many others, Turgenev's novel, within its small compass, demonstrates remarkable prescience about the destinies of the coming generation of Russian revolutionary youth, particularly the nihilists and terrorists, both anarchist-tinged and both inclined, therefore, to put a huge value on their acts as personal statements. Both as description and as forecast, we may say in the idiom of the radicals that *Fathers and Sons* is truer "to real life" than *What Is to Be Done?*

Chernyshevsky's work, which exposes so many of its deeper inadequacies through its surface ineptitudes, is of course only the first crude effort in a prolific tradition. More skillful writers were to ring ingenious variations on the basic theory he set forth. But his failures have served to outline sharply the most troubling creative problem in this tradition: the matter of assimilating the ideological dosage with the fictional illusion of life, or more precisely of rendering plausible—in effect of disguising—the point where the leap is made from the present to the future, or from the actual to the desired.

One other quality of the novel has been evident from the beginning of this inquiry: that it is a thorough exercise in reducing important areas of human experience to political terms. Thus Chernyshevsky's "mastery" over life is in reality a mastery of the political means to change the social order; the fusion of personal life with convictions is actually a subordination of private emotion to the dictates of public attitudes. Finally, it is clear that Chernyshevsky's attempt to discredit "the demands of art," as false and unreal, together with his repeated invocation of the variety and disorder of "real life" to accomplish this end, is then followed by the substitution, under various guises, of the "demands" of revolutionary politics as the organizing principles for the successful work of art. We may not doubt that the politicalizing of the literary process is the final destination of his zigzag journey.

It is in these terms that the novel was received by later representatives of his trend. Plekhanov seems to have discovered a universal value in Chernyshevsky's evocation of the moral code of revolutionaries and of the generalized human striving for a better world:

Who has not read and reread this famous work? Who has not been charmed by it, who has not become cleaner, better, braver, and bolder under its philanthropic influence? Who has not imitated the purity of the principal characters? Who, after reading this novel, has not reflected on his personal life, has not subjected his personal striving and tendencies to a severe examination? We all draw from it moral strength and faith in a better future.[37]

In a similar vein, Georgi Dimitrov, the Bulgarian Communist leader, suggests that, for a believer, the novel had exactly the "aesthetic" effect that Chernyshevsky intended it

[37] Quoted by Vodovozov in the postscript to *Chto Delat?* (p. 464). This, despite Plekhanov's many quarrels with Chernyshevsky as a thinker.

to have. Dimitrov singles out Rakhmetov as a basic influence
on the formation of his own character:

I must say that . . . there was no literary work which influenced
me so strongly in my revolutionary education as Chernyshevsky's
novel. For months I literally lived with Chernyshevsky's heroes.
Rakhmetov was my particular favorite. I set myself the goal of
being as firm, as self-possessed, to temper my will and character
in my struggle with difficulties and deprivations, to subordinate
my personal life to the interests of the great cause of the working
class—in a word, to *be* like this irreproachable hero of Chernyshevsky.[38]

Lenin's feeling of identification with the novel is striking.
A recent memoir records his passionate reply over a Swiss
café table to a colleague who had dismissed it as "primitive":

Will you be careful what you say? . . . How can the monstrous, absurd idea enter your head of calling the work of
Chernyshevsky, the greatest and most talented representative
of socialism before Marx, primitive and ungifted. . . . I declare
it's inadmissable. . . . Under his influence hundreds of people became revolutionaries. . . . For example, he fascinated my
brother and he fascinated me. He ploughed me up more profoundly than anyone else. When did you read *What Is to Be
Done?* It's useless to read it if the milk hasn't dried on your
lips. Chernyshevsky's novel is too complicated . . . to understand and evaluate at an early age. I myself tried to read it when
I was about fourteen. It was no use, a superficial reading. And
then, after my brother's execution, knowing that Chernyshevsky's novel was one of his favorite books, I really undertook to

[38] Quoted by Vodovozov in his editor's postscript to *Chto Delat?*
(p. 470), from Dimitrov's foreword to an unavailable 1935 edition of
the novel. A connection with our own day is established by the British
Marxist, Ralph Fox, who appealed to Western writers in the 1930s
to make Dimitrov, whose self-defense at the Reichstag fire trial he
calls an "example of moral grandeur and courage worthy to stand beside
the greatest in our human history," the hero of a new kind of novel for
our time. (See Ralph Fox, *The Novel and the People* [New York,
1945], pp. 100–107.)

read it, and I sat over it not for several days but for several weeks. Only then did I understand its depth. . . . It's a thing which supplies energy for a whole lifetime. An ungifted work could not have that kind of influence.[39]

Lenin's invocation of Marx and of his own brother, as well as the excited terms of his praise, testify to the depth of its influence. It was clearly instrumental in his conversion to the revolutionary way of life after his brother's death. Valentinov notes elsewhere that before this climactic moment Turgenev was Lenin's favorite writer, and speculates on the reasons for it. Perhaps Lenin loved the life in nature of the nobleman's estate, which we now know was very familiar to him in his youth.[40] But, Valentinov points out, he also must have accepted Turgenev's unfavorable portraits of revolutionaries without distaste.[41] It is remarkably symbolic to find Lenin taking sides in that debate of the sixties when certain fateful choices Russia has felt compelled to make were dramatized more vividly than has ever happened since.

These testimonials from distinguished revolutionaries provide a good sense of the terms of the novel's acceptance by Soviet critics. One authoritative statement connects the novel with Soviet literature's most solemn purposes:

The enormous educational significance which Chernyshevsky's novel, *What Is to Be Done?*, had for contemporary revolutionary youth is well known, forming in the persons of Rakhmetov, Kirsanov, Lopukhov, Vera Pavlovna a well-defined system of social conduct. Thus Soviet literature, exposing the survivals of capitalism and at the same time depicting the positive hero of socialist construction, carries out an enormous educational work. This cognitive-educational significance of literature is disclosed

    [39] N. Valentinov, "Chernyshevsky i Lenin," *Novy zhurnal*, No. 27 (1951), pp. 193–94.
    [40] N. Valentinov, "Rannie gody Lenina. Lenin v Kokushkine," *Novy zhurnal*, No. 36 (1954), pp. 231–35.
    [41] N. Valentinov, "Vydumki o rannei revolyutsionnosti Lenina," *Novy zhurnal*, No. 39 (1954), pp. 222–29.

with special sharpness by Comrade Stalin who defined writers
as the "engineers of souls." In this way, through the specificity
of its content, through its form, and through its function, all
indissolubly linked, literature appears before us as a specific
ideology.[42]

Given the Soviet Marxian premise that *literature is ideology,*
then Chernyshevsky had found the way, before anyone else,
to write a novel that propagated a "specific," healthy, progressive brand of it.

An elementary respect for their own national heritage
prevents Soviet critics from including *What Is to Be Done?*
among the classics of the nineteenth century. By the curious
double standard which regards the great writers of the past
with reverent awe, yet supports a creed for its own literature
which opposes them, Chernyshevsky's novel stands as a
pioneering work in the second tradition, which was to reach
fruition in socialist realism, a significant forecast of that
"higher" order of literature to come.

[42] *Literaturnaya entsiklopediya,* VIII, 190–91.

6
REBUTTAL I
The Theory

The political excludes the artistic because, in order to prove, it must be one-sided. TOLSTOY

On the situation of literature in periods of social stress, Lionel Trilling writes: "Any large, intense movement of moral-political action is likely to be jealous of art and to feel that it is in competition with the full awareness of human suffering." [1] Save that the spokesmen for the "large, intense movement" and the writers themselves believed that they had a common cause on many matters, and that there was, as we have seen, in nineteenth-century Russia a unique responsiveness each to the other's vision, Mr. Trilling's insight is a particularly fruitful one for approaching the historic split of the 1860s.

Though the writers felt themselves in competition with the radicals, they were not indifferent to politics, and felt more or less compelled to choose the most hospitable among three major currents of political protest: the revolutionary socialist, the insurrectionary anarchist, and the evolutionary libertarian. In a sense, they represented a fourth group, a kind of writers' party, but they were completely unorganized, and generally worked in closest association with the libertarian group. Even Dostoevsky who disagreed strongly with the social views of this group, or Tolstoy who held aloof from

[1] Lionel Trilling, "Introduction." in Henry James, *The Princess Casamassima* (New York, 1948), I, xx.

all groups, may be said to have enjoyed the climate of tolerance it engendered.

Considering for a moment the ideological aspects of the controversy, we see why the radicals might look to literature for an energizing influence on the confused men of good will, and why, by the same token, the hesitations, qualifications, and tragic insights of the liberal writers would have local aspects of "defeatism." But we cannot draw much advantage, for example, from the uproar that greeted Turgenev's *Fathers and Sons*. Was the novel a "slander" on the younger generation? Did it harm the progressive movement, benefit the status quo? Was Bazarov a veiled portrait of Dobrolyubov; was he copied from another model; or was he entirely imaginary? Turgenev himself, in his defense of that novel, made many contradictory statements on most of these questions, and we are not equipped to answer them. It may be said, however, that his defense was based on the concept that the author is—and indeed must be—responsive to burning social questions, but must at the same time be free to deal with them as his discipline permitted.[2]

We should fare better in seeking out the assumptions about art from which these charges arise. The public statement of the liberal position was sporadic and unsystematic.

[2] Turgenev was to abandon this position in one important particular in a letter to Saltykov in 1876: "I am ready to confess that . . . I had no right to give our reactionary riffraff the opportunity to seize upon a sobriquet ["nihilist"] . . . ; the writer in me should have made this sacrifice to the citizen—and therefore I acknowledge as justified both my alienation from the youth and all kinds of reproaches. . . . The question that arose was more important than artistic truth—and I should have known this in advance. (I. S. Turgenev, *Sobranie sochinenii* [Moscow, 1949], XI, 305.) This attitude of capitulation was expressed earlier in his *Literary Reminiscences*, though in more modified form. A. Yarmolinsky, his biographer, notes Turgenev's tendency to cater to the ideas of his correspondents. This surrender of a key position in his letter to Saltykov may be accounted for by the expectations of his **stern correspondent**, the unreconstructed radical satirist.

Often we shall find its most effective defense in letters, diaries, and reminiscences. A consistent theory, which meets the radical position at every essential point, does emerge, however, to help us in detaching the central issue from its local origins and from the terms of the contemporary debate.

The issue was joined on three main points: the situation of the artist and his relation to the truth of his work; the aesthetic function of literature; and the attitude toward universal values in art. Closely involved in these three questions are the definitions of the hero as they relate to theories of human nature and to possibilities for exploitation by the writer.

II

The competition between the two groups involved their professional vested interests: the liberals were writers, the radicals—"the literary Robespierres" in Turgenev's phrase— were critics, for the most part. The latter expressed more than the usual resentment at occupying a secondary, mediator's role in the literary process. As self-appointed guardians of a new civic virtue, they exerted enormous pressure on the writers with the aim, finally, of controlling the moral substance of the creative output. In this contest, the two groups invaded each other's disciplines from time to time: Turgenev discussed literature publicly and at length, notably in articles like "Hamlet and Don Quixote" and in his *Reminiscences*; Tolstoy, Dostoevsky, and, later, Chekhov did so too, though less formally; and the radicals, as we have seen, at least once tried to show the writers how it "must be done." But in the course of these incursions, each remained true to his professional interests: the writers entered criticism to defend and clarify their view of the writer's function; the critics wrote novels to illustrate their own critical prescriptions. The conflict between them remained unresolved on this level until decisions by the Communist Party during the early five-year plans vested ultimate control over literature elsewhere than in the creative faculty of the writer himself.

In their defense against the jurisdictional claims of the critics, and in their rejection of all forms of subservience— to politics, to science, to ethical systems, or to predetermined aesthetic effects—the writers invoked an informal ideology of literature's independence from any prescription which threatened to reduce it to the terms of other disciplines. In some alarm, and with characteristic vehemence, Tolstoy wrote on January 4, 1858, to V. P. Botkin:

What would you say if now, when the filthy stream of politics is trying to swallow everything, and to soil if not to do away with art—what would you say about the people who believe in art's independence and its immortality coming together and demonstrating this truth both by deed (the practice of art) and word (criticism), and trying to save what is eternal and independent from the accidental, one-sided, and all-pervasive political influence.[3]

Tolstoy went on in the same letter to propose the formation of a journal, together with Turgenev, Fet, and others, devoted to "artistic enjoyment" and to "taste," indifferent to any "tendency" and to the "demands of the public." His central insistence on art's (and, of course the artist's) independence sustained him in his own work, until the great personal "crisis" before 1880 led him formally to abandon this stand.

The crux of the dispute is in the effort to locate the center of the creative process. For the liberals it is unquestionably fixed in the sovereign moral intelligence of the artist. For the radical it is elsewhere—in life which can always be invoked

[3] L. N. Tolstoy, *Polnoe sobranie sochinenii* (Moscow, 1935), V, 536–37.

to challenge a novel's formal design, in ethical obligations which arise from the needs and suffering of the masses, or in a doctrinal truth which alone directs the writer to "the significant" in experience.

In asserting their independence from the views and aspirations of other men—above all from the tactical needs of an underground political movement—the artists were merely insisting on minimal conditions for the performance of their work, which they conceived as the discovery of the whole truth about human experience. "Truth," unadorned and without qualification, became a battle cry of the group. "My hero is truth," Tolstoy shouted at Sevastopol, refusing to falsify for patriotic purposes any of the human beings he observed there. Art's truth, Turgenev felt, was a special personal vision of experience to which the artist dedicated himself as to a holy mission. The critics simply did not understand the creative process:

They do not imagine that enjoyment . . . which consists of punishing oneself for the shortcomings . . . in the people one invents; they are fully convinced that an author unfailingly creates only that which conducts his ideas, they do not want to believe that to reproduce powerfully and accurately the truth, the realness of life, is the greatest happiness for a writer even if this truth does not coincide with his own sympathies.[4]

Formal discipline is no end in itself—art is not a game— but a means to this greater end. Political truth is not false but "one-sided," simply one aspect of the totality of man's experience. The goal is the rendering, compactly but completely, of the whole of the human condition as one's characters share it. The writer does not address himself to the "significant" truth or to the useful truth or to the probable truth,

[4] From Chapter 5, "À propos de *Fathers and Sons*," in his *Literary Reminiscences*, dated 1868–90 (*Polnoe sobranie sochinenii* [St. Petersburg, 1913], X, 104).

but to the whole of its gnarled and knotty substance. Chekhov, the last and often the most perceptive spokesman for the writers, makes it clear that no limitation within the writer's awareness must be allowed to infringe on the fidelity of his image. Since it is in the artist's mind that order and meaning are discovered in experience, he must clearly be independent (though not necessarily unaware) of the imperatives derived from other disciplines, if he is to meet this challenging and exhausting standard of "absolute and honest truth."

In a sense the writers' claim to autonomy is based on the notion that the act of creation is in itself an act of discovery. Art maintains its own outposts on the frontiers of experience, conducts its own explorations according to its own rules, and presents its findings to the public without referral to any authority outside the writer's conscience. Art bears comparison in this connection with a scientific experiment. Lionel Trilling has compared the fabricated world of the work of art—Marianne Moore's "imaginary garden"—with the artificial situation of the experiment, "which is devised to force or foster a fact into being." [5] Both wings of Russian realism accepted some such view of the creative process. But there is a significant difference between them on this point. It is not that either group really rigged the experiment or allowed the unrestricted play of the experimenter's subjectivity. The distinction is rather to be found in differing standards of selectivity regulating the amount and kinds of data to be taken under consideration. The liberal in spite of his prejudices and predispositions seemed always inclined to permit more data—in terms of variety of character and situation—as raw material to be tested in his experiment. The radical favored

[5] Lionel Trilling, "Introduction," in James, *The Princess Casamassima*, I, xiv.

smaller amounts with a larger share pretested by other disciplines. To the extent that this was so, the outcome always
tended to be predetermined in this kind of fiction, as Chernyshevsky's novel clearly indicated.

The writers' effort to remain true to the logic of the data,
and to organize them without damage or distortion, gave rise
more than once to the peculiar situation in which the writer
struggled desperately, and sometimes unsuccessfully, to con
trol the outcome of his story, and asked in bewilderment
what had gone wrong when he failed. Gogol's Chichikov
(*Dead Souls*), Tolstoy's Levin (*Anna Karenina*), Dostoevsky's Myshkin (*The Idiot*)—all represent intentions unful-
filled. It may be argued that Raskolnikov's questionable conversion violates the logic of the data, and the writer's better
judgment, too, as it is revealed in his working notes for the
novel's conclusions: "Raskolnikov goes to shoot himself." [6]
Ivan Karamazov's state of suspension, far from fulfillment
but as far from defeat, does not express the author's explicit
beliefs as we know them to be. In all these cases the writer
has created someone as strong and assertive as himself, with
an independent identity and destiny. Turgenev is painfully
honest and frankly at sea about his relation to Bazarov. True
to his precept: to present "the whole of the living human
face," he found himself unable to say, after he had done so,
that Bazarov was the creature of his hopes, or even whether
"I love him or hate him." [7] Working out of this ambivalence,
Turgenev endowed Bazarov with a striking combination of
good and bad qualities: he has in his make-up "coarseness,"
"heartlessness," "ruthless dryness and sharpness," yet he is
"strong," "honorable, just, and a democrat to the tip of his

---

[6] F. M. Dostoevsky, *Iz arkhiva F. M. Dostoevskogo. Prestuplenie i
nakazanie: neizdannye materialy*, ed. I. I. Glivenko (Moscow-Leningrad,
1931), p. 216.
[7] Letter to A. A. Fet, dated April 6/18, 1862 (*Sobranie sochinenii*,
XI, 212).

toes." [8] These, at least, are some of the qualities Turgenev discovered in him after the fact. But they were not the result of a calculated balancing of vices and virtues during the act of creation itself. At that moment his governing intention was to exclude arbitrary manipulation and to submit to the logic of his invention. He has described his curious feeling of helplessness before his creation:

It seems that an author himself does not know what he is creating; my feelings for Bazarov—my personal feelings—were of a confused nature (whether I loved him or hated him, the Lord knows!), nevertheless the image came out so defined that he immediately stepped into life and started to act in his own particular way. In the end what does it matter what a writer thinks of his work. It is a thing in itself and he is a thing in himself.[9]

Turgenev would have been a happier man if he had really believed in the separate existences of author and hero. He was never able to disclaim responsibility for Bazarov entirely, but he achieved a degree of detachment that enabled him to penetrate to the real reasons for the clamorous and discordant reception of "his favorite child." The danger lay in his own ambiguity:

If the writer's attitude toward his characters is not defined . . . if the author himself doesn't know whether he loves the character he has set forth . . . then it is thoroughly bad. The reader is prepared to attach to the author imaginary sympathies or imaginary antipathies, if only to escape from the unpleasant "uncertainty." [10]

Fathers and Sons fell, as Turgenev put it, "like oil on the fire." [11] In this superheated time readers "read through"

[8] *Ibid.*, pp. 212–16.
[9] Letter to I. P. Borisov, January 5, 1870 (*ibid.*, p. 259).
[10] From the *Literary Reminiscences* in *Polnoe sobranie sochinenii*, X, 106.
[11] Letter to P. V. Annenkov, June 8, 1862 (*Sobranie sochinenii*, XI, 217).

the novel and groped for direct, immediate identification with the life around them. There was neither the leisure nor the tolerance to honor his real purpose as he explained it to Dostoevsky: "Nobody, it seems, suspects that I tried to present . . . a tragic figure—and everybody comments: why is he so sinister? or why is he so good?" [12]

Turgenev was a victim of the partisan view of truth held by the political extremists on both sides, a view impatient of paradox or ambiguity, hence unwilling to accept the complexity or the contradictions of tragedy. In the radicals' universe allowance was made for obstacles and setbacks but not for doubt or bewilderment. They felt that much larger sectors of the available truth were known than the liberal writers believed. And, in any case, important new discoveries would not, in all likelihood, be made by freely ranging writer-explorers. The writer, in the radical prescription, was expected to deal far more with the given—to illustrate the known, not to seek the unknown. Behind the words "typical," "healthy," "progressive," and "necessary" lay the certainty that such words had fixed and exclusive definitions, and, still further in the background, the implication that these definitions, constituting the essential truth, must be accepted by—or even imposed on—writers.

In deciding what truth is for the writer, certain judgments must be made about what aspects of the truth of human life or what moments in man's life cycle are of greatest fictional interest. For the great Russian novelists ideas and doctrine were not excluded, but were contained in character, and made a function of the whole man. The truth of fiction for them embraced all varieties of love, friendship, and hatred, had as its permanent backdrop the perspective of growth, decay, and death, and, because of the artist's elevation above,

[12] Letter to F. M. Dostoevsky, April 22, 1862 (*ibid.*, p. 216).

and independence from, his characters, included the human facts of fallibility, error, and failure. The radicals, on the other hand, were interested in ideological man. In their view of literary truth—and undoubtedly in their own private moral code—character was a function of doctrine, and men generally were most "interesting" when seen in active response to their social situation. Against the liberal creed of knowledge of life for its own sake whatever the consequences, the radicals opposed an ideology, a body of organized knowledge designed to affect men's future social behavior in a specific way. Since the doctrine was known to be valid, its spokesmen in art could not be permitted to fail, or if they did, for personal reasons, they became simply uninteresting or untypical in the radicals' special use of those words. For the liberal with his eye focused on the individual in all his observable relations with life, this doctrinal view of man was, as Tolstoy put it, "one-sided." Turgenev was undoubtedly reacting against this view when he enjoined young writers to steer clear of any and all "dogma." Also, since an ideological view of the world involved a calculation about the future, literary truth for the radicals must contain that diagram of what is to come, as they discerned it in present events. According to the canons of realism, the future, seen either as the inevitable or as the desirable, must remain an unknown. Possibilities might be stated, but any effort to force character into one of these possibilities had unhappy results, as we have seen in the case of Chichikov, Raskolnikov, Levin, and others.

III

The two views of art contain sharply contrasting assumptions about the aesthetic effect a novel should have on the reader. Radical criticism displayed a parental concern for the *immediate* effect of a literary work upon the reader's conduct and morale. In this setting art becomes a discourse not between equals but between teacher and students, or for that matter, between fathers and children. Turgenev's remark that Chernyshevsky's dissertation set forth a view of art for "immature" people is very shrewd, for these matters are the proper concern of writers of juvenile literature. There is no question here of the author's posing his informed judgment against the reader's own. Rather, a number of fundamental decisions have been taken by self-appointed guardians of morals, and the reader is invited to share them but is not expected to find his own way among them or to reject them. This situation has obtained, of course, to a greater or lesser degree since 1929 in the Soviet Union. Zhdanov poses the issue with devastating clarity in his "Report on the Journals *Zvezda* and *Leningrad*." After belaboring Zoshchenko and Akhmatova for corrupting the ideals of youth, he attacks them further for daring to suppose that "if a man has done a good, artistic, fine piece of writing, his work should be published even though it contains vicious elements liable to confuse and poison the minds of our young people." [13] This at least is frank.

At bottom this attitude rests on the radicals' premise that art's proper aim is the stimulation and direction of action. Chernyshevsky disagreed with Aristotle's view that art "imitates" life and that its instructive value is contained therein: "We imitate in order to act, not in order to know something." [14] In distinguishing between the two schools on this

[13] A. A. Zhdanov, "Doklad o zhurnalakh *Zvezda* i *Leningrad*," *Literaturnaya gazeta*, No. 39 (September 21, 1946), p. 4. This raises the question of a *youth-centered* literature, in effect of a national literature of juvenilia.

[14] N. G. Chernyshevsky, *Estetika*, ed. N. G. Bogoslovsky (Moscow-Leningrad, 1939), p. 234.

point, it is safer to rely on this remark by Chernyshevsky
than to accept his more formal distinction between an art
concerned with practical human strivings and an art directed
toward "enjoyment," with its connotations of frivolity and
indulgence. We are confronted then with an opposition between action to change life, on the one hand, and a general
knowledge about life, on the other, as the ultimate aim of
art, between, that is, a manipulative and a contemplative
aesthetic.

In formulating this view of art the Russian literary radicals
came close to paraphrasing Marx's celebrated prescription
for philosophy: "The philosophers have only *interpreted* the
world in various ways; the point, however, is to *change it*." [15]
In this view, knowledge is measured by its persuasive value.
The liberal would doubtless agree with the radical that art
was indeed a kind of instruction in life. But he would certainly demur at the further step that converts education into
agitation. He might agree that satire led most directly and
most validly to action by arousing disgust with a given state
of things, but he would add that successful satire does not
break its mood of mockery by including a set of instructions
for removing the evils under attack. As in the case of tragedy,
the instruction is primarily an inference to be drawn by the
reader, and any action on his part will proceed from his own
conclusions. The radicals hoped to control the reader's response by drawing the conclusions within the work of
art, and by showing the action they hoped he would
take.

Chekhov defended himself against the same kind of pressures, and may be quoted as a final rebuttal speaker for all
the writers. He is quite explicit in a letter to A. S. Suvorin:

[15] The Eleventh Thesis on Feuerbach (Karl Marx and Friedrich
Engels, *Selected Works* [Moscow, 1951], II, 367).

You are right to require a conscious attitude from the artist toward his work, but you mix up two ideas: *the solution of the problem and a correct presentation of the problem.* Only the latter is obligatory for the artist. In *Anna Karenina* and *Onegin* not a single problem is solved, but they satisfy you completely just because all their problems are correctly presented. The court is obliged to submit the case fairly, but let the jury do the deciding, each according to its own judgment.[16]

Thus Chekhov frees the artist from responsibilities which are, properly, not his at all, and at the same time protects him in his role as observer and organizer of experience. In the final libertarian image he surrenders any claim to legislative, parental controls over the reader's response: it is not for the artist to worry about what the work of art causes people to do. His maximum offering to the reader is a precious, hard-won illumination. The adult reader may come away depressed or elated, with his sense of life clarified or confounded. He may act more resolutely, less so, or not at all. That is the reader's business. Tragedy may numb his will or blight his expectations, but as a sure road to the truth it cannot be by-passed.

We return, finally, to the incompatibility already noted between realism and the projection, in whatever form, of future events. The writers' reluctance—and their inability when they tried—to cross the line between *is* and *should be* did not mean that they were indifferent toward what was to come. Any knowledge of life—particularly the kind of moral investigations in Russia's great writing—should be of use to the prophets and activists who would *change* life. But it was not, largely because the kind of human truth that literature dealt with was too complex, too ambiguous, and

[16] Letter to A. S. Suvorin, dated December 23, 1888 (Anton Chekhov, *The Selected Letters of Anton Chekhov*, ed. Lillian Hellman [New York, 1955], p. 57).

too imprecise to sustain predictions or to promise solutions. The writers felt that it was their responsibility only to show man as he was, and he would change himself.

It was Turgenev who made the most telling comment on the radical orientation toward the future. Bazarov, his own version of the radical personality, was a tragic figure precisely because of his involvement in what was to come. "I dreamt of a dark, wild, large figure," he wrote, "half growing out of the soil, strong, malicious, honorable—and doomed all the same to perish because . . . he stands on the threshold of the future." [17] The source of the radicals' optimism became for Turgenev, since he did not share their faith in the rapid, upward evolution of things, the very source of Bazarov's undoing. The doctrinal motives which constitute Bazarov's commitment to the future become devalued and evaporate in the face of his present personal needs. Thus stripped of his ideals he is confronted with the last responsibility of all large men, of "dying with dignity." [18]

Turgenev's implication that man always looms larger than the doctrine he professes brings up the problem of general truths in art. Radical art is virtually indifferent to universal statement. It operates so fixedly in the glare of the immediate political present and future, and its limited, topical, agitational view of truth is so concerned with the contemporary and the concrete, that there is no opportunity for the artist to concern himself with the timeless. Because of the radicals' materialist distrust of absolutes and permanent categories, their kinds of social generalization do not readily extend themselves through time, since society changes, and its labels are constantly rewritten. Value is conferred on art from without, by the service it performs at any given moment,

[17] Letter to K. K. Sluchevski, April 14, 1862 (*Sobranie sochinenii*, XI, 215).
[18] Letter to A. A. Fet, September 4, 1862 (*ibid.*, p. 219).

and, by all accounts, the modern Soviet reader is still expected to value *Dead Souls* for its exposé of social conditions
and to derive a kind of *ex post facto* indignation from it. Even
the radical hero-type, whom Lenin, Plekhanov, and Dimitrov
found a source of strength many years later, exerted a sec-
tarian appeal, directed mainly to believers. The one value he
expressed, which transcended the specific articles of his faith,
was that virtue is found in complete personal subordination
to a doctrine of revolutionary social change. The one universal tenet of the radical view of literature would seem to be
that it concern itself eternally with the momentarily relevant.
Should the artist achieve a level of universal interest, it must
be regarded as an unimportant by-product of his solemn attention to the present and to the immediate future.

It must not be supposed that in contrast to the radicals'
myopia, the writers deliberately set out to explore the timeless or to search for philosophical absolutes in the manner of
Chernyshevsky's whipping-boy, Vischer. Turgenev was as
topical as a gossip columnist, and Dostoevsky's source books
were as often as not the crime stories in the daily newspaper.
The essential difference between the two approaches shows
up most clearly in their view of character: in the radical prescription character was a function of ideology; in the writers'
practice ideology was a function of, or was contained in,
character. Grounding their conception in the wholly recreated human being, the writers proceeded outward from
that and were free to explore him in all his relations to the
world, to sex, to society, to belief, or to death. When the
radicals and the liberals looked at the same type they saw
him differently: one saw him governed through his reason by
"convictions" or doctrine and powered by the disciplined
emotions that flowed from this combination; the other comprehended the entire human vessel in which reason and con-

viction were contained. The writers anchored their concept
of character in the timeless biological cycle of human life
and the permanent emotional and psychological needs implicit in this cycle. As Chekhov said: "It seems to me that
it is not up to writers to solve such questions as God, pessimism, ... The job of the writer is to depict only who, how
and under what circumstances people have spoken or thought
about God and pessimism." [19] Focused thus on the man and
not the idea, we see that the balance of good and bad qualities
in Bazarov which may well have been "ideologically harmful"
to the revolutionary cause in 1862 is the precise source of his
universal appeal.

Though it was not their primary concern, the writers felt
that the expression of permanent truths was, nevertheless, a
legitimate aim. Tolstoy, addressing the Society of Lovers of
Russian Literature in 1858, not long before the height of the
controversy, divided Russian literature into "two separate
kinds," and summarized some essential differences between
the two aesthetics:

In the past two years it has seemed that political, and particularly denunciatory, literature, which borrowed the media of art
for its purposes and found remarkably intelligent, honorable,
and talented representatives who responded warmly and decisively to every question of the moment, to society's every
temporary wound, would completely absorb the public's attention, and would deprive literature of all its significance. The
majority of the public began to think that the problem of all
literature consisted only in the denunciation of evil, in discussing it, and correcting it. In the past two years I have heard
and read opinions to the effect that the days of the story and of
verse have gone forever, that the time is coming when Pushkin
. . . will no longer be read, that pure art is impossible, that
literature is only a weapon for the civic development of society,
and so forth. One could hear, it is true, during that time the

[19] Letter to A. S. Suvorin, dated May 30, 1888 (Chekhov, *The
Selected Letters*, p. 54).

voices of Fet, Turgenev, Ostrovsky, muffled by the political uproar . . . but society knew what it was doing, continued to
sympathize with political literature alone, and to consider it
alone as literature. This enthusiasm was noble, necessary, even
just. In order to have the strength to make those enormous
strides forward which our society has made in recent times, it
had to be one-sided, it had to become enthusiastic about further
goals in order to reach them, it had to see that single goal ahead.
And actually can one think about poetry when for the first
time a picture of the evil that surrounds us is unveiled before
one's eyes, and when the possibility of putting an end to it is
presented to us? How could we think about the beautiful as we
fell ill? It is not for us who make use of the fruits of this enthusiasm to reproach it. . . . But however high-minded and
wholesome this one-sided enthusiasm has been, like any enthusiasm it could not endure. The literature of a people is its full
many-sided consciousness, in which must be reflected equally
the national love for goodness and truth and the national contemplation of beauty in a given epoch of development.[20]

Tolstoy was convinced that public taste was swinging away
from "civic" problems toward a more balanced appreciation
of the uses of literature:

Society now understood, not from critical articles alone, but
discovered through experience . . . that seemingly simple
truth that, however great the significance of a political literature which reflects the temporary interests of society, however
necessary it is for national development, there is another literature which reflects eternal, universally human interests, the most
precious, heartfelt consciousness of a people, a literature accessible to men of every nation and every epoch, a literature without which no people possessing strength and richness has ever
developed.[21]

Tolstoy concluded that, in spite of his personal preference
for the second kind of literature, the two kinds could and
should coexist, and together would constitute a total "con-

[20] Tolstoy, *Polnoe sobranie sochinenii*, V, 271–72.
[21] *Ibid.*, p. 272.

sciousness" "responsive to the many-sided needs of its society." [22] But there are times of great social stress apparently when literature cannot be exempted from the vital public concerns of its day. This is the escape clause Tolstoy was to invoke for his own retreat into a fiercely limited and tendentious definition of its function; and it is the clause that has become a permanent statute of the Soviet literary code since the First Five-Year Plan.

[22] *Ibid.*

7

REBUTTAL II
Hamlet and Don Quixote

Two kinds of heroes represented the two kinds of literature. In a sense, the crux of the entire argument may be found in the distance that separates Bazarov and Rakhmetov, seen as two views of the same social type, but the full range of the argument involves us finally in *two* opposing views of *two* distinct social types, members of successive generations, which were loosely identified as the "men of the forties" and the "men of the sixties." For this reason, their dispute often had the aspect of a family squabble (between "fathers" and "sons") with all the bitterness born of familiarity. But they differed too in birth, in education, and in the quality of their sensibilities. The earlier generation were, as a rule, disaffected and conscience-stricken members of the serf-owning gentry. They were highly educated at home and abroad, and their basic intellectual endowment was composed of roughly equal parts of French political rationalism and German philosophical idealism. They attached great weight to the schematic principles of the first and the inflated, capitalized abstractions of the second. The end product of their training was most often the erection of a system of "convictions" which they defended in print when they found an opening, or discussed in study circles. They solemnly proclaimed their reverence for art and philosophy as the "loftiest" manifestations of the human spirit. What diffuse political pressure they were able to exert was toward a high-minded reformism. They were talkers and definers, not doers, and, as such, offered a much better recruiting ground for artists than for revolutionaries. Their times, the "leaden" reaction of Nicholas I, contributed more, whether directly or indirectly, to the blunting of their social aspirations than any cowardly evasion of their responsibilities. Even their detractors gave them credit, by and large, for keeping their moral identity intact, even if little or nothing of public benefit issued from it, and, in honoring the purity of their intentions, would accept their defenders' contention that essentially they were men of sensitivity and honor.

Their successors were generally identified with a quite distinct social group: the *raznochintsy*, the classless intelligentsia which was open to anyone who could find his way to an education. They were free of the cultural prejudices of the cultivated nobility, and resentful of its pretensions and apartness. But in spite of their relatively "democratic" origins they were as cut off by their education from the masses they would help as their rivals were by the circumstance of birth. In the major articles of their intellectual creed they were advocates of a doctrine by no means hostile in all respects to what had gone before. Their ideas represented an evolutionary step beyond their predecessors' and often rested on the same intellectual foundations. Thus their commitment to the French rationalists remained intense even as it changed from a well-mannered respect for human rights in the abstract to the belligerent advocacy of Jacobin leveling tendencies. On the philosophical level, though they stopped short of Marx, they followed closely the epochal transition within Hegelianism from idealism to materialism, acknowledging their debt to Feuerbach and others of the left-Hegelians. In their thinking about society they accepted the possibility of violent change. Indebted though they were to the French Utopians, Fourier, Blanc, and Saint-Simon, they found native sources for a socialist economic order which implied a drastic alteration of existing property relations. Science—both natural and social—replaced art as the most trustworthy source of truth, though art, as we have seen, was given a subsidiary role as a publicist of its findings. The men of the new generation portrayed themselves as blunter, less speculative, and more concerned with concrete achievement than with the formal symmetry of their beliefs or the nicety of their expression. Direct, unsentimental, and practical, they were likely to find more meaning in an autopsy report or an economic monograph than in the ambiguities of art.

As they appeared to their partisans, the men of the forties were praised for their intentions, excused for their failures, and viewed generally in a compassionate light. According to their most prominent defender, Alexander Herzen, they were honorable and pitiable victims of an implacably hostile environment. But to their radical opponents nearly every virtue that was claimed for them displayed its unattractive underside. Their vaunted sensitivity was an aristocratic finickiness; their pride in their convictions was simply another aspect of their enormous vanity; and their estrangement from work and activity was not tragic, nor was it even an enforced idleness, but the result of an atrophy of the will and of the emotions that was a natural result of their parasitic economic existence. From this vantage point they were credited with honorable intentions during the darkness of the thirties and forties, when their convictions kept the tradition of dissent from extinction, but were regarded as contemptible for their nonperformance in a period of rapidly widening arenas for action.

The men of the sixties felt that their own champion had

inherited the best properties of his fainthearted predecessor, and had developed correctives for his every fault. The new man, they said, was abrupt, direct, fearless, practical, unsentimental, and selfless. But, as might be expected, each of these qualities had its evil counterpart in the eyes of the older men. The young revolutionary, according to them, was arid, insensitive, crude, and, because of all the virtues he claimed for himself, conceited to the point of arrogance. Indeed, his "rudeness" was one of the points at issue most fruitful for its relevance to the new man's literary possibilities.[1]

All the men of the forties, by the admission of their own defenders, share one important condition: they are alienated men, cut off by a combination of inner failing and outer prohibition from personal fulfillment on any level of private or public endeavor. This condition is intricately—even mysteriously—brought about, as the literature tells us so often, but it unites them all, despite the variety of individual types, in a tragic brotherhood. The younger generation claimed that it had found the way to avoid this unhappy condition. Their elders, of course, were willing to grant them no such exemption and it was their effort to include the young radicals among the alienated that touched off the controversy. Three related arguments may be distinguished, all of which concern the very points at which the radicals undertook to protect themselves against alienation. These took the form, first, of a breathtaking assertion of freedom from the values and institutions of the status quo; second, of an unshakable faith in human reason and the principles it made known to them; and, finally, of a powerful belief

---

[1] Isaiah Berlin traces this rudeness to Belinsky's God-given bad manners and vehemence of expression. Later generations of radicals, he says, cultivated rudeness as a style of behavior, designed to express their disgust with the old ways. See Mr. Berlin's article, "A Marvellous Decade (III), Belinsky: Moralist and Prophet." *Encounter*, V, No. 6 (December, 1956), 39.

in themselves, as the personal instruments of the historical process. Thus armed they proposed to complete the hazardous journey on which the liberals had become lost midway: from integration with the intolerable status quo, thence to a state of estrangement from it through the action of education and of the moral sensibility, and, finally, to a renewed state of integration, through their philosophy of action, with a rational future world of which they were the first heralds. They had found the way to a state of personal engagement, they were convinced, that would sustain them in their struggle with the Tsarist system, because they believed in the justice of their attack and in the inevitability of its outcome.

The radical state of mind with its special defenses against alienation was subjected, however, to a merciless critique, designed to show that it too was vulnerable and precisely at those points where its spokesmen considered it strongest. The radicals' belief in the power of reason, for example, represented a fatal error of judgment, and made them extremely vulnerable to the germs of alienation. Bazarov's convictions did not square with his emotional needs, or, as some felt, were merely a manifestation of his personality unbalance, and he disintegrated as a result of the tension between them. Dostoevsky directed his attack on the new men in *Notes from Underground* at precisely this point. Reason constituted perhaps "one-twentieth" of the human make-up, and served only as a presumptuous excuse for the expression of the capricious, criminal impulses which aspire continually to dominion over man's nature. In the contest between good and evil instincts, reason is but the tool of the animal in man, of the "weak," "rebellious," malicious, destructive side of man's nature.

A good part of Tolstoy's polemic against historians in

War and Peace is directed against an inflated estimate of
the power of the mind. In his blindly determinist view of history, no man is granted the privilege of directing the course
of events, nor of predicting the course they will take. History is the unforeseeable resultant of the minds, will, and
hearts of all who take part in it. Any tendency to overempha-
size the rational faculty is mistaken and dangerous: "If we
admit that human life can be ruled by reason, the possibility of life is destroyed." [2]

In the radicals' defense it should be noted that their concept of reason lacked the arid quality of the French *phi-
losophes*, and that its election to the governing position
in their lives was not an easy or automatic matter. On the
contrary, it was an expensive and difficult, though unavoidable, choice. Chernyshevsky wrote in a letter to Nekrasov:

I myself know by experience that convictions do not constitute
everything in life—the demands of the heart exist, and in the
life of the heart there is genuine joy and genuine sorrow for all
of us. This I know by experience, I know it better than others.
Convictions occupy our mind only when the heart rests from its
joy or sorrow. I will even say that for me, personally, my private
affairs are more significant than any world problem—men do
not drown themselves, or shoot themselves, or become drunkards
because of world problems—I have experienced this and I know
that the poetry of the heart has the same rights as the poetry
of thought—for me, personally, the first is more attractive than
the second. . . . I have allowed myself this frankness not only
to tell you that I look on poetry by no means exclusively from
the political point of view. On the contrary, only by force does
politics dig its way into my heart, which does not by any means
live by it, or, at least, would not like to live by it.[3]

[2] L. N. Tolstoy, *War and Peace*, trans. Louise and Aylmer Maude
(New York, 1942), p. 1256.
[3] N. G. Chernyshevsky, *Polnoe sobranie sochinenii* (Moscow, 1949),
XIV, 320. Compare this quotation with Lenin's famous remark to
Gorky after listening to the *Appassionata*: "It affects your nerves, makes
you want to say stupid, nice things and stroke the heads of people who

The last wistful qualification suggests the final outcome of the tension between heart and mind in his own case.

However reluctantly the decision is made, and however slight is the margin of the heart's subjugation, certain drastic consequences flow from this choice, according to the liberals' critique. Reason is the principal justification for the radicals' sweeping—and to many, terrifying—claim to freedom from all the taboos and restraints of the culture they despised. By their apparent willingness to take human life, to commit "the necessary murder," they had, according to Dostoevsky, discarded timeless moral principles. In their scorn for a particular social order they seemed to others to threaten many of the permanent achievements of human civilization. The freedom to which "all is permitted" could lead only to license, destruction, and anarchy.

But for the radical, deliverance from every oppressive institution and every inhibiting code of the environment was an indispensable precondition for action—the more absolute his opposition, the more drastic his program for change, and the more thorough his rejection of contemporary values. Yet the aim of this break, as he saw it, was never self-indulgence. Reintegrated, as the radicals thought they were, by a combination of personal indignation, social analysis, programmatic doctrine, and "scientific" expectations, their freedom existed within sharply defined limits, and with a narrowly prescribed outlet, similar to a gun barrel, through which it could be discharged. It was a freedom only to be effective or useful, and entirely lacking in easy rewards. Yet within its compass the radical felt himself protected from all the com-

---

could create such beauty while living in this vile hell. And you mustn't stroke anyone's head—you might get your hand bitten off. You have to hit them on the head, without any mercy, although our ideal is not to use force against anyone. . . . our duty is infernally hard." (Maxim Gorky, *Days with Lenin* [New York, 1932], p. 52.)

promises, the contradictory loyalties, and the wracking doubts that led to alienation.

But the nonradicals replied that this sort of freedom ended in an even more drastic kind of alienation. By casting off so many moral and social restraints, by rejecting such a broad cross section of human achievement, by asserting their superiority over so many disciplines of the mind, and by denying their own human needs, the radicals, they felt, paid a fatally high price. Raskolnikov cut himself off from love, from God, from Russia, and from mankind when he dared to act. His awful isolation resulted in a crippling distortion of values. With their eye always on the whole man, the writers believed they had discovered here a point of primary vulnerability.

To the extent that the radicals' defenses were based on doctrine and on expectations, the writers were unimpressed since they shared neither. To the extent that they were made of raw personal courage, the writers were, on the other hand, thoroughly respectful. But to the extent that they involved a monumental and disfiguring self-assurance, the writers were extremely interested, because here again they detected a flaw, that led as surely—and for the same reasons—to alienation as Pechorin's thirst for self-immolation or Rudin's self-delusions. Whether the radicals' defenses were regarded as a general character trait, or as an emotional orientation toward the world, and quite apart from ideological labels, the writers felt they had discovered a new variation of a familiar pattern.

This is the celebrated "rudeness" of the radicals, a term which refers to the quality of their sensibilities, more than it does to their table manners, though these too, we are assured by the gently bred liberals, were deplorable. The arrogance of their posture toward the world, whether viewed

as cause or symptom of their maladjustment, was for the
outside observer the outstanding feature of their personalities. This is the burden of Herzen's harsh personal attack on
the radical youth. Himself one of the least "superfluous"
representatives of the men of the forties and a political
revolutionary to boot, he nevertheless felt himself separated
from the men of the sixties by birth, training, and outlook.
His most famous article on the subject, "The Superfluous
Men and the Men with a Grudge," which appeared in his
journal, *The Bell*, in October 15, 1860, is one of the land-
marks in the quarrel between the generations.[4] He was principally concerned with defending the older men against un-
justified attacks from their overbearing young successors. It
is a sentimental defense of the liberal group, by one of its
members. They were, he insisted, the honorable, well-
intentioned, and far from inactive victims of the savage re-
pressions of the Nicholas era. Their idleness was enforced
by circumstances, and their lethargy concealed sharp suffering. They had become, he confessed, pathological types
toward the end of their ordeal, prematurely burnt out, disillusioned, and "sick in body and soul." [5] But for all their
sins and shortcomings they were guiltless of the insulting
charges directed at them by the "sullen" new men, who were,
if anything, sicker than their forebears. Herzen characterized the new types in vividly uncomplimentary terms. They
were, he said, gravely deficient in sensibility. They were able,

[4] A. I. Herzen, *Polnoe sobranie sochinenii i pisem*, ed. M. K. Lemke
(Petrograd, 1919), X, 413–23. The article is believed to be a response
to Dobrolyubov's review of Turgenev's *On the Eve*. The model for the
radical type whom he compares with a narrow-minded, joyless Russian
preacher of the Middle Ages named Daniel Zatochnik is probably
Dobrolyubov himself. It was written not long after Chernyshevsky's
clandestine trip to London, in the course of which he tried without
success to effect a rapprochement with Herzen.
[5] *Ibid.*, p. 417.

for example, to surmount the defeat of the revolution of 1848 without pausing to weep a single tear for its fallen heroes. There was a sinister "lightness" to all their emotional responses which, combined with the immoral pleasure they found in negation, and the "terrible ruthlessness" of their personal code, made for a most unappetizing kind of person. They displayed a monk's hatred for human frailty; they had the speech, the manners, and the sudden, explosive rages of bureaucrats; and they were, Herzen insisted, hypochondriacs to a man. At bottom he detected the starved egos of ambitious and unsuccessful mediocrities. On their faces were the marks of a "gnawing, short-tempered, and curdled self-love." [6] In spite of the polemical ferocity of his tone, which damages his case at times, Herzen has diagnosed their trouble in a way that was echoed by most nonradical commentators. Although they too were victims of traditionless, Russian barbarism, and their intentions were no less exalted than their predecessors', their essential rudeness made it impossible to admire them, or to share their convictions or their hopes. They were inadequate as people, hence unworthy of the purposes they professed to stand for.

Turgenev, whose indictment of the radical is far gentler than his friend Herzen's, had, nevertheless, to acknowledge the presence of a towering arrogance in the radical type.[7] In Bazarov this quality provides the outlet for his admirable courage and energy and is, at the same time, a crippling malformation of his character. When his doctrinal supports have been worn away and shown to be inadequate, Bazarov lapses fleetingly into a Nietzschean image of himself as a

[6] *Ibid.*, pp. 418–19.
[7] Even Chernyshevsky acknowledges this. But with Rakhmetov, his self-assurance and his abruptness in personal relations are seen as a refreshingly direct and time-saving manner which all his friends understand and appreciate.

kind of superman, before he collapses under the weight of
his swollen ego.[8] When charged with falsification and slander on this point, Turgenev looked beyond Herzen's concrete explanations and sought to explain it in general, psychological terms:

What kind of artist would I be (I don't say man) if I did not
understand that self-confidence, exaggeration of expression . . .
and posing, even a certain cynicism, constitute inevitable attributes of youth.[9]

Turgenev was not always able to remain on this level of
universal comment, oscillating as he did between it and
the specific terms of reference forced on him by his enemies.
But he was firmly established in this mood when he wrote
his subtle and comprehensive essay on literary heroism,
"Hamlet and Don Quixote." [10] It is the final document of
the writers' rebuttal and is the nearest thing there is to a
public manifesto of their position. In it Turgenev clearly
takes his departure from the specific issues of his day, but
he arranges them in new ways, draws refreshingly different
distinctions, and proceeds to a level of universal statement.
The essay purports to be a study of human nature and of
the two polar types that make it up. But it is unmistakably
a writer's view of human nature, and we are aware at every
moment that his classification and analysis are rooted in the
literary possibilities these types present to the working nov-

[8] Turgenev makes it clear in a letter to K. K. Sluchevski that the slip
of a knife that kills Bazarov is not an accident but part of a coherent
tragic design (*Sobranie sochinenii* [Moscow, 1949], XI, 214–15).
[9] Letter to A. P. Filosofovaya, August 18/30, 1874, *ibid.*, p. 288.
[10] First delivered as a speech on January 10, 1860, at a public meeting for the benefit of the Society for the Assistance of Needy Writers
and Scholars, it was then published in the radical *Sovremennik* (No. 1
[1860]), though it received an entirely hostile reception from the maga-
zine's policy-makers. Its appearance is often used to mark the decisive
moment in the break between liberals and radicals. I have used the text
of the public lecture as found in I. S. Turgenev, *Sobranie sochinenii*,
XI, 5–20.

elist. Although his versions of Hamlet and of Don Quixote are plainly intended to comment on the quarrel then going on about character types, his insight raises the entire question of the literary hero to a plane of general aesthetic discussion, which touches on some of the outer limits of the possibilities of fiction. To be sure, the essay was generated out of an intense concern with contemporary problems, but to view it *only* as a narrow "superstructural" reflection of local conditions is to deny its continuing relevance to creative problems.

Turgenev has cast the whole of his elaborate distinction in typically ambivalent terms. There is no favoritism nor invidiousness in his judgments: each type has his virtues; each type has his faults; and both are held within the orbit of his sympathy. He first distinguished between them by noting the relation each man had to his moral code: "The ideal, this basis and goal of their existence is either outside them or within them; in other words, for each of us, either the private 'I' stands in first place or something else which is acknowledged as more exalted." [11] Between egoism and altruism, the apparent advantage lies entirely with Don Quixote because he has faith:

Faith, above all, faith in something eternal, immovable, in truth, in a truth which is outside the individual man, to which it is not easy to give oneself, which demands sacrifices and services. . . . Don Quixote is imbued with devotion to the ideal, for which he is prepared to subject himself to every possible deprivation, to sacrifice his life; he values his life only to the extent that it will serve as a means for the realization of the ideal, for the establishment of truth and justice on earth.[12]

But in the very assertion of his moral nature Don Quixote's great failing is made evident, although it is not enough to devalue the purity of his purpose:

[11] *Ibid.*, p. 6.   [12] *Ibid.*, p. 7.

A constant striving toward one and the same goal lends a certain monotony to his ideas, a one-sidedness to his mind; he knows little, but he need not know much: he knows what his cause is, why he lives on earth, and this is the principal knowledge. At one moment Don Quixote can seem a complete maniac, because the most indubitable materiality disappears before his eyes, melts like wax in the flame of his enthusiasm (he really sees live Moors in wooden dolls, knights in sheep)—at another moment, limited because he does not know how to sympathize easily, or to enjoy himself; but, like an ancient tree, he has struck his roots deep in the soil and cannot change his convictions, nor be shifted from one subject to another; the strength of his moral substance (note that this madman, this wandering knight, is the most moral being on earth) gives special force and grandeur to all his judgments and speeches, to his whole figure, in spite of the comic and the ridiculous into which he perpetually falls.[13]

Don Quixote's strength, then, *is* his weakness. His singleness of purpose requires that he be both deficient in understanding and limited in sensibility, to the degree that he has a well-developed capacity for self-delusion.[14]

Thus far, Turgenev has dealt with the revolutionary as he was. With the introduction of the idea of the comic, however, we become concerned with the observer's response to his image. And not far in the background we sense the preoccupations of the novelist, who is concerned with the face the revolutionary presented to him to write about, and with the problem of rendering his moral purity bearable for the reader by "reducing" it to acceptable terms through the devices of art. The source of the comic is first of all the blindness that characterizes the revolutionary's dedication

[13] *Ibid.*, pp. 7–8.

[14] This searching yet belittling insight could not be expected to endear itself to the radicals for all the gentleness with which it is expressed. At a time when their lives, and more important, their cause, were at stake, they were not disposed to welcome such a condescending evaluation of themselves.

to the cause. In a related sense comedy arises from his commitment to the future: only "the fates" will decide whether the apparent chamber pot on Don Quixote's head will turn out later to be what he had known it to be all along, a helmet of shining armor. Turgenev, here, in taking two of the most antagonizing features of the radical ethos, and making them acceptable through the agency of comedy, assures the reader that the radical is as fallible and as foolish as he. Turgenev says: "A certain allotment of the ridiculous must inevitably be added to the actions, to the character of the people dedicated to a great new cause, as a tax . . . as a calming sacrifice to the jealous gods." [15] We are entitled to interpret "the jealous gods" both as the rules of art and the expectations of the average, nonbelieving reader. The ultimate purpose of the "comic envelope" is to release "a reconciling and cleansing force" through laughter. And, Turgenev adds: "Whom you laugh at you forgive and are ready to love." [16] Turgenev has mediated between the image and the reader, and has brought this encounter to a typically literary resolution. The love toward which Turgenev would lead the reader is composed of equal parts of respect (for the purity of Don Quixote's purpose), of affection, and of pity. Pity, in a sense, is Turgenev's final destination. Through it, the sting of the radical's arrogance is removed. At the same time the reader is detached from that direct identification with the literary figure which the radical aesthetic posited, and is elevated to the writer's superior point of sympathetic (and condescending) vantage. In showing how this type can be assimilated into a work of art, Turgenev has extended the definition of alienation to embrace the revolutionary as well. For he is cut off from awareness, from a rich emotional life, and from a genuine knowledge of evil as

[15] Turgenev, *Sobranie sochinenii*, XI, 18.   [16] *Ibid.*, p. 9.

surely as Hamlet is cut off from action and from love by his
egotism and by his perceptive, skeptical, and hungry intellect.

Hamlet is easier to write about than Don Quixote because he possesses so many of the conventional attributes
of the tragic hero. But the literary problem, as Turgenev
sees it, is substantially the same: to reduce him to a condition in which he arouses the reader's pity. In the case of the
dry, withdrawn Hamlet, who is incapable of love, hence of
being loved, who is barred from action because of the range
of his awareness, the principal obstacles to his acceptance
by the reader are his scornful pride and his apparent lack
of moral commitment. Don Quixote's condition of moral
purity and the consequent foolishness of his mien is exactly reversed in Hamlet's case: it is inconceivable that the
latter be laughed at, and in his anxious, twisting flight from
commitment (until it is too late), he seems to abandon the
possibility of asserting any moral position. Yet as he approaches death it becomes clear that scorn is his kind of
moral utterance, and that the target of his negation is evil.
As he becomes more deeply entangled in hostile circumstance, his pride is shown to be a mask for personal courage and dignity, which dissolves on the point of death into
a quiet humility. By this route he reaches his final destination beside Don Quixote in the pity and understanding of
the observer.

Art, Turgenev seemed to insist, must be granted the
privilege of rendering the activist and the intellectual equal
in the face of death, through the universal solvent of pity.
Certainly the artist may accept neither type at his own
evaluation of himself. The injunction to pity the revolutionary was anathema to the radicals, of course, who could
not see themselves in the whole context of their depriva-

tion, sacrifice, and self-delusion. Yet it is Chernyshevsky's refusal or inability to account for, or to contain, or to rise above their sense of superiority that makes his heroes unacceptable to the reader who does not share their creed. The human faults Turgenev perceived are there, but because the author has failed to explore them fully or to show them as sources of vulnerability, as well as of strength, the novel fails to supply that kind of total illumination that is art's function. Dealing with his heroes, the writer must insist on his claim to occupy an eminence above and independent of the ideas and values that sustain them. He must reject the assumption that any man's social reality is entirely congruent with his human reality and must see him in all his dimensions. Finally, he is obliged to detach the reader's emotion from the character's assertion of his own views. The hero in Turgenev's formula ends as an object of contemplation, not of emulation, more to be pitied than imitated. There is instruction in his fate but it is not the same lesson the hero, himself, would have the reader learn.

The revolutionary, no less than any other type, can best be explained in art's terms through defeat. His fallibility and his suffering are the surest means of access to understanding his total condition, whether he is proud, isolated, and tragic, or single-minded, deluded, and comic. Here, Turgenev has transcended the political categories with which he began his analysis and has suggested a scale for the reclassification of Russian hero-types. The proud, self-centered, and conventionally heroic figure who dares to act in defiance of his surroundings appears both within and without the movement of extreme political dissidence. Thus the Pechorins and Bazarovs, as well as the Stavrogins and Prince Andreis yet to come, are brothers beneath their ideological labels, and are, in turn, joined by the bond of

suffering with the mock-heroic Onegins, Rudins, even with
the quixotic Myshkin, and, conceivably, at the far end of
the scale of heroism, with the monstrous antihero of *Notes
from Underground.*

The writer's job is done, Turgenev suggests, when he has
explored, clarified, and generalized human suffering. But the
radical responds to suffering with the blunt and urgent
question which is echoed so often by Russian intellectuals:
what is to be done about it? It is not misreading Turgenev's
essay, perhaps, to propose, in a final look at it, that the Hamlet and Don Quixote figures also stand for the artist and the
revolutionary respectively, the first dedicated to awareness
at all costs, the second to action at all costs, and that both
share a common painful destiny. Turgenev's proposal, if
such it may be considered, could not be accepted by the
radicals. They saw their own suffering as a tiny sacrifice when
set against the misery of the mass, and, if it contributed to
the alleviation of the general misery, it was irrelevant, even
shameful, to dwell on it. If the writer replied that the revolutionary nevertheless suffers as all men do, and that by
the drastic, though high-minded, decisions on which he bases
his life he invites a new and more awful kind of suffering,
the agony, say, of an Ivan Karamazov, which art cannot fail
to record, the radical might respond that Ivan's private hell
is not typical or useful, or even, in his sense, truthful, and
that it fades into triviality when set against the consuming
agony of a nation.

II

The great controversy of the decade between 1855 and
1865, which illuminated so many crucial questions in the
history of the Russian intellect and imagination, did not
have a conclusive outcome on all its many levels. The events

of 1917 came closest to deciding the fundamental political questions at issue. The First All-Union Congress of Soviet Writers in 1934, though it too appeared to make an irrevocable choice between a free and a proprietary approach to literature, lacked the finality of the Bolshevik seizure of political power. The creed of Russian classical realism continued to show itself after 1934, as it had between 1917 and 1934, sometimes with the apparent indulgence of the political magistrates, at other times to their surprise and discomfort. The images of the hero continued to reflect the tension between the two approaches to literature.

In the intervening years between 1865 and 1917 the literary competition continued in new forms, corresponding to new conditions, but unchanged in its essentials. The new man went through a number of metamorphoses after the decline of the radical democrats, making his major reappearances first in the Narodniks' "little band of heroes," then as the early Bolshevik who, in turn, became the "new Soviet man." In the nineteenth century the radical continued to be viewed by many writers with detachment or outspoken hostility. Dostoevsky's *Possessed*, and Chekhov's *Ivanov* are among the better known works that contain unflattering portraits of the activist or the man of "progressive convictions." The literary portraiture of the alienated man, on the other hand, was to reach new heights of complexity and richness in the years that followed the decade of controversy: *War and Peace, Anna Karenina, The Death of Ivan Ilyich, The Idiot, The Raw Youth,* and *The Brothers Karamazov* were yet to be written.

Chekhov carried the alienated man, in his mock-heroic aspect, to a kind of apotheosis, in response, perhaps, to the general antiheroic trend in modern European realism. If this attitude had been as prevalent in Russia in the mid-

century as it was in Western Europe, there might not have
been the persistence of the large, taciturn, self-enclosed figures, whether rebels or revolutionaries or madmen, whom
Turgenev epitomized in his image of Hamlet. Certainly
Tolstoy was expressing this antiheroic current when he
wrote in *War and Peace*:

For an historian considering the achievement of a certain aim,
there are heroes; for the artist treating of man's relations to all
sides of life, there cannot and should not be heroes, but there
should be men.[17]

His only hero, as he had said earlier, was truth; and when he
repeated the same thought to Gorky years later in more
general terms—"Heroes—that's a lie and invention; there
are simply people, people, and nothing else" [18]—he was taking a positive stand against the new heroic romanticism
Gorky was advocating.

In the decades after 1865, the contest between the two
schools had no decisive outcome: political extremists did
not gain control of the great instrument of Russian realism;
the writers kept the realist creed alive and in active service,
through the death of Chekhov and beyond. But there were
notable defections from their position. Turgenev, who was
distressed by the clamor he touched off through his inter-
ventions in the controversy, lapsed into a state of confusion.
A great loss to literature was registered when it became apparent that he had been jarred loose from the delicate balance of ambiguities that had sustained *Fathers and Sons*
as well as "Hamlet and Don Quixote." His petulant satires
against the new generation of radicals made it clear that he
had surrendered important positions to the radical view of
art, even as he opposed radical political ideas. A polemical,

[17] Tolstoy, *War and Peace*, p. 1356.
[18] Maxim Gorky, *Reminiscences* (New York, 1946), p. 54.

topical view of the truth had replaced the Olympian claims he had earlier asserted for the artist's kind of truth. And when he labored and brought forth his own "positive hero," the sluggish Solomin of *Smoke* (1867), so well armed against failure because he ventured so little, a "helper" not a "leader," he had permanently impaired his vision by making his art the servant of his inconsequential political views. Tolstoy was the most dramatic "turncoat," of course, and his repudiation of art was, characteristically, more deliberate, more drastic, and more flamboyant. "Art is a lie," [19] he told Gorky. Earlier he had written *What Is Art?* (1897) to set the narrow boundaries within which art could be trusted to deal with essential moral truths. Turgenev's retreat and Tolstoy's desertion testify to the urgency with which the social question forced itself on all men of conscience in prerevolutionary Russia. There was a point of fundamental choice, apparently recognized by all, between the concerns of artist and revolutionary. To decide that in the face of suffering of a certain quality, quantity, and intensity, art became expendable, was a tragic but not always an impossible choice for Russian men of letters.

The radical critics worked on the margins of the great creative currents of the age, exerting a steady pressure of conscience, often posing the questions the writers undertook to explore. It was when the alliance between them broke down, when the tactical requirements of political action asserted themselves too urgently, that the artist and the revolutionary were thrown into direct competition for "the awareness of human suffering." Each was forced to default on one premise of his alliance: the revolutionary had to compromise with the expedient choices that the social crisis offered him, the writer to fall back on that neces-

[19] *Ibid.*

sary "compromise" with his civilization without which he
could not function. The rupture in the 1860s was costly,
resulting in disillusion and bitterness. More robust spirits
like Tolstoy and Dostoevsky maintained themselves intact
as artists against the ferocious pressures of the next two decades, until Tolstoy, independently, felt himself driven to
make that ultimate choice between art and action which he
had acknowledged twenty years before. When he did, he
found himself involved in the creation of a positive, emblematic hero—in this case, himself. For the power of his
doctrine flowed from the example of his own moral life,
which was to radiate outward until it was accepted by enough
men to bring about the nonviolent, but nonetheless total,
overthrow of the social order. Tolstoy was reflecting the belief, so deeply ingrained in the Russian consciousness since
the time of the *bogatyr*, that the surest promise of their
release from intolerable suffering was the appearance of a
new kind of moral personality, not a Messianic leader, but a
more general type, susceptible of imitation, whose personal
qualities would contain and express the means to that
liberation.

8
MARXISM, REALISM, AND THE HERO

Among the qualities inherent in matter, motion is the first and foremost, not only in the form of mechanical and mathematical motion, but chiefly in the form of an impulse, a vital spirit, a tension. KARL MARX, *The Holy Family*

Marxism, John Strachey has said, is not merely a body of ideas, but a separate "country" of the intellect. One visits it in pursuit of the answers to a single, delimited question—in this case the connections between Marxian ideas and the properties of realism—at the risk of returning with incomplete findings, rendered useless by loss of context. In any case, one is automatically exposed to the charge of "distortion," both from the nationals of that country, and from outsiders who have never crossed its borders. Yet the matter cannot be sidestepped. Marxism makes up the bulk of the Soviet intellectual inheritance according to all official comment on the matter; the Soviet habit of scholastic dependence on past intellectual authorities makes it imperative to inquire into the literary consequences of Marxism. The little Marx and Engels had to say about literature itself has been piously, exhaustively, and repeatedly explored by Soviet critics in search of a viable "literary policy."

I

A fundamental polarity in the Marxian concept of human behavior is defined in two of Marx's most familiar notions.

The first summarizes his view of man as a determined creature:

The mode of production of material life conditions the social, political and intellectual life process in general. It is not the consciousness of men that determines their being, but on the contrary, their social being that determines their consciousness.[1]

The second emphasizes man's role as a free, conscious, and responsible agent, as the "maker of his own history." A great distance separates these two ideas and very different consequences have flowed from the varying emphases Marxists have put upon them. But for Marx and Engels there was apparently no formal contradiction between them. They are found side by side in the same sentence in a state of harmony which certainly is intended to express more than a verbal resolution of the tension between them. In the Third Thesis on Feuerbach, Marx wrote:

The materialist doctrine that men are products of circumstances and upbringing, forgets that it is men that change circumstances and that the educator himself needs educating.[2]

The unity that contains these contradictory propositions can be described briefly: man's capacity to acquire true objective knowledge of his history, of his social milieu, and of all his real relations with his environment leads to a state of awareness that permits—indeed, requires—action. "Freedom," Engels said, ". . . consists in the control over ourselves and over external nature which is founded on knowledge of natural necessity."[3] Man becomes the hastener of history, struggles to master it, and, when he achieves that

[1] Karl Marx and Friedrich Engels, *Selected Works* (Moscow, 1951), I, 329.
[2] *Ibid.*, pp. 365–66.
[3] Friedrich Engels, *Herr Eugen Dühring's Revolution in Science* (New York, 1939), p. 125.

mastery, gains control over his destiny. As Vernon Venable, writing on the central "dilemma of inevitability," has pointed out, man, himself, "the needing organism, purposive human activity . . . is a nuclear causal factor"[4] in *determining* history's course.

Soviet experience has shown that the search for a "correct" solution to this perpetual problem has affected every area of thought and action at one time or another—political strategy, philosophy, education, psychology, literature, art, and economic theory, to name some of the important ones. The opposition between Bolshevist and Menshevist tactics before the revolution, the historic debate of the philosophers in 1929 between the "mechanists" and the "dialecticians,"[5] and the drastic reversals in psychological theory after 1929[6] reflect conflicts between Marxian sects according to the construction each has put upon this troublesome unity of conceptual opposites. In the Soviet vocabulary today the principal schism is described as between "Leninism" and "Plekhanovism." One of Lenin's major contributions to Soviet Marxian theory is now said to be his redefinition of man as the conscious, responsible, and disciplined maker of his own history, as opposed to Plekhanov's emphasis on man as the creature and passive beneficiary of the historial process. It was Stalin who extended Lenin's notion of conscious political partisanship to every field of intellectual endeavor, in-

[4] Vernon Venable, *Human Nature; the Marxian View* (New York, 1946), p. 190. I should pause here to acknowledge my debt to this excellent work, particularly for its elucidation of the ethical question in Marxian theory.

[5] See Julius F. Hecker's summary of the debate in *Moscow Dialogues* (London, 1934), Dialogue XIV, pp. 157–73.

[6] Cf. Raymond Bauer's *The New Man in Soviet Psychology* (Cambridge, 1952), particularly Chapter 2, "Two Kinds of Marxism," and Chapter 6, "Consciousness Comes to Man."

cluding literature and art, and such self-contained activities
of the human intellect as astronomy and musical composi-
tion.

Applied to the scholarly and creative disciplines, the dilemma is expressed in another kind of antithesis: as the
opposition between a science of history and of society, on the
one hand, and a summons to revolutionary struggle, on the
other. Marx made his famous distinction between the function of the philosopher as *interpreter* or *changer* of the world,
insisting that the second had become his true vocation.[7] Yet
if we apply this distinction to Marx's and Engels's own
careers, it is clear that though they played both parts, the
best years of their lives were spent investigating social
phenomena, not in devising revolutionary strategies. Hecker
distinguishes two peaks of the activist phase within the
history of Marxism—1848 and 1917.[8] Marx's most productive years, between 1850 and his death in 1883, were largely
spent in the British Museum, not on the barricades. According to Marx's example, each adherent of his system had to
make a decision about the importance he would assign to
knowledge as against action. Thus the Marxist chooses between two approaches to experience, two kinds of truth:
one objective, analytical, and descriptive, the other selective,
tendentious, and agitational. Obviously the first is more congenial to scholarly investigation and is, at the same time,
closer to the determinist pole in the Marxian dichotomy.
The investigator of a given historial event will explore all
lines of causal development, including the role of human
consciousness, because all events in the Marxian materialist
view of the universe are assumed to be determined when

[7] Eleventh Thesis on Feuerbach. Marx and Engels, *Selected Works,*
II, 367.
[8] Cf. Hecker, *Moscow Dialogues,* pp. 134–35.

seen in the past. Even the Marxian "accident," an intersection of two or more lines of causal development, which could not have been foreseen by the historical actors at the time, becomes a determined event as soon as it is completed. The pragmatic agitator is less interested in the past, though he knows that he is history's instrument and has its momentum behind him.

It is more than a question of the uses the Marxist shall make of his time or of the *kinds* of information that will serve his purposes. In theory, all information must be accessible to the revolutionary movement at some level in its hierarchy of command, as it was to Marx in the British Museum, but it is not necessarily to be shared with the entire rank and file in undigested form. Before he passes it on he sifts it to discover what it tells of coming events, and "interprets" it to square with certain basic attitudes of the rank-and-filers and to stiffen their wills and arouse their emotions. The scholar-determinist might venture to extend his findings into the future in the form of a "scientific" prediction, but the moment he looks up from the data he is expected by his alter ego, the agitator, to exert all the influence he can on the most controllable causal agency in the historial process—the human mind. Would this not result in an abrupt and bewildering change of key in any single work? Actually, in the Marxian classics the two kinds of truth are always present in some kind of synthesis. Marx and Engels did not often face problems of revolutionary strategy, or permit themselves to predict the immediate how and when of social change, but their great analytical works are charged with emotion and constitute in their totality a generalized call to arms.

Lenin, the activist and strategist, drastically altered the emphasis by insisting on the indissoluble unity and interdependence of "theory and practice." [9] Practice poses the questions and tests the answers theory returns in a close and continuous interchange. Bound by a rigid standard of practical application, theory is not granted the right to explore freely, or to wander any great distance from immediate political tasks. Lenin is concerned, of course, with *political* theory and practice, but this approach to knowledge has been extended at times to many intellectual spheres in the USSR through the limitless definition of what is political, that is, of what affects the power or security of Party and state.[10]

How does the Marxian polarity manifest itself in those writings of Marx and Engels which bear on problems of the literary imagination? It is already clear that the "agitational" truth of Marxism, with its emphasis on stimulus and persuasion, resembles the views of the Russian radical critics at several points: the attitude toward the future, the doctrinal view of truth, and the consequent posting of a rigid standard of selectivity. It is also evident, I think, that the

[9] See V. I. Lenin, *Materialism and Empirio-Criticism* (Moscow, 1952), pp. 190–96, for a typical discussion of this matter. Raymond Bauer has very acutely traced the consequences of Lenin's epistemology in its Soviet application. For his account of the successive steps by which the Marxian notion that knowledge must be tested by use (Marx's Second Thesis on Feuerbach) became the doctrine that usefulness to the Party is the final determinant of all truth, see Bauer, *The New Man in Soviet Psychology*, pp. 103–6.

[10] It is on the levels below the one where policy is made that writers, scholars, commentators, and other "toilers of the brain" are exposed to the dangers of overemphasizing one or the other aspect of Marxian truth. Thus, a history of philosophy may be charged by *Pravda* with "objectivism," or "the passive reflection of events," and its author subjected to a torrent of abuse on that account. On the other hand, when a linguist, say, or a geneticist, says he has found a superior "Marxian" or "Soviet socialist" approach to his discipline, the passage of time may reveal that in his agitational zeal he has paid inadequate attention to the objective data, or to the special requirements of his field, and that his leadership has brought the Soviet section of his branch of science to the point of intellectual bankruptcy.

opposition between investigation and agitation corresponds
closely to the tension we have already noted in literature between "is" and "should be." Shall literature, then, be primarily concerned with interpreting or changing the world?
And, in this connection, is there any formula for the literary
hero? The central division in Marx's thinking, we may note
here, manifests itself in a suggestive way on this very question. When asked by his daughter in a parlor game to name
his favorite heroes, he responded with two: a hero of action
—Spartacus, and a hero of thought—Kepler.[11] Should the
literary hero be Spartacus or Kepler, or both, or neither, or
no one? In any case, how free should the artist be to explore
his universe?

II

The scattered observations Marx and Engels made on
literature are impressive for their range. Their cultivated
tastes bear the imprint of a solid nineteenth-century humanist education, and the general tone of their approach
differs markedly from that of the Russian radicals in its lack
of suspicion or hostility toward the literary imagination. The
question to determine is whether or not their random remarks on the subject fit together in any kind of scheme, and
where, if at all, the scheme connects with deeper currents
of Marxian thought. In this connection the issues brought
to light in the Russian literary debate offer a useful set of
testing devices. Marx and Engels may not belong under either
heading, but a tendency in either direction is important because of the close attention Soviet intellectuals affect to pay
to the founders of their tradition.

Marx and Engels insisted, of course, that literature, to-

[11] A. V. Lunacharsky, ed., *Marks i Engels ob iskusstve* (Moscow, 1933),
p. 208.

gether with all other products of the human intellect, has its being within an ideological superstructure, the content of which is ultimately determined by the economic and political structure of society. But, once they had established the *primacy* of the economic factor, they felt constrained in several subsequent utterances to correct the tendency of their interpreters to make the socioeconomic situation not the *ultimate* but the *sole* determinant of the shape and substance of "intellectual products." Engels, on two occasions, attempted to set general limits to the efficacy of the economic factor as the governor of man's spiritual life. In a letter to Conrad Schmidt in 1890 he discussed the philosophy and art of the Enlightenment in these terms:

I consider the ultimate supremacy of economic development established in these spheres too, but it comes to pass within conditions imposed by the particular sphere itself: in philosophy, for instance, through the operation of economic influences . . . upon the existing philosophic material handed down by predecessors. Here [the] economy creates nothing absolutely new, but it determines the way in which the existing material of thought is altered and further developed, and that too for the most part indirectly, for it is the political, legal and moral reflexes which exercise the greatest direct influence upon philosophy.[12]

Engels is arguing here against a too simple view of the relations between economics and culture. The inference may be drawn from the phrase "existing material of thought," that every discipline of the mind has a history of its own, laws of its own development, concerns which are unique to it, and the power to exert its own causal influence on men and events. On the last point Engels is quite explicit:

Political, juridical, philosophical, religious, literary, artistic, etc., development is based on economic development. But all these

[12] Karl Marx and Friedrich Engels, *Selected Correspondence, 1846–1895* (New York, 1942), pp. 483–84.

react upon one another and also upon the economic base. It is not that the economic position is the *cause and alone* active, while everything else has only a passive effect. There is, rather, interaction on the basis of the economic necessity, which *ultimately* always asserts itself.[13]

Confronted with the achievements of the Greeks, Marx went further:

It is well known that certain periods of the highest development of art stand in no direct connection with the general development of society, nor with the material basis and the skeleton structure of its organization. Witness the Greeks as compared with modern nations or even Shakespeare.[14]

Soviet Marxists, in general, have ignored these qualifications and have assumed an extremely direct and restricted relation between base and superstructure. The permanent, all-determining war between the classes is inevitably present in all works of the mind and imagination, whether or not the human agent is aware of it, and is the key to their meanings as well as the touchstone of value-judgments about them. Every work of art presents itself to the critic as an expression, in rationalized or direct form, of class interest. The Soviet Marxist does not say that literature partakes of ideology or has a relationship to it, or is influenced by it. Literature to him *is* ideology or, even more narrowly, every literary work is a form of class consciousness. I. Nusinov leaves little room for qualification in a typical definition of the Soviet attitude on this matter:

In class society where all human consciousness and behavior is defined by class being and conditions of class struggle, all human social activity, including all conscious activity, serves the tasks of class struggle. Literature, like any other ideology, takes the form of class consciousness serving class self-definition. In

[13] Letter to H. Starkenburg, January 25, 1894, *ibid.*, p. 517.
[14] *Literature and Art* (New York, 1947), p. 18.

this is to be found the common ground of social genesis and social function which literature shares with other ideologies.[15]

Before 1929, the work of art, seen as a reflection of its social milieu and of the class attitudes of its author, was analyzed by Plekhanovist criticism to reveal—or "to unmask"—its ideological essence and its relation to progressive and regressive social forces at the time it was written. This was the critic's primary function—the "sociological moment" —of the act of criticism. The critic then moved on to the second, or "aesthetic moment," the critical estimate of the work's formal properties. At its most absurd this approach turned into a search for the writer's birth certificate. And, though much of the nonsense in this attitude was swept away by the attack on "vulgar sociologism" in the late twenties, the close, uncomplicated connection between art and society went unchallenged.

With the shift of emphasis to conscious, willed behavior after 1929, the base-superstructure framework was simply stood on its head. It was assumed, apparently, that the largely unconscious process of reflection which had been brought to light by Marxist analysis had only to be reversed, and made conscious, so that the artist not only reflected the base but deliberately worked to influence those who were changing it. Literature was no longer a form of passive ideological reflection, but an active, "healthy," controlled ideological instrument, not a mirror any more but a weapon. Stalin's massively simple definition of the relation between base and

---

[15] I. Nusinov, "Literatura," *Sovetskaya entsiklopediya*, VI, 404. Nusinov defines characteristics which distinguish literature from other forms of "thought." The main distinction he makes between poetry and science is Belinsky's, not Marx's, namely, that the artist thinks in "images," the scientist in propositions. Lukács considers it one of the greatest achievements of "Russian democratic-revolutionary criticism" that it "advanced to a point where the social genesis and the aesthetic value of a literary work were hooked up with each other." (George Lukács, *Studies in European Realism* [London, 1950], p. 116.)

superstructure emphasizes the instrumental character of disciplined consciousness, and doubtless has served to justify every restriction on Soviet intellectual life. In his article on the linguistics controversy of 1950, he wrote:

The superstructure is generated by the base but this by no means signifies that it merely reflects the base, that it is passive, neutral and indifferent to the fate of its base, to the fate of classes, to the character of the system. On the contrary, having put in an appearance, it then becomes a most active force which contributes vigorously to the formation and consolidation of its base, takes all steps to assist the new order to drive former classes into the dust and liquidate them.

It could not be otherwise. The superstructure is created by the base to serve it, to help it actively in taking shape and growing strong.[16]

In this view of the proper goals of human spiritual activity, there is no reason to doubt that the work of art will be valued above all for its ideological leverage. From the absolute preeminence of the social task—the remaking of the base— is derived the society's entire system of rewards and punishments, of restriction and permission. No one is exempt, including the writer. Marx and Engels never faced the problem of building the new order. All they had to say about art is subject to this qualification, but there is a dramatic contrast, nevertheless, between modern Soviet attitudes and Marx's remarks in 1842 on the writer's freedom:

The writer, of course, must make a living in order to have the opportunity to exist and to write, but he must in no way exist and write in order to earn a living. . . . The writer, in no way, regards his work as a means. It is an end in itself; it is so little a means either for him or for others, that when necessary the writer makes sacrifices to its existence, when necessary, his own

[16] J. Stalin, "On Marxism in Linguistics," in *The Soviet Linguistic Controversy* (New York, 1951), p. 70. The primacy of social issues, a sense of disciplined struggle, service, and partisanship are all suggested here.

existence, and, like the preacher . . . he takes as his principle: "Obey God more than men," men among whom he includes himself with his human needs and desires. . . . The first freedom of the press consists in its not being a trade.[17]

This passage has greatly troubled Soviet commentators. M. Lifshitz, one of the principal curators of the Marxian inheritance, has devoted a good deal of time and ingenuity to interpret it so that it loses all validity as a general statement about the situation of the writer. His qualifications are designed to prove that all its meaning is derived from Marx's personal situation and from the tactical political needs of the movement.[18] Its lasting significance, he insists, is to be found in the remark about literature as a "trade," which finds a logical extension in Lenin's famous article in 1905, "Party Organization and Party Literature," a violent attack on the bourgeois writer as a hireling of reactionary political forces who makes a business out of literature. Lifshitz's interpretation, with its suggestion that Lenin is merely completing Marx's thought, overlooks the fact that Lenin not only ignored Marx's view of the artist's autonomy but, at important junctures, completely reversed it.[19]

This questionable interpretation could be validated only if Lifshitz were able to show that Marx ever said that art should subordinate itself to political, or other alien, interests. There is no such reversal of attitude in Marx's later remarks, and their humanist temper suggests that he always honored the differences between the concerns of the artist and the political activist. Not that the autonomy of art ever meant

[17] He was defending his own newspaper from political censorship in Germany when he was editor of the Jacobin *Rhenish Gazette*. The quoted passage is taken from Marx and Engels, *Literaturnoe nasledstvo*, ed. Franz Mehring (Moscow, 1907), p. 225.
[18] See his article "Marx," in *Literaturnaya entsiklopediya* (1932), VI, 886–87.
[19] See Chapter 10 for a full discussion of Lenin's article.

irresponsibility. The great writers of the past were never free
of the pressures, nor blind to the issues, of their time. But
there is no tendency in Marx to proclaim that the "correctness" of a work is the source of its value, nor that progressive
political commitment is any primary obligation of the writer.
The literary achievement *per se* of Shakespeare, Aeschylus,
Cervantes, or Dante—to name his favorites—is the mark of
their greatness and the source of their value. The great
writers of the past are giants among men who bear impressive witness in their persons and in their work to the wonder
of the human potential. And, though their work may reflect
the general excitement and vitality of an age, Marx and
Engels never try to connect them more intimately with the
contending factions in their society.[20] In discussing contemporary writers, with whom they had sharp, doctrinal
quarrels, or whose relationship to class alignments was the
opposite of their own, Marx and Engels were strongly inclined to respect the man as an artist. Political considerations
were deliberately set aside. Goethe, who, Engels felt, displayed a distressing ability at times to accommodate to the
worst values in his society, was, nevertheless, at other moments in his career "a defiant, ironical, world-scorning genius." [21] Heine, whom he knew and disagreed with, was always

[20] Engels's remarks on Dante are in point here: "The close of the
feudal Middle Ages, the threshold of the modern capitalist era, was
marked by a gigantic, colossal figure. It was an Italian, Dante, who was
both the last poet of the Middle Ages and the first poet of modern times.
Today, a new historical era is unfolding. Will Italy give us the new
Dante, who will mark the hour of birth of this new poletarian era?"
(*Literature and Art*, pp. 76–77.) Comment on other great moments in
the history of culture exposes the same general assumption: that the
excitement of an era of change is the best soil for great art. Ancient
Greece is an exception, in that its art rests on the perfect fusion of social
values with patterns of mythological belief.

[21] See *Literature and Art*, pp. 81–83, for the whole of his opinion.
Engels carefully qualifies the negative aspects of his judgment. Goethe
is "too universal," "too active," "too fleshly," "too sharp-sighted," to

spared Marx's terrible wrath.[22] In the case of Balzac, Engels again demonstrated his belief that art and politics are separate domains, simply by disconnecting the writer's political intentions from his literary achievement.[23] Balzac told the truth, Engels felt, despite his royalist aspirations, because he reflected the major currents of social change in France exactly as Marx and Engels had, by other means, discovered them to be. Indeed, this is the usual interpretation given to this passage by Soviet commentators: art may tell the Marxist truth despite the social preferences of the writer. But Engels's point has a number of other implications that must be unsettling to any advocate of prescriptive control over literature. Engels makes it clear that the value of a work of art is not a necessary function of its social genesis or of its political intentions, and, further, that if it is a well-made work of art without notable historical falsity, it is *ipso facto* valuable and true. Balzac disclosed what he did because he was a great artist, not an indoctrinated socialist, or a confused royalist, and, in his devotion to his calling, he betrayed or set aside his lesser allegiances. Finally it would seem reasonable to infer that, if great works of art proceed from bad political intentions, then bad works of art may issue from the best of intentions, and that in the end, talent and integrity—"the courage of the true artist" [24]—are all.

stand accused of cowardly flight from his dilemma. His final weariness is the result of a defeat inflicted on him by the environment he despised but required in order to fulfill himself. Engels is careful to point out that his judgment proceeds "neither from moral nor from partisan . . . but chiefly from aesthetic and historical standpoints." The artist shall be judged by his work, apparently, and shall be granted immunity on that basis from the furious political abuse reserved for lesser men.

[22] Marx said in a letter to Engels, that like Horace, Heine was "at bottom a cur in a political sense." "Yet in other respects," he added, "the old wretch is very lovable" (*ibid.*, p. 107).

[23] See Engels's letter to Margaret Harkness, written in April (*ibid.*, pp. 41–43).

[24] *Ibid.*, p. 41. From the same letter to Margaret Harkness.

The celebrated discussion of realism and tendentiousness confirms this view of Marx's and Engels's true feelings about art. As materialists they were disposed to favor realism, and as social scientists they adhered to a rigorous canon of verisimilitude in their judgments on the recreated world of fiction. In addition, the realist writer must generalize, and in his generalization cannot fail to comment on his world:

> Realism, to my mind, implies besides truth of detail, the truthful reproduction of typical characters under typical circumstances.[25]

There is no doubt, too, that the "typical" in a novel must coincide at some point with their own analysis of society. To this extent their ideas parallel those of the Russian radical democrats. Engels was even willing to criticize lesser works that were submitted to him for comment on the ground that they did not square with his own analysis of a specific social milieu.[26] But when the question of conscious tendency in the novel was put directly to Engels, his acceptance of the idea was so qualified that it offered little encouragement to the untalented petitioners who sought his support. He stated his position not as an advocate, but negatively, as one who was "not at all an opponent of tendentious poetry as such." [27] To illustrate his position, he named his models:

> The father of tragedy, Aeschylus, and the father of comedy, Aristophanes, were both decidedly tendentious poets, just as were Dante and Cervantes; and the main merit of Schiller's *Craft and Loves* is that it is the first German political propaganda drama. The modern Russians and Norwegians, who are writing splendid novels, are all tendentious.[28]

Protected by the breadth of his definition and by the great figures he invoked in its support, he was willing to grant, not

[25] *Ibid.*
[26] See his letter to Margaret Harkness in this connection (*ibid.*, p. 42).
[27] *Ibid.*, p. 45. From a letter written to Minna Kautsky in 1885.
[28] *Ibid.*

that all great works of art are tendentious, nor that all works of art should be tendentious, but that some great works of art have not ceased to be great because they have been tendentious. The order of values implicit in this statement seems unmistakable: works of art may be both great and tendentious, but the artist who imitates them might attempt the second only if he achieved the first. The propagation of "healthy," "correct," "progressive" ideas is nowhere declared to be the writer's preeminent obligation. If his work is "to serve," the implication is clear, it will do so by being true to its own nature, by performing its persuasive function unobtrusively, through the fictional material itself. Engels is clear on this point: "The more the author's views are concealed the better for the work of art," [29] because "the tendency should flow by itself from the situation and action without being explicitly formulated." [30] He was prepared to admit tendency into the work of art under certain conditions, but he was unwilling to say what *kind* of tendency, nor even that it was essential.

Engels's most explicit statement about art's potential value to the socialist movement stopped far short of the prescriptive strictures of the Russian radical democrats. His qualifications tend to associate him much more closely with their opponents' position in the controversy of the sixties, particularly in their unwillingness to impose an explicit educational or inspirational function on art:

A socialist-biased novel fully achieves its purpose, in my view, if, by conscientiously describing real mutual relations, breaking down conventional illusions about them, it shatters the optimism of the bourgeois, instils doubt as to the eternal character of the existing order, although the author does not offer any definite solution or does not even line up openly on any particular side.[31]

Apparently any gifted and honest writer could penetrate the fog of bourgeois rationalizations and come upon the

[29] *Ibid.*, p. 42.   [30] *Ibid.*, p. 45.   [31] *Ibid.*

Marxian truth about the real relations that bound men together. But this was service enough for art to perform. The
artist was a welcome ally but he was free of any obligation
to subordinate his work to agitational considerations. Engels
not only granted the artist this exemption, he insisted on it.
It seems clear, too, that Marx and Engels tend to associate
literature with the objective, analytical, not with the agitational, world-changing, phase of their own theory. Even
when art makes use of their analytical concepts it must conceal them, and must state its "case" in the terms traditionally
proper to its medium.

The realism they favored had, by its nature, to deal with
the past. It was perfectly proper, Engels told Margaret
Harkness, to write of the working class's "convulsive attempts . . . to attain their rights as human beings," because
these efforts "belong to history and may therefore lay claim
to a place in the domain of realism." [32] But Engels declared
himself opposed to any entanglement in the future: "The
writer is not obliged to obtrude on the reader the future
historical solutions of the social conflicts pictured." [33] His
obligation toward history's dialectic was not to concentrate
on its emergent phase, but only to record its history up to
the present. On this crucial point, the advocates of an agitational realism can find no sanction for the inclusion of
prediction and promise which is central to their aesthetic.

[32] *Ibid.*

[33] *Ibid.* On this point, Soviet critics rely on other evidence to support
their view of the future. Paul Lafargue reported: "Marx looked upon
Balzac, not merely as the historian of the social life of his time, but as
a prophetic creator of character types which still existed only in embryo
during the reign of Louis Philippe, and which only reached full development under Napoleon III, after Balzac's death." (Quoted in *ibid.*, p.
139.) This second-hand report does resemble the ideas of the Russian
radicals and the socialist realists. But it should be pointed out that
Balzac's prescience is seen as an additional attribute of his genius, and
is nowhere advocated by either Marx or Engels as a quality to be deliberately cultivated.

The response of Marx and Engels to a number of politically emblematic heroes was entirely consistent with the standards and attitudes explained above. In Engels's criticism of Minna Kautsky's novel, *Old and New,* which he praised for its precision and "naturalness," he found the hero absolutely unacceptable:

In truth he is too faultless, and if at last he perishes by falling from a mountain, this can be reconciled with poetic justice only in that he was too good for this world. It is always bad for an author to be infatuated with his hero, and it seems to me that in this case you have given way somewhat to this weakness. Elsa still has traces of personality although she is also somewhat idealized, but in Arnold personality is entirely dissolved in principle.[34]

The author has violated the integrity of her story because, as Engels told her, "you felt the need of publicly declaring your convictions, of bearing witness to them before the whole world." [35] The declamation of principles was no substitute for the creative and lifelike handling of character. By making her protagonist a flawless representative of her own aspirations, she had lost control of him by surrendering "that fine irony which demonstrates the power of the writer over his creation." [36]

Marx, too, considered political heroism in literature, and found similar grounds for rejecting the two examples that came to his attention. Revolutionaries, he felt, were valid subjects for the artist. But, he also seems to suggest, if they are done badly they need not be done at all. Marx's comment on two obscure French novels in no way implies that a shabby piece of work might gain his approval on political grounds alone. He wrote:

[34] *Ibid.,* p. 45.   [35] *Ibid.*
[36] *Ibid.,* pp. 45–46. It is this "ironic" control that the modern Soviet writer has lost, too.

Nothing is more desirable than that the people who stood at the head of the revolutionary party, either before the Revolution, in secret societies or in the press, or later in official positions, be finally depicted in strong Rembrandtian colors, in all their living qualities. Hitherto these people have never been pictured in their real form; they have been presented as official personalities, wearing buskins and with aureoles around their heads. In these apotheoses of Raphaelite beauty all pictorial truth is lost. The two books under review do get rid of the buskin and aureole. . . . They go into the private lives of these people, showing them in carpet slippers, together with their whole entourage of satellites of various kinds. But that does not mean that they are any nearer a true and honest presentation of persons and events.[37]

Marx's reasons for dissatisfaction are suggested in the word "Rembrandtian." As elsewhere in his and Engels's remarks about art, an unqualified classical standard of excellence formed the basis of their judgments. Its ingredients are depth, color, richness, vitality, and energy; and when these qualities are present the result is a unique kind of "pictorial truth." No lapse from this standard was to be condoned for the local gains which might be derived from the *merely* favorable portraiture of revolutionary heroes. There is certainly nothing in what they say to suggest that political virtue is, in itself, a source of artistic excellence. It was a legitimate—even "a desirable"—subject for art, but it must always be measured against a Shakespearean or a Dantean or a Rembrandtian standard.

There was no departure from this approach—and no support, therefore, for Soviet attitudes on these matters—on the two other occasions on which Marx and Engels discussed the literary hero. Both men wrote long letters to their colleague, Ferdinand Lassalle, about his play *Franz von Sickingen*, a tragic drama of the civil wars in sixteenth-century

[37] *Ibid.*, p. 40.

Germany. In their severely qualified praise of the play three points deserve mention: their acceptance of the tragic mode, their suggestive formula for adapting it to the Marxian view of history, and the further exposure of their Shakespearean standards of judgment.

On the first point Marx was perfectly explicit: "I can therefore only express my full approval of making this the central theme of a modern tragedy." [38] The trouble came in working out the theme, the tragedy of an inopportune revolutionary, of a man of conviction and energy, who saw the need to act but was doomed to defeat because of the discrepancy between his personal aspirations and his situation in history.[39] Engels described the central conflict in abstract terms as "the tragic collision between the historically necessary postulate and the practical impossibility of its realization." [40] Sickingen died, Marx said, because as a knight he was the "representative of a perishing class" and could not, therefore, make an alliance with the peasantry which would have fulfilled his morally praiseworthy but historically unrealizable purposes.

In their criticism of Lassalle's treatment of his theme, Marx and Engels again invoked a standard of Shakespearean complexity and vitality. The historical data were correct and the principal characters were correctly identified with social forces, but thinness of characterization meant the absence of that indispensable union of the general and the particular through which ideas are expressed in literature. Sickingen, Marx said, "is drawn too abstractly," and failed, there-

---

[38] *Ibid.*, p. 46.   [39] *Ibid.*, p. 55.
[40] *Ibid.* This formulation of the tragic possibility in a determined universe has had little attention from Soviet Marxists. The thought that the revolutionary is always, in some sense, *inopportune*, that he lives in a state of dangerous tension between his expectations and the historical process, has been very little used by Soviet writers. Leonid Leonov is the only one who has sensed Marx's idea here and exploited it with any success. (See Chapter 13.)

fore, to participate in the drama as an active moral personality. He was, rather, the unhappy "victim of a collision
independent of all his personal calculations." [41] In their
critique of the play, Marx and Engels returned repeatedly
to the idea that sterility of characterization robbed the play
of dramatic interest and intellectual significance. Dialogue
sounded like "lawyers' speeches"; the character Mina was
turned into "a doctrine of rights"; individuals were made
into "the mere mouth-pieces of the spirit of the times";
"argumentative debate" should be replaced by "motives more
lively, active, spontaneously occupying the foreground . . .
through the course of the action itself." [42]

Marx summed up his objections to the play's lifelessness
in the epithet "Schillerism." As an antidote, he proposed to
Lassalle simply that he "Shakespearize more." [43] Engels
echoed this thought more politely: "You could without harm
have paid more attention to the significance of Shakespeare
in the history of the development of the drama." He went
on to predict a future synthesis of the "great intellectual
depth and conscious historical content" of German drama
with "Shakespearean vivacity and wealth of action." [44] But
until this was achieved, we may conclude, the absence of
"Shakespearean vivacity" would always invalidate the Ger-

[41] *Ibid.*, p. 48.

[42] These judgments are taken from the letters written by both men
in 1859 to Lassalle (*ibid.*, pp. 46–56). The ideas expressed in these
letters are so similar as to be uncanny, unless, of course, they had discussed the play together and agreed on the line to be taken. Engels is
politer and more detailed, but both men interlard their criticism with
extravagant praise, perhaps to flatter an important colleague, or perhaps
because, as Engels pointed out unctuously, the Socialist movement
would gain from the play's success, and "we are all very pleased at every
new proof that whatever field the party enters it always shows its superiority." (*Ibid.*, p. 56.) The severity of their criticism, nevertheless,
indicates that neither Lassalle nor "the party" would profit anything
until extensive revisions had been made.

[43] *Ibid.*, p. 52.   [44] *Ibid.*

man intellectual contribution. Marx's and Engels's uncompromisingly high standards did not discourage their sympathizers from attempting to forward history's course by the calculated use of imaginative fiction. In resisting their disciples' efforts in this direction, it is clear that Marx and Engels were not merely expressing a cranky personal preference. Marx's remarks on the lasting value of Greek art indicate that he spoke out of a broad view of the separate histories of art and society. The question at issue was the general one posed by Marxian evolutionism: does a higher stage of social development guarantee higher forms of art? All the aesthetic evidence, Marx felt, pointed to a negative conclusion.[45] But this, in turn, raised another important question: wherein is the permanent appeal of Greek works of art? The answer, Marx said, "lies in understanding why they still constitute with us a source of aesthetic enjoyment and, in certain respects, prevail as the standard and model beyond attainment." [46] Marx avoided a direct answer to this question

[45] Marx and Engels touched a number of times on the question of the *kind* of social situation (as distinct from the *stage* of social evolution) that was most favorable for art. The great intellectual currents that swept through Europe with the disintegration of the Middle Ages Marx associated generally with the beginnings of the capitalist era. At the same time he was aware of national differences: Dante, da Vinci, Shakespeare, Luther, Cervantes, for example, bore the stamp of their milieux. Yet he never attempted to establish close connections between these men and the rising middle class. The ferment attendant upon a colossal shift in economic power seemed, in the case of the Renaissance, at least, to furnish favorable conditions for great art. In the eighteenth century, and to a certain degree in the nineteenth, the artist seemed to succeed best in a stance of protest against the moral falseness of his society. Neither of these conditions were present in Greek society where the serenity and security of shared values and beliefs— the real source of Greek art was mythology, Marx said—furnished a different set of conditions for the artist. It is a pity Marx never brought his powers of generalization to bear on these problems of cultural history.

[46] *Literature and Art*, p. 19. Lifshitz's treatment of these two questions is interesting. In answer to the first he refers to Hegel. At different

by invoking one of the overworked clichés of his century. Greek civilization was not the "adolescence" of mankind, as Hegel asserted, but its "natural" childhood, the spontaneity, innocence, and vitality of which were as ephemeral in history as they were in man's life. Evasive as his answer was, it permits several inferences which challenge both the Russian radicals and their Soviet legatees at several important points. In the first place, by disconnecting the value of works of art from their relative place in the evolution of history, Marx completely undermines Timofeev's grotesque assertion that Soviet art is more valuable than prerevolutionary art because it expresses a "higher" form of social development.[47] Second, Marx did not suggest that art's value depends on the "progressive" or "reactionary" attitude it assumed toward contemporary social struggles, which is the only explanation the modern Soviet aesthetic gives for the permanent appeal of classical works of art. On this problem, Marx and Engels are much closer to Tolstoy's remarks in 1858 that great art is accessible to all peoples in all times,[48] and seem to insist that all art be measured against the greatest men have made. Finally, Marx's use of the analogy of childhood to explain Greece's greatness directs our attention to his and Engels's sense of the underlying human unity of history, subsuming all the stages society passes through, and suggests that art's permanent anchorage is in the indestructible wealth of the human being, which it expresses and celebrates.

It has already been pointed out that Marx and Engels

---

moments in history, he says, the ratio between alienation and integration in a given society varies quite independently of that society's position on the ladder of social evolution. Thus a healthy Greece is perfectly capable of producing a greater art than, say, a disintegrating capitalism. The second question, the matter of universal value in art, Lifshitz ignores (see his article "Marx," in *Literaturnaya entsiklopediya,* VI, 888–90).

[47] See above, p. 26.   [48] See above, pp. 123–25.

associate imaginative literature with interpretation, not with change. The prose realism they favored in their own time dealt most properly and most successfully with events in the past and touched on the future—whether as prediction or inspiration—only at grave risk to itself. For these and other reasons it is clear that Marx and Engels were not disposed to connect literature with the activist phase of their theory. Perhaps the wonder is that they never did. Literature was of great personal concern to both men, but it was less than a secondary interest in their intellectual lifework, a source sometimes of the apt example or the trenchant quotation. Beyond that it was largely a private matter, discussed in correspondence or in conversations with friends. It is a tribute, perhaps, to the soundness of their education that they resisted the temptation to make literature an instrument of their mission. They were no less embattled at times with the world than the Russian radical democrats, who showed no such scruples. Their reluctance to make use of literature tends strongly to align them with the position of the realists, not with their radical opponents, in the mid-century debate in Russia.

Engels's hope that the literature of the future would contain "great intellectual depth" and "conscious historical content" represents their maximum claim that literature possess social utility. The presence or absence of these elements would give the Marxist critic grounds for a kind of ideological judgment. But an adequate emphasis on the third and balancing ingredient—"Shakespearean vivacity"—would, presumably, keep literature free from any crippling subordination to doctrine. Marx and Engels surrendered all major claims to political dominion over it, by indicating that the presence of ideology would never be permitted to compensate for the absence of artistry. Their prescription, if such it can be called, was mild and general: any morally honest exploration of the capitalist world would bring to light the disturbing truth about it. This knowledge might arouse indignation, hope, or disgust, but apparently the reader's response was not to be directed beyond these generalized emotions. At no time did they cross the line into the realm of political uplift favored by Chernyshevsky, Dobrolyubov, Lenin and Zhdanov.

It is not possible here to survey the monumental labors that have attended the Soviet exegesis of Marx and Engels on the arts. But a general trend is evident: the gradual replacement of Marx and Engels by the Russian radicals as guides to "literary policy." Soviet disenchantment with their original Marxian literary bequest has made itself increasingly evident since 1934. The "pre-Marxist materialists," as the Russian radicals are still called, were found to have greater and greater relevance to the Soviet scene. Lenin's central notion of art's "partisanship" in the social struggle, whether he knew it or not, reflected a position much closer to Chernyshevsky's than to Marx's. Zhdanov's failure to mention Marx and Engels once in his 1946 review of the Soviet literary scene is a conclusive sign of their eclipse as commentators on cultural matters. In a recent article, "Lenin and Soviet Art," G. Nedoshivin suggests the thinking that lay behind Zhdanov's omission:

Beginning with the middle forties of the last century, they [Marx and Engels] examined fundamental problems of art as a form of ideology, elucidating questions pertaining to realism, especially in the conditions of bourgeois society, and analyzing the status of literature under the domination of capitalist relations. Although the works of Marx and Engels contain truly profound observations concerning the opportunities Socialism opens for the development of creative art, they naturally could not formulate a finished theory on the development of art after the Socialist revolution and the launching of the practical con-

struction of Socialism. The historical background of the nineteenth century could not provide the material for any such
theoretical generalization, and the two great thinkers concentrated on an analysis of the substance of art in the conditions
prevailing in class society in general and bourgeois society in
particular. . . . And in connection with this many general questions of aesthetics which Marx and Engels dealt with in their
time had to be subjected to a more profound treatment in the
light of the new situation.[49]

So the argument runs. One notes the narrow superstructural view of art, which assumes, first, that art will undergo
a metamorphosis in close, mechanical response to changes
in economic conditions, and second, that this process can
be directed by a single "theoretical generalization." Marx and
Engels have been trapped in their own system, and dismissed as prisoners of their times. The losses implicit in this
view of culture include much that Marx and Engels valued:
diversity of form, continuity of tradition, spontaneity of
creation, and universality of interest. Although his reasons
are open to challenge, Nedoshivin is right at least in noting
the incompatibility between classical Marxian and Soviet attitudes toward literature. "Shakespearean vivacity" must fare
ill in the grim climate of official uplift described in the
following excerpt (typical of many) taken from a recent
editorial:

Cultural advancement that leads to an abundance of spiritual
values for the people has always been regarded by the Communist Party and the Soviet Government as one of their major
tasks. The great leaders of the Soviet people, Lenin and Stalin,
always attached exceptional importance to literature and the
arts, emphasizing their immense part in molding the minds of
millions and accelerating the process of socialist development.
    To fulfill this mission every work of art, no matter in what

[49] G. Nedoshivin, "Lenin and Soviet Art," *Soviet Literature*, No. 1
(1952), pp. 142–43.

sphere, must above all give expression to the advanced ideas of the times, to the genuine spirit of the people, it must correctly reflect the needs of society and respond to the hopes and aspirations of the masses, the real makers of history.[50]

The whole of the humanist heritage, so reverently regarded by Marx and Engels, is swept away in this flood of jargon. And all the ways art has discovered for exploring man's condition are reduced to a single formula. The same editorial points out that in order "to fulfill his mission the artist must produce works which help to bring out the finest traits of the Soviet character." [51] The final issue of this doctrine is the new Soviet man, his eye all agleam with official virtue. Marx and Engels have contributed nothing to this closed system with its single, predetermined outcome, not because of the limitations imposed on them by "class society," but because they shared few of the assumptions that support it.

It is Lenin who is credited today with the "profound treatment" of Marxian ideas on art which Soviet critics see as an extension beyond—and any outsider must see as a departure from—the original premises. The "principle of political partisanship" in literature, although it was ultimately to find more congenial sanctions in the theories of the radical democrats, was derived by Lenin from another area of Marxist theory. The Soviet Spartacus, whom Marx and Engels never foresaw, has Marxian blood in his veins. We must examine the choice Lenin made between the humaneness of Marxism's basic moral intentions, and the harsh ethic of the class struggle, which he was convinced was the only way to fulfill those intentions.

[50] "Soviet Literature and Art on the Upgrade," *Soviet Literature,* No. 12 (1951), p. 134.
[51] *Ibid.*

9

COMPLETE AND
INCOMPLETE MEN

The Marxian view, after Lenin, that man is an historical creature whose social matrix is the only source of his grievances
and aspirations serves an interest in manipulating him in
those terms. But Marx and Engels themselves have a view of
mankind far broader than considerations of malleability and
manipulation: it involves a concept of human nature itself.[1]
Their distrust of essences and fixities makes them reluctant to
define such a vast and imprecise thing as human nature. But
they cannot wholly avoid the matter, cannot, that is, assume
that man's *only* identity through time is physical, or that
he is, at any historical moment, *only* an aggregate of cultural
traits; and they do make allowances for that entity which the
British Marxist, Christopher Caudwell, has called the human
"genotype," "man as he is born," "the common human
creature." [2]

Venable suggests that, though it does not constitute a
formal philosophical commitment on the matter, the use of
the terms "human" and "human reality" by Marx and
Engels acknowledges the existence of a common fund of
traits, needs, and potentialities. They are not metaphysical
essences, but they exist, nonetheless, as "relative historical

[1] See Vernon Venable, *Human Nature; the Marxian View* (New York,
1946), Chapters I and II.
[2] Christopher Caudwell, *Illusion and Reality* (London, 1946), pp.
124 and 136.

constants, empirical common denominators, which emerge for sufficiently long periods of time to furnish the ordinary social meanings of nouns." [3]

Marx and Engels have generally associated the term "human" with the generous ethical purposes that enclose the whole of their system. Venable has defined those purposes simply as "the amelioration of the human lot." [4] Engels is almost lightheartedly imprecise and undogmatic on this score: "The urge towards happiness is innate in man, and must therefore form the basis of all morality." [5] The entire apparatus of theoretical Marxism has presumably been created to serve this universal need of "the common human creature," and it is in this moral substratum that the Marxian views of art examined in the preceding chapter would seem to have their permanent roots. As Caudwell put it: "Art cannot escape its close relation with the genotype whose secret desires link in one endless series all human culture." [6] In the Marxian view, great art reflects the wholeness, the creativity, and the passion men enjoy at certain privileged moments in history. The artists themselves seem at times to have represented the supreme expression of this potential. [7]

Are there clues to the nature of the fully developed Marxian man which were not disclosed in the comments by Marx and Engels on specifically literary matters? He is characterized, in the first place, by a complete and active set

---

[3] Venable, *Human Nature*, p. 24. [4] *Ibid.*, p. 26.

[5] Karl Marx and Friedrich Engels, *Selected Works* (Moscow, 1951), II, 346.

[6] Caudwell, *Illusion and Reality*, p. 206.

[7] Engels said of Goethe: "[He] did not like to deal with 'God': the word made him uncomfortable. He felt himself at home only in the human, and it was this humanity, this emancipation of art from the fetters of religion that determined Goethe's greatness. In this respect neither the great writers of antiquity nor even Shakespeare are up to him." (Karl Marx and Friedrich Engels, *Literature and Art* [New York, 1947], p. 80.)

of appetites, senses, and emotions, for which the fullest expression is sought through his relations with the external world:

Man adopts his all-sided being in an all-sided manner, in other words, as a total man. Every one of his *human* relations with the world: seeing, hearing, smelling, tasting, feeling, thinking, contemplating, willing, acting, loving; in short, all the organs of his individuality as well as the organs which in their immediate form are common to all.[8]

If these activities represent the common denominator of the human endowment, a rough measure of a society's worth may be taken by the degree to which men are permitted to exercise them. Again and again capitalism is condemned in precisely these terms by Marx and Engels because it denies the fulfillment of this basic human minimum. The list of frustrating conditions is a familiar one: division of labor, the reign of money ("universal whore . . . universal procurer of human beings and people"),[9] "naked, shameless, direct brutal exploitation," [10] and so forth. Man's alienation from his full human potential, as it is brought about by these destructive forces, appears as a greater crime in their eyes than the immediate suffering inflicted by hunger, cold, disease, or overwork.

Marx and Engels clearly felt that the blight of alienation was much more virulent and widespread under capitalism than it had been in most, if not all, past historical epochs. At the heart of their indictment of the present system is a vision of man crippled, fragmented, shriveled by the conditions of his economic existence. Marx and Engels repeatedly point out that this unhappy, stunted creature represents an absolute decline in the density and richness of human experience, because of the reduction, through enforced and prolonged disuse, of his given human capacities.

[8] *Ibid.*, p. 61.   [9] *Ibid.*, p. 34.   [10] *Ibid.*, p. 37.

A much truer measure of man's creative potential is found in the human giants of the Renaissance, for example, or in the ancient Greek heroes. The key motifs of human existence at its fullest were the wholeness and versatility of man's interests and achievements, and the grandeur of his claims on life. As a sketch of the Marxian human ideal, Engels's extravagant remarks on the man of the Renaissance are worth quoting at length:

It was the greatest progressive revolution that mankind has so far experienced, a time which called for giants and produced giants—giants in power of thought, passion, and character, in universality and learning. The men who founded the modern rule of the bourgeoisie had anything but bourgeois limitations. On the contrary, the adventurous character of the time inspired them. . . . There was hardly any man of importance then living who had not traveled extensively, who did not command four or five languages, who did not shine in a number of fields. Leonardo da Vinci was not only a great painter but also a great mathematician, mechanician, and engineer, to whom the most diverse branches of physics are indebted for important discoveries. Albrecht Dürer was painter, engraver, sculptor, and architect, and in addition invented a system of fortifications. . . . Machiavelli was statesman, historian, poet, and at the same time the first military writer of modern times. Luther not only cleaned the Augean stable of the Church but also that of the German language; he created modern German prose and composed the text and melody of that triumphal hymn which became the Marseillaise of the sixteenth century. The heroes of that time had not yet come under the servitude of the division of labor, the restricting effects of which, with its production of one-sidedness, we so often notice in their successors. But what is especially characteristic of them is that they almost all pursue their lives and activities in the midst of contemporary movements, in the practical struggle; they take sides and join in the fight, one by speaking and writing, another with the sword, many with both. Hence the fullness and force of character that makes them complete men.[11]

[11] *Ibid.*, pp. 23–24.

History does not repeat itself in the Marxian universe; there is no nostalgia in this admiration for Renaissance heroes, nor any suggestion that these particular types would ever again be duplicated. But if epochs of great social metamorphosis provided the richest soil for large-scale individuals, there was a hope that the transition to socialism might produce men of equivalent *stature*, if not of identical qualities.[12] Marx also felt that these exciting periods of large-scale human figures were invariably moments of great art:

It has been observed that great men appear in surprising numbers at certain periods which are characterized by the efflorescence of art. Whatever the outstanding traits of this efflorescence, its influence upon men is undeniable; it fills them with its vivifying force.[13]

These high points of artistic and human greatness form an historical pattern which is distinct from the stages of social development. Let us note the major phases of the first process. It describes, in general terms, a steady decline from the Renaissance—the last stopping place, they felt, in modern history for the men of truly heroic stature—to the depths of the factory system, and then gives promise of rising again with the establishment of socialism's "truly human culture," to a level equivalent, at least, to history's previous high points. Their language is of particular interest because of the frequent connections it reveals between art, morality, and human dignity. Among their caustic remarks about the new aristocracy of sausage makers and button manufacturers, one characterization of the petite bourgeoisie sums up all the others, and measures one of capitalism's dominant personality types against Marx's standard of human worth:

[12] See Engels's remarks on Dante, above, p. 159, footnote 20.
[13] A marginal note made by the young Marx in a copy of Johann Jakob Grund's *Die Malerei der Griechen*, quoted in Mikhail Lifshitz, *The Philosophy of Art of Karl Marx* (New York, 1938), p. 44.

If the decline of former classes—such as the knight, for instance—could furnish material for magnificent works of tragic art, the *petite bourgeoisie* naturally provides nothing but feeble manifestations of fanatical malice, nothing but collections of phrases and sayings in the manner of Sancho Panza.[14]

This wretched class was so spiritually bankrupt that Marx and Engels would not grant it even the pathos of its own descent. They returned to this thesis again and again. In one oft-quoted statement Marx sets the noble vision of man in Greek mythology against the antipoetic, antihuman conditions of capitalist institutions and technology:

Is the view of nature and of social relations which shaped Greek imagination and Greek [art] possible in the age of automatic machinery, and railways and locomotives and electric telegraphs? Where does Vulcan come in as against Roberts and Co.; Jupiter as against the lightning rod; and Hermes as against the Crédit Mobilier? . . . Greek art presupposes the existence of Greek mythology, i.e., that nature and even the form of society are wrought up in popular fancy in an unconsciously artistic fashion. . . . Looking at it from another side: Is Achilles possible side by side with powder and lead? Or is the *Iliad* at all compatible with the printing press? [15]

Marx obviously feels that in these juxtapositions he is recording an absolute loss. But he would violate the logic of his theory of history if he proposed then to roll back capitalism's enormous advances in social organization and technology, or to create by some cultural alchemy a new mythology (Marx hated pseudo-classicism), or if he despaired entirely of the future of art. The only route open led forward, and history moved on it toward harmony and fruitfulness. As Marx and Engels saw it, capitalism at the height of its powers embodied an absolute contradiction on this matter

[14] Karl Marx and Friedrich Engels, *Sur la littérature et l'art*, ed. Jean Fréville (Paris, 1936), pp. 123–24.
[15] Marx and Engels, *Literature and Art*, pp. 18–19.

of human fulfillment. While it had registered gains in many areas, gains unprecedented in human history, it had done so at tremendous costs, including the near death of art and the mangling of the human being. But in the very process, capitalism had generated the forces that would destroy it, and would, eventually, restore man to his true poetic dimensions. At this point the upward movement of the humanist phase is joined with the process of social change. In *The Holy Family*, Marx describes the act of awareness by which the worker transcended his degraded situation:

Since the abstraction of all humanity, even of the *semblance* of humanity, is practically complete in the full-grown proletariat; since the conditions of life of the proletariat sum up all the conditions of life . . . today in all their inhuman acuity; since man has lost himself in the proletariat, yet at the same time has not only gained theoretical consciousness of that loss, but through urgent, no longer disguisable, absolutely imperative *need*—that practical expression of *necessity*—is driven directly to revolt against that inhumanity; it follows that the proletariat can and must free itself. But it cannot free itself without abolishing the conditions of its life. It cannot abolish the conditions of its own life without abolishing *all* the inhuman conditions of life of society today which are summed up in its own situation.[16]

It may be said that the ethical impulse exposes itself in the early work as antecedent to all the later "scientific" justifications for the overthrow of capitalism. In any case the industrial worker by his destructive acts will point the way to man's discovery—or *re*discovery if we consider the glories of human achievement in the Renaissance as a kind of norm to *return* to—of his incalculably rich potential.

Marx and Engels diligently avoided precise predictions about the socialist future. But when they did occasionally permit themselves moments of visionary anticipation, their

[16] Karl Marx and Friedrich Engels, *The Holy Family* (Moscow, 1956), p. 52.

remarks, again, are in the humanist key. When he was still young, Marx felt that the first condition for conquering man's alienation was "the abolition of private property," which could not fail to result in the "complete emancipation of all human senses and aptitudes" and "the vindication of real human life." "Communism," he wrote, "is humanism brought about by abolishing private property"; it is "the real materialization for man of his being." [17]

Nearly all of their remarks on the Communist future are put not in the terms of economic predictions but of the humanist ethic, and point unmistakably to the restoration of man's wholeness on something like the Renaissance scale. The ultimate *moral* principle of the Communist order, "from each according to his abilities, to each according to his needs," will be enacted when man will have eliminated all the contradictions that separate him from others and from his own potential capacities. The differences between city and country living conditions will be overcome, and the discrepancies in status and rewards between the workers of hand and of brain will disappear as well. But this is only the beginning. The effects of the division of labor presumably will disappear and the demoralizing cash nexus will be replaced by a truly human standard of value. Man will be brought into a true unity with nature, with his fellow men, and with society. From all this, man will emerge with a new creative individuality which will be sustained, not contradicted, by the egalitarian collectivity in which it will have its being. In contrast with other societies which are plagued with the division of labor, Marx sketches this idyllic picture of man in the future society:

In Communist society, where nobody has one exclusive sphere of activity but each can become accomplished in any branch he

[17] *Literature and Art*, pp. 61–62.

wishes, society regulates the general production and thus makes it possible for me to do one thing today and another tomorrow, to hunt in the morning, fish in the afternoon, rear cattle in the evening, criticize after dinner, just as I have a mind, without ever becoming hunter, fisherman, shepherd or critic.[18]

With the resolution of *all* the contradictions of capitalism in the new order, art's emancipation will parallel the restoration of man to completeness. Lifshitz interprets Marx to mean that the artificial separation between the fantasy of poetry and the harsh realities of daily existence will disappear: "Communist society removes not only the abstract contradiction between 'work and pleasure,' but also the very real contradiction between feeling and reason, between 'the play of bodily and mental powers' and 'the conscious will.' "[19] Marx himself felt that the distinction between the professional artist and the laity would disappear:

The exclusive concentration of artistic talent in a few individuals and its consequent suppression in the large masses is the result of the division of labor.[20]

If Marx intended to say that every man might be his own da Vinci, he could hardly have made more extravagant claims. If he intended less than that, he has still implied that art will somehow be made available to all in the grand redistribution of material (and spiritual) goods and services. There is little reason to doubt in this connection that the vision of the "whole," "human" man, made free and enriched by the socialist revolution, was an effective agitational device. But the persistence with which this vision reappears at critical moments in his thought makes it difficult to dismiss the concept as the fabrication of a propagandist. It

[18] Karl Marx and Friedrich Engels, *The German Ideology*, ed. R. Pascal (New York, 1939), p. 22.
[19] Lifshitz, *The Philosophy of Art of Karl Marx*, p. 93.
[20] *Literature and Art*, p. 76.

seems quite clear that this notion is the nearest thing we can find to an embodiment of the innermost ethical purposes of Marxian theory.

The image of the whole man—if there is an outline of him distinct enough to justify use of the term—would seem to offer another model for Soviet imitation. But the information about him is so general and so imprecise he can hardly be said to have an identity of his own. At his most distinct he combines the general virtues of a few Renaissance giants with less discernible resemblances to Marx's own Promethean image of himself. In his hypothetical existence in the Communist future this individual is least tangible, no more than a bundle of abstract qualities. This is hardly a usable image. It lacks the human immediacy of even the Russian radicals' diagram for the new man. The elements that are consistent in it are nevertheless interesting and worth recording as a standard for evaluating the Soviet view. The greatest stress is laid on his freedom from crippling inhibitions. His integrated many-sidedness guarantees a broad receptivity to experience and an equally great intensity and generosity in his response to it. Above all, he is conceived as a very large and autonomous *individual*, self-directed in his choices and acts. In the many ways he is associated with aesthetic and ethical universals, he is ill-suited to the expediencies of revolutionary action, and to the disciplined, self-sacrificing code that sustains it. If the whole man is the *end* of the process of social change, he is material of dubious value for the struggle that must precede that distant eventuality. He is the beneficiary of social change, not its maker. For the period of transition we must posit a different sort of human being—an *interim man*, who is a means toward an end, not an end in himself, a man who will accept all kinds of restrictions on his demands on life in order to make himself over, like Chernyshevsky's Rakhmetov, into history's instrument.

II

The Marxian Utopia, with its roseate vision of man, "whole, integrated, and free," has little connection with the actual moral dimensions of the operating Soviet hero. It has merely given us a standard for ultimate (and invidious) comparisons. It is the "realm of necessity," preceding "the realm of freedom," that concerns us now. We need only recall a few of the conditions which various Marxist thinkers have attributed to the final stage—the withering away of the state, the free and equal distribution of goods according to need, the change-over from the government of people to "the administration of things"—to realize how far Soviet reality is from this destination. In the Marxian design, the era of necessity has the character of a period of transition. In that term are included the years of prerevolutionary struggle, the revolution itself, and all the subsequent years of Soviet history, in which the iron requirements of necessity are defined (as Soviet spokesmen view it) by three primary conditions: the technological lag, the economy of scarcity, and hostile encirclement. Our final question here is this: what clues are there in Marx to the nature of the interim man who has dominated these transitional years? The answers are not to be sought in the humane intentions which support the image of the whole man, but in the specific ethical imperative which Lenin and others have derived from them.

The Marxian imperative may be phrased in the Kantian idiom: "So act, that thy act forwards the historical process." Thus formulated, it is clear that every condition of the act is established by history itself, and by man's position in it. Class struggle is the central fact of history and the touchstone of all moral choice. Since one half of the warring universe, the proletariat, is the power behind history's forward thrust toward a saner, healthier future, and is the instrument which will destroy all obstacles in the way, the primary *ethical* obligation is to support the efforts of that class to free itself. These efforts are exerted in an atmosphere of ruthless, no-quarter conflict: "That man must fight, that there is no hope of human liberation without fight, is thus the very essence, the central command of materialist ethics." [21]

From the outset we are advised to expect the harsh stringencies of a military life. Venable has characterized this internal imperative of Marxian theory as an ethic of "action, pugnacity and partisanship." [22] Its initial premise of total commitment sets aside many of man's normal ethical concerns: the personal as opposed to the class nature of moral problems, the responsibility for making *individual* choices between complex alternatives, and the attendant agonies of doubt and ambiguity that beset the individual who is unsure of history's direction, or of its intentions toward him.

Yet there is a concept of freedom in this moral doctrine, which insists that involvement in the simultaneous battle for the inevitable and the good is binding on all men who learn of its existence. This freedom, which depends on the "recognition of necessity,"

does not consist in the dream of independence of natural laws, but in the knowledge of these laws and in the possibility this gives of systematically making them work toward definite ends. Freedom of the will therefore means nothing but the capacity to make decisions with real knowledge of the subject. Therefore the freer a man's judgment is in relation to a definite question, with so much the greater *necessity* is the content of his judg-

[21] Venable, *Human Nature*, p. 179.   [22] *Ibid.*, p. 204.

ment determined; while the uncertainty, founded on ignorance, which seems to make an arbitrary choice among many different and conflicting possible tensions, shows by this precisely that it is not free, that it is controlled by the very object it would itself control.[23]

It is a "law-abiding" freedom, then, based on a scientific kind of knowledge which dictates a *single* course of action to all who analyze history correctly. All other kinds of freedom are illusory since they do not hasten history toward its morally desirable ends. It is a freedom that is concerned exclusively with man's ability to act effectively, to apply the correct leverage to history, and to manipulate men and events toward those ends. In its concentration on this kind of efficacy whole areas of human experience are declared irrelevant: in exchange for the chance to act purposefully, the Marxian must accept an unlimited burden of restraints on his personal freedom as most men define it. Man is free when he acts in the only way possible. Man may feel that he is "free" to do almost anything—to act, to dream, to reject, to accept. But he is not free to do away with the objective world simply by closing his mind to it. Even when he "rejects" the world he is making a decision which has consequences on the balance of contending forces, merely by withholding his energies from active commitment. To act in concert with the embattled proletariat is the only truly compelling obligation of modern life; all others are illusory, immoral, or antisocial.

In this monolithic view of moral behavior, the most important moment is the act of "recognizing" the necessity. This act is informed by a number of elements, the first of which is scientific insight into the laws of history and into the configuration of historical forces at any given moment.

[23] Friedrich Engels, *Herr Eugen Dühring's Revolution in Science* (New York, 1939), p. 125.

Secondly, it is presumed that this knowledge will dictate a rational course of action. Thirdly, there is a strong emotional component: men are impelled by their disgust and anger to act in accordance with their convictions. This assumption is based on the certainty that most men live in something close to absolute misery, that they are wretchedly and unnecessarily unhappy. Anger is stimulated and given focus by emotional exhortations to replace the intolerable present with a more rational future.

It is quite clear that an ethical imperative based on such a diffuse mixture of analytical, doctrinal, and emotional knowledge cannot be logically or universally binding. Marx and Engels were not particularly concerned with closing their system here. They felt that, so long as the analysis of society remained valid, and the fact of suffering dominated most men's experience, their own empirical findings would be confirmed. Men would, by one route or another, come to accept a concept of revolutionary duty similar to theirs.

The question arises: what place is there for a humane, questing literature in this schematically arranged universe, where virtue is made synonymous with disciplined, militant behavior, where each of the human actors is fortified with incontrovertible assurances of the justice of his cause? The first answer that comes to mind is that, except perhaps for a declamatory poetry like Mayakovsky's, there is none. This may in the end be history's answer, but it has been a surprisingly long time in coming. The delay has been a result of the writers' ability to preserve a vantage of their own, whether by privileged dispensation, or by calculated deception, which has permitted them to make their own comments on the human drama of history. What, then, are the proper subjects for a writer who sympathizes with Marxism, but wants to remain true to the traditions of his art?

Here Plekhanov's attempt to describe the formally binding element in the Marxian ethic is illuminating. In his
schematic formulation of the problem of the hero in history, he says of the man who is sympathetic to the Marxian
cause that "being conscious of the absolute inevitability of a
given phenomenon can only increase the energy of a man
who sympathizes with it and who regards himself as one of
the forces which called it into being." [24] Plekhanov translates
his idea into an algebraic formula: if the inevitable and
desirable event A will be brought about by the sum of
forces S at the time T, then the individual who desires A
but does not add a, the force of his own energy, changes the
formula to $S - a$, and A's occurrence will be postponed or
blocked.[25]

However rudimentary and foolish this may seem (even to
Marxists) it points to a basic distinction between two kinds
of men. The writer in search of dramatic conflicts might
confine his attention to the model revolutionary, the individual whose own energies are entirely identified with the
historical demiurge. But he would probably find greater dramatic interest in the man who knows that A is inevitable
but that he will not live to see it, or the man who discovers
that A has been indefinitely delayed, or the man who finds
that his work for A is wrecking his physical or mental health,
blighting his emotional life, alienating him from treasured
emotional ties, or destroying his moral image of himself.
There is no answer to this problem in prerevolutionary Marxian thought, but the official Soviet solution is clear-cut: the
man who is unable to submerge himself in the flux of history,
who fails to "understand" its direction, who is paralyzed by
a tension between his private and public life, or who for any

[24] George Plekhanov, *The Role of the Individual in History* (New
York, 1940), p. 19.
[25] *Ibid.*, pp. 19–20.

other reason, except physical annihilation, becomes an honorable casualty of the revolutionary struggle is simply not interesting—not typical, significant, or true in the special sense those words have had in the Russian utilitarian tradition since Belinsky. Plekhanov's distinction contains grounds for excluding an enormous range of human experience, particularly of that anguished kind that revolutions cannot fail to create. There are the seeds, too, of a basic quarrel between the writer and the magistrate. Plekhanov's sinister little equation is extended to the writer himself, and he is compelled to identify *his* strength and skill with all other human and historical energies. There is, in fact, no *theoretical* obstacle in Marxism to the enforced submergence of the writer along with all other like-minded men. The protections against it are informal or pragmatic: the kind of respect for the writer expressed by Marx and Engels was also present in the background of many of the early Bolshevik intellectuals, of Plekhanov, Lunacharsky, Trotsky, and, though it yielded at crucial moments to political expediency, of Lenin himself. But beyond good taste, there is nothing to withstand the iron logic of the Marxian argument.

What in the abstract are the human costs and rewards for the individual who chooses to spend his life in the harness of history? It is clear that the man who accepts the restrictions of Marxian freedom surrenders most of the other kinds of freedom that Marx, himself, celebrated in the past and anticipated in the Communist future: freedom from violence, and from confining disciplines, freedom to explore the universe at leisure, and endlessly to amplify one's responses to it. But this discrepancy is in the nature of things, and to act as though one were confronted with a choice between the interim view of morality and its end product is to engage in self-deception. They come in an ineluctable sequence, never the second before the first, and so long as capitalism survives and Communism is not yet built, the realm of true human freedom exists nowhere on earth, not for the most privileged bourgeois individualist.

Even if there is no choice, will not the conscious historical actor, sure of his mission in the necessity of things, undergo terrible deprivations and find new personal rewards? Will he not pay a prohibitive human cost for his many acts of self-renunciation, and for the consequences of his obligatory hostility toward large sections of the human community whose crime, so far as he is concerned, is defined simply by their position in the system of property relations? Marx and Engels were willing to make no such admission. The chances of human fulfillment were certainly no less in a career of engagement than they were in an attitude of unconcern toward the daily ravages of the class enemy. And if it was a warrior's existence that was promised to the recruit, the very justice of the struggle would more than compensate for the wounds he suffered.[26] That the fight contained its own reward and was a surer road to human health than any kind of acquiescence in the order of things is suggested by Marx's view of the revolutionary in combat with his environment:

By . . . acting on the external world and changing it, he at the same time changes his own nature. He develops the potentialities that slumber within him and subjects them to his own control.[27]

[26] Venable gives his own version of the Marxian answer to this question: "The downtrodden, the expropriated, the dispossessed, feel revolution as emancipation, not as limitation, and in respect not merely to its ultimate outcome for humanity at large, but in respect to its daily act for the subjugated themselves." (*Human Nature*, p. 189.)

[27] Karl Marx, *Capital; a Critique of Political Economy*, ed. Friedrich Engels, trans. Samuel Moore and Edward Aveling (Chicago, 1906–9), p. 198.

The distinction between the interim man and the whole man would seem to be very nearly lost in this view of the historical actor. Marx apparently thought that man starts his journey back to wholeness from the very moment he begins to do battle with his environment. Actually, there was no reason for Marx to be particularly aware of the two kinds of men which are implied by the two distinct phases in his thinking about morality. The revolutionary awakening was just beginning. Why should he emphasize—if indeed he was aware at all of—the variety and intensity of the suffering that stretched ahead of the Marxian revolutionary at a time when Marx, himself, was only beginning to divine the direction the road took? He welcomed the forthcoming battle himself (his definition of happiness was simply "to fight" [28]), but he was never the director of an embattled revolutionary army, never responsible for its strategic disposition, for its discipline, or for its morale. The Communist future was unimaginably remote. For the practical strategist's approach to these problems we must turn finally to Lenin.

III

As the theorist of actual revolution, Lenin shifted the emphasis to the activist pole within Marxian theory more drastically than anyone had before him. His union of theory and practice tended unmistakably to put the former at the service of the latter, and to limit men's intellectual horizons to the immediately attainable future. All his energies were applied to systematizing and simplifying human experience in order to expose the controlling levers of history and to direct man's strength to the single task of pulling them. He also tried to prove to men that they had no obligation superior to that

[28] See the account of the parlor game he played with his children (*Literature and Art*, p. 145).

task. As indifferent to the formal categories of ethical theory as Marx and Engels, he nevertheless was the advocate of a strenuous, extremist, and exclusive moral doctrine. In the act of creating the Bolshevik Party apparatus he gave institutional form to the classical Marxian "ethic of action, pugnacity and partisanship," and established the principal conditions, perspectives, and goals of what has been considered ethical behavior ever since in the USSR. Everything he had to say about the function and organization of history's human instrument has a bearing on what was to follow.

One quotation contains a clear outline of the new heroism and the restricted conditions under which it would find expression:

And first of all the question arises: how is the discipline of the revolutionary party of the proletariat maintained? How is it tested? How is it reinforced? First, by the class consciousness of the proletarian vanguard and by its devotion to the revolution, by its perseverance, self-sacrifice and heroism. Secondly, by its ability to link itself, to keep in touch with, and to a certain extent, if you like, to merge itself with the broadest masses of the toilers. . . . Thirdly, by the correctness of the political leadership exercised by this vanguard, and of its political strategy and tactics, provided that the broadest masses have been convinced by their own experience that they are correct. . . . Without these conditions all attempts to establish discipline inevitably fail and end in phrasemongering.[29]

Most of the determinants of Communist behavior are contained in this passage: first of all, the overriding concern with discipline, and, together with that, the virtuous personal qualities that guarantee its maintenance and find their *only* expression as a function of it. It is a regime which makes unlimited demands on the adherent's allegiances, his time, and his energy, and welcomes the harsh asceticism, the hardened

[29] V. I. Lenin, *"Left-Wing" Communism, an Infantile Disorder* (New York, 1940), pp. 10–11.

will, the habits of self-renunciation and self-limitation that this kind of discipline bespeaks. There is the notion, too, that there are two *kinds* of people, the leaders and the led, and that the Bolshevik is urged "to link" or "to merge" himself ("to a certain extent") with the masses so that he can most effectively exhort, agitate, persuade—in short, manipulate them toward predetermined ends. Though in its pre-revolutionary statement this approach has a suggestion of man-to-man argument in it, the exchange is never based on the belief that all opinions have equal value. With the Party's accumulation of power, the essentially parental nature of this relationship became hardened and clarified.[30] The "vanguard" needed, and still needs, to know the temper and grievances of the masses, to make an informed estimate at any given moment of the "possible" (the art of which was and is their consuming concern) in their pursuit of goals which are not open to debate. The third element to note in Lenin's quotation is his definition of the nature of the truths in the name of which leadership is exercised. The key word is "correctness," with its overtone of scientific infallibility, and its implication that a single tactical doctrine is absolutely true—even if only for a short time—after which a new version of the *absolute but temporary* truths that govern the Communist's every utterance and action will be laid down. Of the ingredients that determine what is "correct"—and the place where that uncompromising word is defined is the actual locus of power—the grievances and expectations of the

[30] This is not to suggest that force simply replaced argument; agitation is still a primary activity of the Party member. The change that came with the revolution's victory can be summarized this way: before 1917 the Bolshevik leader hoped to persuade the masses to do what he wanted them to do; after 1917 he set out to persuade them to do what had been decided they *had* to do. He now had gained physical control over his adherents. Whether he used it or not, his relations with his followers were changed.

masses are one, the theoretical teachings of Marxism are another. But the dominant concern is political warfare of a merciless kind manifest in the constant use of the language of "strategy and tactics" with all it suggests of command and obedience, of maneuver and deception, and in the end, of course, of all the limitations a condition of warfare imposes on the whole human being.

War is the arena of virtuous behavior in this transitional phase, as Marx suggested, and it is not governed by rules of any kind. The combat is murderous, without quarter or scruple. Anything less would jeopardize the cause itself:

> Everyone will agree that an army which does not train itself to wield all arms, all the means and methods of warfare that the enemy possesses, or may possess, behaves in an unwise or even in a criminal manner.[31]

Since the enemy's "vanguard" was the Tsar's secret, political police, the first occupants of the battlefield, it may be assumed that these unenlightened minions of the status quo established the moral climate in which the struggle took place. Bolshevik virtue was animated in the nature of things by murderous hostility, and armed itself with weapons of counterterror equivalent in effectiveness to every tactic of political terror the experienced and inventive political police could devise. There were other categories of weapons, of course—techniques of instruction, organization, and agitation, even the polite duplicities of parliamentary "struggle" —but the illegal methods, since they involved ultimate weapons, and were the determinants not of victory or defeat, but of survival or extermination, were central in the Leninist design.[32]

---

[31] Lenin, "Left-Wing" Communism, an Infantile Disorder, pp. 76–77.
[32] The lawlessness of the Dostoevskyan rebel or of the Nietzschean "free spirit" lacks the Marxian revolutionary's grounding in history,

It often seems that Lenin had set aside forever the Marxian whole man in favor of the hardened political monolith. In occasional acknowledgments, however, he indicates that he, too, is working in the larger humanist scheme of Marxism, and that the self-limited human instrument he desires *is* indeed only an interim man. There is an echo of the Marxian classics in his assurance that the development of genuine industrial unions will lead

to the abolition of the division of labor among people, to the education, schooling and training of people with an *all-around development and an all-round* training, people *able to do everything*. Communism is marching and must march towards this goal, and *will reach it*, but only after very many years. To attempt in practice today to anticipate this future of a fully developed, fully stabilized and formed, fully expanded and mature Communism would be like trying to teach higher mathematics to a four-year-old child.[33]

The interim man will presumably last, in Lenin's view, during the "very many years" of tutelage, working as teacher, disciplinarian, exemplar, foster-parent, and turnkey. As he pointed out more than once, the human problem was at the heart of all the reasons that would make the period of transition such a long one:

We can (and must) begin to build Socialism not with imaginary human material invented by us, but with the human material bequeathed to us by capitalism.[34]

---

but neither is irrelevant to the "illegal" situation of the Bolshevik at this time. Nietzsche's warning is in point: "He who fights with monsters should be careful lest he thereby become a monster. And if thou gaze long into an abyss, the abyss will also gaze into thee." (*Beyond Good and Evil*, in *The Philosophy of Nietzsche* [New York, Modern Library], p. 87.)

[33] *"Left-Wing" Communism, an Infantile Disorder*, p. 34. Note the parental image at the end of the quotation.

[34] *Ibid.*

By every indication, he regarded this "human material" as a sorry lot, and the forging of a new image of man out of it was, for all the Bolshevik optimism about the plasticity of human nature, a titanic job during which the vanguard presumably would never abandon its superior vantage.

Now, we may ask once more what fictional possibilities this individual presents to the writer? Or to put it more broadly: with the world divided into the convenient black and white of a for-or-against morality, with a narrow concept of political efficacy, always described in military terms, as the governing standard of truth, what hope or encouragement is there for literary truth? In the first place, it is legitimate, perhaps, to apply the Marxian thesis that man changes and is changed by circumstances to the moral climate of the pre-October Russian revolutionary. If it is true that a master circumstance of his life is the battle with the secret police, then he must be equipped to meet them on their own terms. He must be inured to the harsh, secretive, austere, distrustful life of the underground conspirator and secret agent. He must be eternally armed against betrayal, by others or by himself. He must live, in a sense, "beyond good and evil," ready, on occasion, to lie, steal, or kill for his cause, to outrage his own moral sense, a greater sacrifice of self than any other deprivation he undergoes. In this climate it is not difficult to imagine that the nourishing flame of the world-historical purpose often flickers low or burns out, as it does in Gorky's brilliant story, "Karamora" (1924),[35] about the moral disintegration of a Party member turned informer; or, on the contrary, grows to a fanatical white heat destructive of everything that comes near it. Necessity may be the road to liberation, but it is a harshly formative, if not actually disfiguring, taskmaster while one lives in its service.

[35] In Maxim Gorky, *Best Short Stories*, ed. Avrahm Yarmolinsky and Baroness Moura Budberg (New York, 1947).

There is the moral disease, contracted in underground struggle, when deception and violence begin to have a narcotic effect on men, and make addicts of them. Both revolutionary and police agent are susceptible, though they catch the sickness differently. The brutality of the fight perverts the revolutionary's idealism and turns it, mysteriously, into its opposite. For the police agent, a man with a job to do, it is simply one of the occupational hazards of his work. The moral diagnosis is the same whether Holy Russia or the socialist state is the ultimate object of allegiance, or whether the infected Communist is an underground conspirator or a colonel of the MVD.

Plekhanov's equation has already raised the question of the revolution's honorable casualities, the men who fail through doubt, or fallibility, or inner collapse. One variation could be added to the hypothetical situations that were suggested by it, perhaps the most tragic of all: the case of the man who accepts the obligation to hasten history, but disagrees about the means to accomplish it, who persists in his disagreement to the point of an open break, and then is destroyed because his acts are said to threaten history's instrument, the Party, with disintegration. The mere mention of recent candidates for this role—Trotsky, Bukharin, Radek —suggests the inappropriateness of this theme for Soviet writers. It might be said that Soviet literature will reach maturity when it is willing to produce a drama based on the lives of one of these men. Not that Trotsky and the others are, necessarily, tragic heroes, but the Soviet refusal to see the pathos of its own power struggles is a measure of the immaturity of its art. The "death of kings" has simply been banned from the list of approved themes.

But it is not to the tragic deviant alone that the writer need direct his attention. Even the "adjusted" revolutionary must collect his share of scars, must at some time weigh the balance of costs and rewards in personal terms. Even the believing writer, who at the same time honors his craft as something more than an instrument of agitation, would, one would think, find fruitful sources of dramatic tension in the accumulation of experiences that go to make up that balance. And, though the costs and the scars have been emphasized here (because they are underplayed in most of the subsequent literature), certain rewards as well are available to the practicing revolutionary. In addition to the satisfaction of service and of power, there are moments of transcendent harmony and triumph when history's power galvanizes all its servants. Lenin had known the aesthetic experience of revolution:

History generally, and the history of revolution in particular, is always richer in content, more varied, more many-sided, more lively and "subtle" than even the best parties and the most class-conscious vanguards of the most advanced classes imagine. This is understandable because even the best vanguards express the class consciousness, will, passion and imagination of tens of thousands, whereas the revolution is made, at the moment of its climax and the exertion of all human capacities, by the class consciousness, will, passion, and imagination of tens of millions.[36]

This lyrical experience of communion is echoed, presumably, on a lesser scale in the local triumphs of a Communist's life, and must provide him with the memories to be treasured. A longing for the richness of the civil war experience created an ungovernable nostalgia in many Soviet citizens who felt that their lives had become meaningless in the details of peacetime routine, in the corruption of the New Economic Policy (NEP), or in the pointless dislocations of forcible collectivization.

All that we have said so far of the literary use of the revolutionary experience has assumed the existence of a large measure of freedom for the writer—sympathizer or not—to

[36] *"Left-Wing" Communism, an Infantile Disorder*, p. 76.

concentrate on its human aspects, to see it wholly, and to rearrange it without falsification, according to the traditional properties of his medium. Now we must consider the final movement of encirclement, cutting off all escape: the direct application of the Leninist ethic to the writer himself. It is this potential, resident in the Leninist reading of Marx and Engels, that threatens to turn the writer into something they had never imagined—an engineer of the human soul, salaried, disciplined, and subject to dismissal, and worse, for faulty blueprints.

10

LENIN AND GORKY
The Turning Point

The people need heroes. GORKY

No fewer than six attitudes toward literature, some of them contradictory, have been discerned in Lenin's writings.[1] Soviet critics have had to make the most of these disparate views, stressing one at the expense of the others, but never moving beyond them.[2] Although, taken together, they indicate that Lenin sensed the fundamental antitheses between the Russian classical writers and the radical critics, his most consistent emphasis was functional, and his contribution to the utilitarian tradition is his declaration of the principle of outright political partisanship in literature. The most severely functionalist document in the Leninist heritage is his article "Party Organization and Party Literature," published in November, 1905,[3] which has become the basis of every

[1] See Stanley Edgar Hyman, "Christopher Caudwell and Marxist Criticism," in *The Armed Vision; a Study in the Methods of Modern Literary Criticism* (New York, 1948), pp. 168–208. These are: (1) "the attitude of simple functionalism, . . . that art is a weapon in the class struggle and must be recruited to help make a revolution"; (2) "the analytic Marxist view that art reflects social reality but in many respects transcends both it and the creator's views"; (3) "a puritanic resistance to the sinfulness of art"; (4) "the tired businessman's philistine conception of art as a soothing relaxation"; (5) "the social utilitarian view that art is a form of wealth, to be made accessible to the masses under socialism like any other form of wealth"; (6) "a number of reservations and hesitancies about the other five compounded of his own rich personal respect for the creative artist, devotion to tolerance and personal freedom, and a sense of humor."
[2] *Ibid.*, pp. 196–97.
[3] V. I. Lenin, *Sochineniia*, 4th ed. (Moscow, 1947), X, 26–31.

recent effort to subjugate literature to political interests.[4]

Many critics have questioned its significance on the grounds that it is so much a product of local circumstances that it had little influence at the time it was written, and less in later years.[5] Others have said that when he used the word *literatura* he was talking about the Party press, not about imaginative writing. Still others have challenged his credentials as a literary critic and have discredited the article on those grounds.

Of course, in an atmosphere where the uses of the past are confined to a selective, Talmudic referral to authority, ideas are validated differently than they are when their evolution is undirected and their worth established in competition with other ideas. Lenin's article is important for the literary future because it was Lenin who wrote it, and because of the immense authority it now has in the USSR. When the accredited contributors to a society's stock of wisdom are so limited in number, any theoretical redefinition by a major prophet like Lenin may take on a lasting magnitude out of all proportion to its intrinsic worth.

The question of the ambiguity of the meaning of *literatura* may be set aside here with the observation that, although the Russian word means both journalism and belles-lettres, the mere existence of uncertainty about Lenin's intentions is the most revealing point of all. Actually from several comments Lenin made on works of fiction it is quite clear that,

[4] In his 1946 "Report" Zhdanov uses it to justify unprecedentedly narrow strictures against the artist. He cites it as the next major moment in thinking about art after the radical democrats. (See "Doklad o zhurnalakh *Zvezda* i *Leningrad*," *Literaturnaya gazeta*, No. 39 [September 21, 1946].)

[5] Franklin Reeve has shown recently that Bryusov, the poet, was very much alive to the significance and to the danger of Lenin's argument. Franklin Reeve, "Politics and Imagination," *American Slavic and East European Review*, XVI, No. 2 (April, 1957), 175–89.

when he was in his "functionalist" mood, he actually made
no distinction between the two kinds of *literatura*.[6] As to
the range of the article's applicability, since we are not concerned with its "correctness" as a guide to Soviet literary
policy, we note only that extravagant emphasis has been
placed on it in recent years, most notably by Zhdanov in
1946. But, considered with respect to the continuity of the
utilitarian tradition, the article has great significance. Even
at his most tactical, Lenin was seldom unaware of theoretical
matters, and the article may be read, despite all qualifications, as the most sweeping statement of the contempt for
literature inherent in Soviet Marxism. There are familiar
echoes from the Russian past, too, in Lenin's concept of literary partisanship, although here it is given a narrowness and
rigidity of statement that even the radical democrats stopped
short of. The article takes on added significance from the fact
that it contains some recognition of the delicacy and complexity of the literary process, stemming, no doubt, from
Lenin's intelligentsia background. Even in this inhospitable
atmosphere the opposition to the utilitarian trend receives reluctant recognition. At one moment Lenin seems to propose
that the best of the two traditions be fused, but he makes no
serious effort in the end to resolve the fundamental contradiction between them.

The emergence of the Party and its press from underground illegality late in 1905 provided the local occasion for
the article which poses the strategic question: now that the
Party press has passed the "cursed time of Aesopian language,
of literary servility, of slavish language, of intellectual serfdom," [7] what use shall be made of the new freedom? Lenin's
answer touches on so many of the permanent issues from

[6] See p. 224 for his "tactical" estimate of Gorky's *Mother*.
[7] Lenin, *Sochineniia*, X, 26–27.

the Russian past, his testament is so authoritative, so characteristic of recent Soviet thought on these matters, that it deserves intensive analysis.

The first statement of his thesis is in absolute terms:

Literature must become permeated with Party spirit. To counterbalance bourgeois morals, the bourgeois entrepreneurial and huckstering press, to counterbalance bourgeois literary careerism and individualism, "noble anarchism," and the pursuit of profits—the socialist proletariat must advance the principle of Party literature, must develop this principle, and must establish it in reality to the fullest degree possible.[8]

Lenin leaves no doubt that this principle is entirely a function of political concerns. The degree of subordination it demands of literature is, perhaps, unprecedented, short of certain anarchist prescriptions for the abolition of the written word.

In what does this principle of Party literature consist? Not only that for the socialist proletariat the practice of literature must not be a source of profit for persons and groups, but that, in general, it must not be an individual matter, independent of the whole proletarian cause. Down with non-Party writers! Down with superman writers! Literature must become a part of the general proletarian cause, the flywheel and screw of a single whole, of the great social-democratic mechanism, set in motion by the conscious vanguard of the entire working class. Literature must become a part of organized, systematic, unified Social Democratic Party work.[9]

After this, there would seem to be little left to say. But Lenin anticipates the rebuttal he knows his opinions will provoke:

There will be . . . hysterical members of the intelligentsia, who will raise a howl to the effect that such a comparison belittles, benumbs, "bureaucratizes" the free struggle of ideas, freedom of criticism, freedom of literary creation, and so on and

---

[8] *Ibid.*, p. 27   [9] *Ibid.*

so on. The fact of the matter is that such howls would only be an expression of bourgeois-intelligentsia individualism. There is no argument that literature, less than anything else, will yield to mechanical alignment, to leveling, to the supremacy of the majority over the minority. There is no argument . . . that the guarantee of the greatest range of personal initiative, of individual inclination, the range of thought and fantasy, of form and content, is unconditionally necessary. All this is indisputable.[10]

There echoes in this candid summary of the intelligentsia's probable objections most of the basic points made by Turgenev, Tolstoy, Chekhov, and others in defense of the free practice of their craft. Yet the original thesis still stands. He sees no contradiction in stating that

literature must certainly and necessarily become indissolubly connected with other parts of Social Democratic Party work. . . . The organized socialist proletariat must look after all this work, control all of it, introduce into all its work, without a single exception, the living stream of the living proletarian cause.[11]

With this point established, Lenin remains responsive to the Hegelian rhythm, nevertheless, and endeavors to resolve the two propositions in a kind of synthesis. The problem is essentially an administrative one, he seems to say, and needs only patient attention to it by all concerned:

We are far from the idea of preaching any kind of uniform system, or solution to the problem by means of a few resolutions. No schematism can be considered in this area. . . . The point is that our entire Party . . . should be aware of this new problem, should state it clearly, and should undertake everywhere to solve it. Emerging from the captivity of feudal censorship, we do not want to go and will not go into the captivity of bourgeois-huckstering literary relations. We wish to form, and we will form, a free press not only in the police sense, but also in the sense of freedom from careerism . . . also in the sense of freedom from bourgeois-anarchistic individualism.[12]

[10] *Ibid.*, p. 28.   [11] *Ibid.*   [12] *Ibid.*, p. 29.

In the second half of this passage (from the word "Emerg-ing . . ."), and in the swift transition between the two parts of it, we are able to distinguish the essential *non sequitur* in all subsequent Marxian thinking about art—the deceptive key-change, the illegitimate merging of incommensurable orders of thought. Up to this point Lenin has been concerned primarily with the opposition between freedom and control as it concerns the functioning Party artist. Then suddenly, without warning, he has translated this antithesis into the terms of the unrelated *political* opposition between the bour-geoisie and the proletariat. With his transvalued definition of freedom he reaches the peak of his intellectual sleight of hand. For if we follow him to the end of his list of the nega-tive freedoms it is impossible to avoid the conclusion that "freedom from . . . bourgeois-anarchistic individualism" is, in essence, freedom from every right and privilege the artist has demanded for himself since ancient Greece, that it is, indeed, freedom from freedom itself. Bourgeois freedom is slavery; proletarian "control" is freedom.

But Lenin was not satisfied with this formulation of the problem. In his new version, however, he amplifies the spe-cious key-change and uses it to carry him triumphantly out of the otherwise insoluble dilemma. He begins by restating the original antithesis in very similar terms. Continuing his argument from the remark about "bourgeois-anarchistic in-dividualism," he observes defensively:

The last words will seem to be a paradox or a joke on the readers. What! Some member of the intelligentsia, a passionate partisan of freedom will shout, What! You want the subordina-tion to the collective of such a fine individual matter as literary creation! You want the workers to decide questions of science, philosophy, aesthetics, by a majority vote! You deny the abso-lute freedom of absolutely individualistic intellectual creation!

Calm yourselves, gentlemen! In the first place we are considering Party literature and its submission to Party control. Each is free to write and speak as he pleases without the slightest limitation.[13]

It would appear then that all was well. Lenin recognizes the right of all writers who chafe at Party discipline to remove themselves from it and to write as they please. But he has approached the crux of the issue between the needs of the artist and the needs of an absolutist political group. In 1905 he could dispose of it with a pluralist solution, because there was no need at this time for him to face all the consequences of holding political power. If the opposition between these needs is absolute, Lenin felt free to say in 1905, let each go his own way. But there is a new note in his next formulation of the polarity between artist and revolutionary. He suggests that the freedom of choice he has just granted the writer is, itself, spurious; that this is a freedom only to write irresponsibly or dishonestly:

Every free union, among them the Party, is free to dismiss those members who make use of the Party label to preach anti-Party views. Freedom of speech must be complete. I am obliged to concede to you, in the name of freedom of speech, the full right to shout, to lie, and to write as you please. But you are obliged to concede to me in the name of the freedom of unions, the right to exclude or to break with people who talk this way and that way. The Party is a voluntary union which inevitably would disintegrate ideologically and then materially if it did not cleanse itself of members who preach anti-Party views.[14]

At this point there is a note of plain suspicion of the freely judging intellectual, but on the whole it is a reasonable statement of a more or less gentlemanly standoff, a reasonable statement for any political leader to make to freely committed followers. Though we know now that it is a provisional arrangement, one would think that it might have

<hr/>

[13] *Ibid.*   [14] *Ibid.*

served as a final comment on the matter as things stood in
1905. Not so. Lenin is not content with this: the note of
partisanship must be struck again, and the original thesis
must be reestablished in its purity. The conflict between the
classes is again superimposed on the issue of control versus
freedom. His crude for-or-against morality rearranges the
elements of the argument in such a way that all virtue and
the only valid freedom are found to reside in the proletarian
cause. By the same token, the freedom Lenin has just granted
the dissident artist is found to be false, nothing but a mask
for the "free" writer's status as a kept hireling of the class
enemy.

Mister bourgeois individualists, we must tell you that your talk
about absolute freedom is only hypocrisy. In a society based on
the power of money, in a society where the mass of workers
begs and a handful of the rich live like parasites, there cannot
be real genuine freedom. Are you free of your bourgeois publisher, mister writer? from your bourgeois public which demands
framed pornographic pictures from you. . . ? Actually this absolute freedom is a bourgeois or an anarchist phrase. . . . It is
impossible to live in a society and be free of that society. The
freedom of the bourgeois writer, artist, actress is only a masked
dependence on the money bag, on bribes, on banknotes.[15]

Lenin has abandoned all efforts to analyze the knottiest
problem of all, and has retreated inside the political certainty
that all who cannot be persuaded to be with you are unavoidably and implacably against you. All men are reducible
in moral terms to their class allegiances and their creative
product can only be judged in those terms. At this point
Lenin might have permitted himself the honesty Tolstoy
showed when he faced the bitter fact that art and social
change are, in a final sense, incompatible activities, and that
if the latter is to gain absolute ascendancy, the former must

[15] *Ibid.*, p. 30.

be considered expendable. But Lenin wanted it both ways, and in the following pronouncement, with its sudden reversal of hitherto accepted meanings, there is a fateful setting of the future course of the Russian literary tradition. Socialists, he says, will unmask the "hypocritically free" literature of the bourgeoisie and will set against it "a truly free literature *openly* connected with the proletariat":

This will be a free literature because not profit or career, but the idea of socialism and a sympathy for toilers will win over more and more new forces to its ranks. This will be a free literature because it will serve not a sated heroine, not the boring "upper ten thousand" suffering from obesity, but the millions and tens of millions of toilers, who make up the flower of the country, its strength, its future. This will be a free literature impregnating the most recent word of humanity's revolutionary thought with the experience . . . of the socialist proletariat. . . .

To work, then, comrades! Before us is a difficult and new but great and noble task—the organization of a broad, many-sided diverse literature in close connection with the Social Democratic workers' meetings. All Social Democratic literature must become permeated with Party spirit . . . only then will Social Democratic literature . . . know how to carry out its duty, only then will it know how even in the framework of bourgeois society to tear itself loose from bourgeois slavery and to merge with the truly advanced . . . revolutionary class.[16]

We have already noted the deceptive altering of the terms of the discussion. In a sense it proceeds out of the arrogance of the political revolutionary who insists—who, indeed, must insist—that his "made" universe contains not a portion of the truth or of virtue, but the whole of it, including the only meaningful definitions of freedom, and the only formula for creating a truly great literature. But his formula rests on the major fallacy in Soviet Marxian thinking about art: that art's worth is coterminous with its ideological value.

[16] *Ibid.*, pp. 30–31.

Much of the Soviet future is forecast in the final passage. First, there is the familiar idea that a "free," and presumably a great, literature, will express those qualities only through service to an idea and to the needs of the suffering masses. There is, in addition, the *mystique* of the *narod*, "the flower of the country, its strength, its future," the same *narod* which was, as Lenin repeatedly observed, such poor human material for social change that it had to be harnessed into a relationship of parental control so harsh that it was to require the indefinite suspension of many of the rights, privileges, and amenities of the most advanced civilizations. There is, too, the orientation toward the future, toward *should be* and *shall be*, conceived as the end of a long upward process of education, in which literature will be assigned a major share of the task of propagating healthy, correct, energizing ideas. Through the entire article runs the certainty that this will be best accomplished through "controls," exercised in the name of politically conceived goals.

On the level of theory, whether or not he realized it, Lenin has completed the encirclement of the free intellect. He has accomplished it simply by extending the ethical imperative of revolutionary Marxism to the artist, with no allowance made for his professional needs. The fact that there is no formal barrier in Marxian theory to the assertion of a principle of conscription [17] may now be translated into that other more ominous formula that neither Chernyshevsky, nor Lenin, nor, with few exceptions, the later Communist theorists have had the honesty or the perspicacity to admit,

---

[17] It is true that in 1905 Lenin considered the writer a volunteer in the Social Democratic cause who was free to resign and "lie" for the bourgeoisie. But he has asserted the Party's right to control the writers who come under its discipline, has asserted the principle of political partisanship, as modern Soviet Marxists claim. In the one-Party state today the writer still has the "freedom" to refuse to accept controls, but it is a freedom that leads only to silence.

namely, that when the needs of revolution collide with the
needs of art, the latter will always be denied.

In his thinking about art, Lenin has made an absolute
choice within two sets of polar opposites that were isolated
in the examination of Marxist theory. In the first place, he
has clearly chosen future-oriented agitation over scientific
investigation, and he has placed overwhelming emphasis on
the harsh, one-sided command of interim revolutionary ethics
as against the generous vision of man as a versatile, creative,
many-sided creature—a vision implicit in the long-range
Marxian perspective. Lenin is predictable in these choices
since they are part and parcel of his pioneering changes of
emphasis within the whole world of Marxism. He was a
changer, not an interpreter, of the world, and, drastic as his
emphasis was, the conclusions he drew in this article are not
in the end surprising. But we must note, since he is unwilling
to do it, the disastrous consequences for the poet or the
philosopher in the advocacy of a standard of political efficacy
as the ultimate measure of truth.

This article may be said to mark the junction of the two
principal currents of the Russian revolutionary tradition as
it is concerned with imaginative literature. The waters are
muddy, it is true, and Lenin makes no explicit acknowledgment here of his dependence on the Russian radical
democrats, but their accent is unmistakable in the article,
particularly in the final prescription for a socialist literature.
The concepts of service to an idea and to the masses, of
orienting art always toward a better future, and of educating
men explicitly in their social responsibilities are nowhere to
be found in the classical Marxist writings on art. Since they
have been present in the Russian tradition since Belinsky,
there is every reason to attribute them to Lenin's native inheritance, to Chernyshevsky, above all. Finally, Lenin has

made an unequivocal choice within another crucial set of polarities, this time not Marxist but indigenous, that of knowledge versus political utility as the principal end of literature, as these ideas were developed in the mid-nineteenth-century debate in Russia.

At the risk of imposing too great a symmetry on very complex material, it is possible to outline the general terms of the merger between Marxism and radical democratic thought, as it affects literature. The complicated apparatus of Marxian determinism, with its claims to confirmation in the process of history and in nature itself, with its documented analysis of social injustice, and its proposals for action (as Lenin derived them from Marx and Engels), all replaced or supplemented the vaguer notions of "progress," "natural truth," and the rudimentary critique of social decay in the thinking of the Russians. Both bodies of ideas rested on the concept of an upward moving, dialectically operated universe, which the partisans of both had learned from Hegel. Brought together, as they were, by this shared belief, radical democratic ideas about literature seem to have survived the Marxian reinforcement to their assumptions, without fundamental change. There was, after all, a vacuum in classical Marxism on the matter of literature's role during the epoch of transition, which the Russian utilitarian theories were perfectly designed to fill. The wonder is that it took Soviet theorists so long to recognize the jigsaw neatness with which they fit together. Of course, early Soviet critics came into disturbing contact with the contrary, that is, the classical, or anti-utilitarian, trend in Marx's and Engels's remarks on art. Some of the critics may have been spellbound by the belittling designation, "pre-Marxist," which Plekhanov and others placed on the Russian radicals' ideas. Others may have inherited scruples from the classical past about controlling art and the artist as drastically as Chernyshevsky proposed. In any case, it was not until after 1932 that the prerevolutionary critics rose to a position of influence on a level with Marx and Engels. By 1946 they seemed to have gained absolute ascendancy. When the grand merger had been effected it became clear that the binding force between them was the supremacy of the activist, political ethic in both sets of ideas.

Hegel to the contrary, history does not often organize itself into the form of dramatic tragedy. But if I may borrow the analogy, this moment (1905) deserves to be seen as the climax (albeit a hidden one) of the dramatic contest between the two factions within the Russian literary tradition, the moment of the fatal reversal of direction for the affairs of the protagonist, here thought of as the ideas of the classical tradition. Although it took years for this to become apparent, all else that follows is, in a sense, a denouement. The climactic moment was not apparent to the actors, but Lenin's article, together with Gorky's *Mother*, the novel that appeared a short time later as if to illustrate his doctrine, mark a watershed in the history of Russian thought. If these two documents announce the beginning of a new tradition, as present-day Soviet critics claim, they also contain a veiled death sentence for the old. It may be that the sentence will not be carried out in the end, but for the trained ear Zhdanov's "Report" has the ring of an epitaph.

II

Gorky had written to Chekhov as early as 1900: "The time has come when the heroic is required." [18] Gorky felt this generalized need throughout his creative life: he found dignity and defiance, tenderness and courage, wisdom and

[18] Maxim Gorky, *Reminiscences* (New York, 1946), p. 99.

saintliness in the lower depths of Russian life. His lifelong moral quest took the form of a search for heroes. He seems to have projected his own intense, almost virginal, sense of moral purity outward into the crowds he moved through, in a constant search for the men whose strength, humility, and independence he could admire. His searchlight picked them out of the most unexpected places. His gallery of heroes is varied and colorful—tramps, thieves, prostitutes, hermits, smugglers—and, although it is always threatened by sentimentalism, few of the portraits are blurred by the playing down of compensating vices, or by minimizing the filth, corruption, or despair that framed the reflected glint of virtue. In the tension of these contrasts, Gorky's notes of human affirmation establish their veracity. The function of these unlikely heroes was a simple one: to provide reassurance that man's dignity survived all vicissitudes, that there was hope. Nilovna, the heroine of his novel *Mother*, described the nourishing effects of contemplating virtue in others, in the broad, extra-political terms that characterize most of Gorky's own search:

She knew men who had emancipated themselves from greed and evil; she understood that if there were more such people, the dark, incomprehensible, and awful face of life would become more kindly and simple, better and brighter.[19]

He did not limit his search to a single class, or look for a single set of admirable qualities through the range of castes and classes in Imperial Russia. He found a successful tragic design, for example, in the career of the energetic, self-made bourgeois who was destroyed by the wealth he had accumulated. In his autobiography he tended to celebrate all kinds of dissenters, from the Old Believers to the most extreme elements of the revolutionary movement. When his quest

[19] Maxim Gorky, *Mother*, trans. Isidore Schneider (New York, 1947), p. 248.

centered momentarily on the rising Social Democratic Labor Party in the first decade of the twentieth century, and his long, uneven, affiliation with that movement began, the generative force of a new kind of literature was created. It did not matter that *Mother*, the single novel he devoted to this theme, had no sequel, or that he shied away from the treatment of revolutionary political virtue in fiction in later years. The novel's publication in 1907 crystallized and gave literary expression to the fateful tendencies Lenin's article promised. The dangers that are forecast by this event may be summarized as the substitution of a programmatic, declamatory optimism for the undogmatic exploration of human life and suffering which had been the major preoccupation of the classical writers. The new novel promised, as Chernyshevsky had done in his novel, a way to end suffering. The issue of the positive hero becomes central again and is, according to the faction that welcomed the changes *Mother* initiated in Russian writing, the element that most solidly links the past with what is to come. In the novel's Bolshevik hero, Pavel Vlasov, we are told that Gorky

continues the tradition of classical revolutionary-democratic literature, which created a series of freedom-loving heroes . . . but at the same time includes in it completely new material [so that] the image of Pavel Vlasov is the ancestor of the gallery of heroic images in Soviet literature: of Ostrovsky's Pavel Korchagin, the heroes of Fadeev's *Young Guard*, and a number of others.[20]

Mother contains two formulas often found in later Soviet fiction: the conversion of the innocent, the ignorant, or the misled to a richer life of participation in the forward movement of society; and the more important pattern of emblematic political heroism in the face of terrible obstacles. The

[20] L. I. Timofeev, *Sovremennaya literatura* (Moscow, 1947), p. 52.

first theme is embodied in the figure of the mother, whose life is transformed by affiliation with the revolutionary movement, and the second in the grim figure of her son, Pavel. Actually the two themes are interwoven, with Pavel acting as the principal agent in restoring his mother to a life of dignity and purpose. This relationship also illustrates the kind of inspiriting effect the image of Pavel is intended to have on the sympathetic reader.

Pavel's inspirational value derives from the moral qualities he displays and the kind of purposeful activity in which he displays them. When courage, endurance, strength of will are exercised in certain kinds of tactically "correct" political behavior, during the May Day parade, for example, it is always a calculated effect he aims for. His later defiance of the Tsarist court reflects a public, not a private, emotion in the sense that it is not a personal defense, but an occasion to instruct the masses in the workings of the hateful system. Pavel acts on this, and on all other occasions, out of two supplementary kinds of knowledge that make up class consciousness: the abstract generalizations about society learned from his precious books, plus the documentation of working-class misery which is daily before his eyes. Thus equipped with emotion and knowledge, Pavel goes forth to permanent battle with the status quo.

This, at least, is the way we are asked to read the novel. It may be read quite differently, however. The novel's conflict is posed between moral absolutes and the writer's attitude toward the conflict is not that of an observer but of a partisan who is, himself, engaged in the bitter class warfare. In this rigid opposition there is no opportunity for the emblematic good man to move in the area between good and evil, or to be involved with, tempted by, or overcome from within by evil. He may reproach himself for lacking the en-

durance he needs to carry out the tasks history has set for
him. He may search his soul to find the courage he needs.
He may examine the reasons which brought him to his
exposed position. But he will not question the position itself.
Evil is tangible and external, and all man's resources are
needed to combat it. Since, according to the formula in
Mother, the good man is the most distant from evil, he cannot yield to it without forfeiting his position in the novel's
moral hierarchy. Pavel's revolutionary colleague, the Ukrainian, Andrei Nakhodka, asks a question which is vital for the
revolutionary and suggests at the same time a fruitful approach for the writer to the tensions of revolutionary activity.
After he has confessed to the murder of a police spy, he asks,
in effect, what crimes he will commit in the name of the
revolution, what violations of his private moral code are
permissible (or bearable) for the dedicated man.[21] But
Nakhodka is too weak, too susceptible. He is a good-hearted
follower, but not the leader Pavel is. In Pavel's eyes such
questions have a certain validity, but they do not really concern *him*, and can always be resolved in the terms of his
political-moral absolutes.

But the ease with which he does resolve them seriously
challenges his adequacy as a literary portrait. He is, among
other things, a fanatical moralizer and prophet. It may be
argued that these qualities have been forced on him by the
stringencies of his situation, or that they are inevitable costs
of his kind of life. In any case they are there—we know because Gorky, perhaps unwittingly, shows them to us—to be
accounted for, overcome, or read into any final assessment
of his human worth. At the very least they are barriers to
awareness, if not to action. By failing to record his hero's
limitations fully Gorky has provided grounds for seriously

[21] See Gorky, *Mother*, pp. 140–50.

questioning his human and literary judgment in this matter.

The politicalizing of Pavel's emotions is very nearly complete. The following rapture is brought on by uttering the introductory word "Comrade" to a crowd of listening factory hands:

When Pavel had thrown out the word to which he was meant to attach a deep and signficant meaning, his throat contracted in a sharp spasm of the joy of fight. He was seized with the invincible desire to give himself up to the strength of his faith, to throw his heart to the people. His heart kindled with the dream of truth.[22]

Despite the extravagantly bad writing and the hints of psychological imbalance, this passage, together with many others like it, is important because it describes the deepest emotional satisfaction of the political man. When his mother argues that he should not expose himself to danger by carrying the banner in the May Day parade, Pavel answers: "I must do it! Please understand me! It is my happiness." [23] She is silent, and he continues in the vein of his grand political passion, hinting now at a taste for martyrdom: "You oughtn't to be grieved. You ought to rejoice. When are we going to have mothers who will rejoice in sending their children even to death?" Told by his mother that she speaks out of love for him, he answers: "There is a love that interferes with a man's very life," [24] and then, later, "I want no love, I want no friendship which gets between my feet and holds me back." [25] When Nakhodka, whose humane awareness is in inverse proportion to his political effectiveness, reproaches him for his harshness, and for acting the hero in front of his helpless mother, Gorky the writer has brought to light a legitimate conflict of values. Pavel's pomposity,

[22] *Ibid.*, p. 68.   [23] *Ibid.*, p. 137.   [24] *Ibid.*, p. 138.
[25] *Ibid.*, p. 139.

rigidity, and fixity of purpose, with their suggestions of sub-limation and megalomania, are predictable consequences of his personality and of his way of life, as given. But Gorky the propagandist betrays his persuasive insight, a few moments later, by extracting a quick apology from Pavel. For the rest of the novel the insight is forgotten. Gorky's uncritical approval of Pavel is unmistakable as the latter grows into the most effective political leader in the area. Finally, when Pavel rises to speak at his trial: "A party man, I recognize only the court of my party and will not speak here in my defense," [26] he has become in his own eyes the selfless incarnation of the public cause, without doubts, hesitations, or concern for personal loss, and Gorky, having surrendered his control over the character, can only agree.

The matter of tension between private and public life appears constantly, but it is resolved with one exception in favor of the latter. Sacrifice and suffering are often mentioned but seldom shown, and never explored to any depth. Consider the example of the design for marriage which Pavel's wife outlines to his mother:

He's free at any moment. I am his comrade—a wife, of course. But the conditions of his work are such that for years and years I cannot regard our bond as the usual one, like that of others. It will be hard, I know it, to part with him; but, of course, I'll manage to. He knows that I'm not capable of regarding a man as my possession. . . . I love him very much and he me . . . we will enrich each other by all in our power; and if necessary we will part as friends.[27]

Gorky records this solemnly, without irony, or any sense that it is any less than what will be accomplished. The two women sit enclosed in each other's arms: "It was quiet, melancholy and warm." [28]

[26] *Ibid.*, p. 363.   [27] *Ibid.*, p. 378.   [28] *Ibid.*, p. 381.

Nikolai, another revolutionary, whose marriage was broken up by the exigencies of exile and underground conspiracy, rationalized his loss in harsher terms:

Family life always diminishes the energy of a revolutionary. Children must be maintained in security, and there's the need to work for one's bread. The revolutionist ought without cease to develop every iota of his energy; he must deepen and broaden it; but this demands time. He must always be at hand, because we—the working men—are called by the logic of history, to destroy the old world, to create a new life. . . . No revolutionist can attach himself to an individual—work through life side by side with another individual—without distorting his faith; and we must never forget our aim is not little conquests, but only complete victory! [29]

Only once does raw human experience force its way through the web of political rationalization. Nakhodka's anguish at the casual blow which turned out to be an act of murder bespeaks real inner conflict. He knows the conventional terms in which the crime can be justified, and he recites them with an air of conviction:

It so happens that we sometimes must abhor a certain person in order to hasten the time when it will be possible only to take delight in one another. You must destroy those who hinder the progress of life, who sell human beings for money in order to buy quiet or esteem for themselves. . . . If it happens sometimes that I am compelled to take their stick into my hands, what am I going to do then? Why I am going to take it, of course, I will not decline.[30]

He has the right, even the duty, to act in that way. But this explanation is only "logic," he says, it has nothing to say to the conscience:

I go against logic for once. I do not need your logic now. I know that blood can bring no results, I know that thin blood is barren, fruitless. . . . But I take the sin upon myself, I'll kill

[29] *Ibid.*   [30] *Ibid.*, p. 148.

if I see a need for it. I speak only for myself, mind you. My crime dies with me. It will not remain a blot upon the future. It will sully no one but myself—no one but myself.[31]

The crime which is justifiable in public terms is nevertheless unacceptable to Nakhodka's moral sensibility. It is the most terrible and destructive act of self-renunciation the revolutionary can be asked to carry out, even though he believes, as he does it, that it is in the name of the time when "free men will walk on the earth" and "life will be one great service to man":

In your forward march it sometimes chances that you must go against your very self. You must be able to give up every thing— your heart and all. To give your life, to die for the cause—that's simple. Give more! Give that which is dearer to you than your life. . . . I will tear my heart out, if necessary, and will trample it with my own feet.[32]

Despite the congealed rhetoric, this is intelligible moral utterance, exposing grounds for the deepest division between the individual and his cause, including permanent banishment from the Utopia to come. One need not agree with his definition of the dilemma to see in this the germ of genuine tragic conflict, the real drama of the revolution's honorable casualties. Gorky does not develop it further. Pavel, who, with his mother, remains in the center of the stage, understands and sympathizes: "Andrei won't forgive himself soon," he says, "if he'll forgive himself at all." But he reduces it again to the comforting blacks and whites of the political morality which Andrei has for a moment seen through:

He killed a man unwittingly. He feels disgusted, ashamed, sick. . . . But they kill off thousands calmly, without a qualm, without a shudder of the heart. They kill with pleasure and with delight.[33]

[31] *Ibid.*   [32] *Ibid.*, pp. 148–49.   [33] *Ibid.*, p. 153.

And then, true to the basic cadence of the book, Pavel dissolves his doubts in the strain of political evangelism that disfigures so much of the novel. Addressing his troubled mother, he says:

If you felt the abomination of it all, the disgrace and rottenness, you would understand our truth; you would then perceive how great it is, how glorious.[34]

With this the mother's doubts are set at rest, and the episode is ended.

Gorky's optimism, at this time, about the revolutionary's capacity to endure hardship of all kinds, without moral damage, is summed up in some observations that the mother, by now a hardened revolutionary, makes to a comrade:

There's a great deal of hardship, you know. People suffer; they are beaten, cruelly beaten, and everyone is oppressed and watched. They hide, live like monks, and many joys are closed to them, it's very hard. And when you look at them well you see that the hard things, the evil and difficult, are around them on the outside, and not within.[35]

But even by the most ungenerous estimate, the virtues of monks do not contain Gorky's sense of human possibilities. It was this fact, perhaps, that prevented his ever again attempting a large-scale fictional treatment of the revolutionary movement.[36]

WE are confronted here with problems already made familiar to us by *What Is to Be Done?* The hardheaded

---

[34] *Ibid.*, p. 154.   [35] *Ibid.*, p. 385.
[36] The dramatic use made of revolution in *Egor Bulychov* and *The Artamanov Business* is more characteristic of Gorky. In both works it appears at the very end as an offstage turbulence which implies that an impersonal vengeance has caught up with the sinful, doomed, but dramatically interesting merchants, whose end it announces.

visionaries of *Mother*, like the self-confident new men in
Chernyshevsky's novel, have their minds fixed firmly on the
emergent future. They are struggling to forward a trend
which, they are convinced, is both inevitable and infinitely
preferable to the unbearable present. Gorky makes no attempt to hide his own partisanship in this contest. Completely identified with his protagonists, he is as committed
as they are to the overthrow of life as it is, in the name of
a compelling vision of life as it should be. But the question
again arises: how can the conflict between future and present
be dramatized within the confines of the realistic novel?
Apart from the many "utopian" speculations in the novel,
the desirability of the future can be suggested only indirectly,
through the intensity of the characters' dedication to it.
Otherwise the affirmative case must be set forth in declamatory assertions by the hero or his lieutenants. In spite of the
endless, florid talk about the better world their personal
struggle brings closer, what these men are fighting against is
always more vividly realized than what they are fighting for.
Their anger is thus better motivated than their invincible
optimism. In a novel of repeated tactical defeats this assurance is communicated only by defiant speeches.

The source of their optimism is a political truth founded
upon abstractions. That the historical force championed by
Pavel and his comrades is somehow benign is an assumption
outside the novel which may or may not be accepted by the
reader. Gorky's abandonment of a more traditional novelist's
vantage for overt political commitment, therefore, prejudices
any claims the novel may have to universal interest. The
novel of open political partisanship can be acceptable only
to like-minded readers. The only possibility of reaching a
more indifferent audience rests in the acceptability or credibility of the human material—above all, of the hero—in the

novel. And we have seen, I think, that the partisan blight
has effectively neutralized his (or their) appeal.

The general difficulties we have indicated—involvement
with the future, motivation by doctrine, and this writer's
close identification with his heroes and with their cause—
have one marked effect on the texture of the novel: it is
shaped, down to the smallest technical details, by the spirit
of political evangelism. It is not only that the climax of
the novel is declamatory (Pavel's speech before the court),
or that all the characters' actions and utterances are shaped
by political considerations. The dialogue often resembles a
verbal exchange of newspaper editorials, written in the turgid
rhetoric which also disfigures Gorky's pamphleteering. The
expository passages, the dramatic passages, the physical descriptions of the characters and of nature are likewise permeated with evangelism. As the mother goes down under
the strangling fingers of the police spy at the novel's end
she shouts a slogan, "You will not drown the truth in seas
of blood." [37] When Pavel has overcome her doubts about
the essential justice of Nakhodka's act of homicide, "The
mother arose agitated, full of a desire to fuse her heart into
the heart of her son, into one burning, flaming torch." [38]
Class virtue manifests itself in the bodies, postures, faces,
above all in the eyes of the characters. The eyes of the class
enemy are muddy, bleared, or shifty, but, in the midst of his
courtroom speech, "Pavel smiled, and the generous fire of
his blue eyes blazed forth more brilliantly." [39] At times
Gorky comes very close to self-parody: "You'd better put
on something; it's cold," one character remarks; and the
other answers, "There's a fire inside of me." [40] This is not
simply bad writing but a striking example of the fusion of

[37] Gorky, *Mother*, p. 402.   [38] *Ibid.*, p. 154.
[39] *Ibid.*, p. 364.   [40] *Ibid.*, p. 239.

form and content. At the heart of the matter is Gorky's total partisanship. Under its influence all literary and human truth—even the truth of the physical universe—becomes subordinated to a single dogmatic view of political truth.

The history of this novel's reputation is voluminous. We may note only the major trend here: what was at first, in the opinion of critics, a very questionable piece of work is now considered the foundation of socialist realism. Lenin at his most functionalist is reported by Gorky to have told him while it was still in proofs:

Yes, I should hurry up with it, such a book is needed, for many of the workers who take part in the revolutionary movement do so unconsciously, chaotically, and it would be very useful to them to read *Mother*. "The very book for the moment." [41]

Gorky's biographer in English reports that Gorky himself was extremely displeased with it: "Gorky . . . has come to agree with most of his critics, namely, that the novel suffers from weakness of characterization and too obvious didacticism." [42] His critics included many authoritative Soviet voices in the 1920s. Plekhanov and others found the novel schematic, sentimental, didactic, and ideologically false. The reversal of this generally held verdict coincided with the promulgation of socialist realism in 1932, with all that this meant for the setting of new standards of literary judgments on the leading personages in the novel. I. Bespalov's article on Gorky in the *Literary Encyclopedia* (1929) has this to say:

Most vividly developed in *Mother* are the mother, Andrei Nakhodka, and Rybin. Pavel is presented schematically and somewhat bookishly.[43]

[41] Maxim Gorky, *Days with Lenin* (New York, 1932), p. 6.
[42] Alexander Kaun, *Maxim Gorky and His Russia* (New York, 1931), p. 557.
[43] I. Bespalov, "Gorky," *Literaturnaya entsiklopediya*, II (1929), 652.

In later judgments Andrei's and Pavel's positions are generally reversed. The Ukrainian is seen as a loyal, if fallible, lieutenant, but Pavel is the "first among equals." Timofeev's textbook for secondary schools notes Pavel's resemblance to Chernyshevsky's Rakhmetov, and praises his image as the incarnation of Bolshevik virtue. He is endowed with "will, intelligence," and "firmness of character." These traits in turn sustain his chief political attribute: "clarity of goal, readiness to surmount all obstacles for the achievement of this goal." [44] This judgment echoes scores of others, which find in Pavel a point of junction of the old and the new, the first successful image of the positive Bolshevik hero, and the first successful solution of all attendant creative problems. At the heart of these opinions is the assumption that the contemplation of Pavel's image by the reader will stimulate him to emulate the hero's actions and thoughts, and coincidentally to respect Pavel's position as a representative of Communist leadership.

Gorky knew that his approach to literature implied important departures from classical realism. In his letter to Chekhov about the need for "the heroic," Gorky exposed some of the thinking that underlay this demand:

So there you go, doing away with realism. And I am extremely glad. So be it! And to hell with it! . . . Everyone wants things that are exciting and brilliant so that it won't be like life, you see, but superior to life, better, more beautiful. Present-day literature must definitely begin to color life and as soon as it does this, life itself will acquire color. That is to say, people will live faster, more brilliantly.[45]

Bespalov goes on to say that even though the core of Nakhodka's ideological views is anarchist in substance and Christian in form, he is a better propagandist and a more compelling literary figure than the "rationalist Pavel Vlasov." Ideological correctness has not yet become the sole measure of truth.

[44] Timofeev, Sovremennaya literatura, pp. 83–84.

[45] Gorky, Reminiscences, p. 99.

The "realism" that must give way to the "heroic" was neutral, he felt, hopeless, and rooted in the present, in life as it is; the "heroic" that was to replace it was not escapist, but functional, in that it was to quicken and change men's lives and set them in motion toward an unspecified vision of life as it should be. On the single occasion when this general feeling was translated into political myth-making, he invested the "color" and the promise in Pavel and the other Bolsheviks. This lapse has been seized upon and made the theoretical basis of "socialist romanticism," the ingredient of socialist realism which directs the writer not to a general heightening of experience as Gorky originally intended, but to the celebration of the emergent future exactly as it is defined in the Party program and in the five-year plans. This is the obligatory step beyond the present, beyond reality, beyond realism, and beyond the empirical truth that the figure of the Soviet hero must express. Pavel Vlasov is valued as an *ideological* portrait, made up of hope, doctrine, and tendency as much as he is of flesh and blood. Thus the grounds for doubting his human validity are built into the very basis of the theory he stands on.

In a sense, Gorky and Lenin collaborated in this first demonstration of Soviet literary partisanship. Perhaps in Lenin's, certainly in Gorky's, case, it did not represent their only or their final thought on literature. But it set an example of the extreme prescriptive potential in Soviet Marxism which, even at that time, had the critical inheritance of the Russian radical tradition solidly grafted onto it. It has provided primary documentation ever since for the most extreme applications of this theory to Soviet writing.

11

LEATHER MEN

> . . . *people whose revolutionary class consciousness has already grown into an emotion, an unbreakable will, has become an instinct like hunger and love.* GORKY

Postrevolutionary literature makes it clear that the civil war is the brightest and most fearsome experience in the memory of Soviet man. Many who lived through its worst moments remained fascinated by it and continued to value it for the intensity of its emotion, even as they forgot the suffering, the brutality, and the suspension by all factions of minimal standards of human justice. Every man enacted the private drama of his own expectations within the national tragedy. Many found the revolution stillborn when the bloodletting finally ended; others had been recast in its furnace, and never lost their taste for the easy release of rage and violence. Many more went home numb, hiding their psychic wounds, and sought relief in the cadences of peacetime existence.

The Soviet Russian imagination has never ceased to regard those years as the climactic moment of its own history, and has never found a suitable substitute for it as a source, not simply of fictional material, but of genuine spiritual adventure. Of the four later novels we shall examine in a final survey of the range of the Soviet literary expression, two, *Road to Calvary* and *The Silent Don*, deal almost entirely with the civil war, and in the other two, *Road to the Ocean* and *The Making of a Hero*, civil war experiences have shaped characters and situations which are also explored in later years.

One finds in the early civil war novels a disorder and lack of control over the material which may be attributed to two factors: the extraordinary resistance of the material itself, rich though it was, to conventional literary organization; and a tendency on the part of the writers to celebrate violence, riot, and disintegration for their own sakes. Had they been disposed to make leisurely explorations of character, the moral conflicts, complex though they were in a certain sense (within the family, within the village, as well as between armies and social classes), were posed so absolutely and settled by such violent means—often by the blow of a saber—that they had few opportunities to do so. Few have succeeded as Sholokhov did in *The Silent Don* in assimilating the entire experience into a grand literary design. In the early works about the civil war, the writers hewed close to a vein of personal reminiscence, accepted a broad standard of partisan virtue (although the departures from it are often the most interesting moments), and attempted a minimum of literary invention.

The Soviet writer has never been entirely free of doctrinal "guidance," but in the 1920s he worked under less pressure than he has at any time since. In 1925, government and Party formally declared hands-off in art, and the many unofficial literary groups then clamoring for supremacy exerted so much pressure from so many directions that they tended to neutralize one another. The views of these groups reproduced the spectrum of theories lying between the prescriptive and the exploratory extremes that have already been isolated in the Russian national tradition. Some of the schools, it is true, are beyond its limits: the formalists who considered the preoccupation with human value to be outside the proper concern of criticism; the Plekhanov-oriented "sociologists" whose "unmasking" of the class essence of past literary works was an academic, not a critical or creative, concern; the Mayakovsky-led experimenters with "the word" whose primary concern was with poetry. But within our spectrum the debate continued, between the On Guardists as the spokesmen for the harshest tendencies in the prescriptive aesthetic and the diffuse group known as the fellow-travelers, partially organized in the Serapion Brotherhood, whose spokesman was Alexander Voronsky.

Voronsky's aesthetic was one of the few theories of the Soviet era which was not *primarily* directed toward finding a place for art within the fixed and absolute limits of class warfare. From Tolstoy and Proust he derived the central assumption of his theory—that art essentially was a form of cognition, not of agitation:

Before everything else art is knowledge of life. Art is not the arbitrary play of fantasies, of feeling, of moods, art is not an expression of the subjective sensations, or experiences of the poet. Art does not set itself the goal . . . of awakening "good feelings" in the reader. Art like science perceives life. Art and science have one and the same subject—life, reality. But science analyzes, art synthesizes; science is abstract, art concrete; science is directed to man's reason, art to his sensuous nature.[1]

Voronsky, an old Bolshevik himself, had, of course, to come to grips with the problems of the class-divided universe and of the relation between art and ideology. But his formulation avoided two extremes: first, the view that the artist tropismatically expresses the ideology of his class by virtue of his birth or of his class conditioning, and that this reflection is the most important element in his work; or, second, the view that the artist is obliged to become a conscious spokesman for the interests of the "advanced" class, the

---

[1] *Literaturnaya entsiklopediya*, II (1929), 313.

proletariat. The artist, as well as the scholar, reflects his findings through a "psychological class prism."[2] But his researches are undirected, are not valued simply because they reflect class interest, and their objective pursuit constitutes his first obligation to his class. Reality exactly as he discovers it to be is his primary area of operation.

This summary of Voronsky's views indicates that the nonprescriptive strains in the Soviet intellectual legacy found hospitality in the early days, and that accommodation was thought possible between two basic human activities, free investigation of the world and the making of revolution. It is not surprising that a majority of the most gifted writers drew together under the shelter of this doctrine. Variety in theme, frankness in treatment, and ambiguity in outcome are qualities that have often been noted in this early fiction. It is reasonable to assume that the more adventurous of the writers found support for their freedom of movement in Voronsky's rejection of narrow political claims made on them by the Proletkult–On Guard–RAPP axis.

In this air of relative nonconformity no single doctrine was preeminent, and no single design for the literary hero prevailed. In fact, the concept of the hero as an important structural device or didactic instrument was not widely discussed in the critical debates of the time.[3] Trotsky and Voronsky, for example, both expressed dissatisfaction with the various images of Communists that had appeared in

---

[2] *Ibid.*, p. 312.

[3] A symptom of the general indifference to the matter is found in the brief entry under "Hero" in the *Bolshaya sovetskaya entsiklopediya*, XVII (1929), 451–52. Hero is defined as an ancient Greek concept which reappeared in the figure of the Christian saint, and as a device of neoclassic tragedy. In the *Literary Encyclopedia*, the problem is briefly treated under the heading "Obraz" (VIII [1934], 190–91). The treatment, which reflects the (then) new doctrine, socialist realism, also looks like a last-minute insertion in a long article, most of which echoes the ponderous terminology of Plekhanovist literary scholarship.

novels, but neither they nor anybody else proclaimed that the creation of the shining image of the Communist hero was a preeminent obligation of the Soviet writer. All factions were concerned with defining the nature of literature itself, and with making a literature worthy of the new epoch, whether a radically different one, a "proletarian" literature, or, if this was a daydream (as both Trotsky and Voronsky maintained), then a literature which incorporated the best of the past in its investigation of the new Soviet reality. The most explicit treatment of the hero problem is contained in the doctrine of "the living man," a very general notion which echoes the classical past in its overall injunction to show the Communist with all his faults and the class enemy with all his virtues.[4]

Whatever there is of interest on the hero is to be found in the literature itself. Free from hounding by any single omnipotent, critical group, the writers explored a number of disparate solutions. Non-Party writers like Fedin, Kaverin, and Olesha dealt sympathetically with the tragic "maladjustment" of the prerevolutionary *intelligent* who could not comprehend the disorder of a world in revolution. In this connection one occasionally finds discussions about "the superfluous man," but it had become clear by 1929 that this was a declining trend, that the new "new man," the Bolshevik, had established himself at the center of Soviet literature.

II

The most celebrated essay on heroism from these early years is Dmitri Furmanov's *Chapaev*, published in 1923, a book which has survived all doctrinal reversals, and is now established as a Soviet classic. Though it is usually classified as a novel, it is really a diary with the thinnest of fictional

[4] See below, pp. 270–76.

disguises—the author has simply changed his own name—
and has all the immediacy and incoherence of history directly
observed at a volcanic moment. Judged in terms of its fictional pretensions, it is episodic and formless. The war between Red and White is the background, but the real conflict, as it appears fitfully in the narrative of events, is between
the attitudes that make for victory over the external enemy
and the personal inadequacies and organizational shortcomings that threaten victory. There are two heroes, the legend-
ary guerrilla leader, Chapaev, and his commissar, Klychkov
(Furmanov). Their relationship, their initial antagonism
and ultimate partnership, is the focal point of the human
story and, at the same time, the source of a crude symbolism.

The distribution of skills and energies between the two
heroes is as expected: Klychkov, the Party man, the "rationalist," is the guardian of policy and discipline, but he lacks
the military skills and is not himself a primary source of
revolutionary energy. His faith in his Party's knowledge of
the laws of social change is absolute. His disciplined allegiance to those who are directing the process of change
endows him with a self-assured wisdom in the name of which
he focuses and manipulates the skills and energies of others.
His work is leadership; he deals with men's attitudes, their
morale, their understanding of the cause, and their allegiance
to it.

Chapaev, the source of the book's color, embodies a different set of heroic virtues. His elemental strength, his colorful
boasting, and his instinctive qualities of leadership recall the
heroes of Russian folklore, or the strain of peasant anarchism
represented in the past by Bolotnikov, Razin, and Pugachev,
leaders of the great *Jacqueries* of the seventeenth and eighteenth centuries. The alliance between the two men, the
commissar and the peasant guerrilla leader, which is central in

the book, has extra significance because of the unintentional disclosure that their "partnership" conceals a subtle inequality which ends in the subjugation of one by the other.

Klychkov's premise—"that politics is the mainspring of the civil war"—defines his function and his personality as well. He is convinced that his work of inspiring troops, regulating human relations, expediting, planning, explaining policies, and imposing order on undisciplined emotion is the *sine qua non* of victory. Military skills are merely the techniques of the struggle; Klychkov manipulates the men who direct the strategy and fire the guns. "Political work" is the very heart of the matter:

The political department was like a huge sponge continually absorbing the innumerable reports, facts, and wealth of experiences that came pouring in from the various units and from the surrounding population; and then, having assimilated this experience—at all kinds of conferences, meetings, etc.—it would exhale it again, through the medium of its organizers and agitators, in the form of countless leaflets, proclamations, instructions, and directives.[5]

In the execution of his mission as one of the "torchbearers, mouthpieces, teachers," of the revolution, Klychkov shows himself to be quick, flexible, determined, patient, ruthless, tactful, or deceptive, as the situation demands. He aims above all things to gain control over himself and over others. When his inner life is touched on, it is the story of the perfection of self-discipline, and of the systematic conquest of his emotions. In this respect, lapses from his standards of political virtue are more revealing than his adherence to them. His first hours under fire are spent in abject cowardice in the baggage train, far from the front where his duty requires him to be:

[5] Dmitri Furmanov, *Chapaev* (Moscow, 1934), p. 205.

Oh! Shame, unspeakable, unutterable shame! It was bitter to
realize that his heart had failed him in the first battle, that he
had fallen short of his own expectations. Where had been the
boldness, the heroism of which he had dreamed so much when
he was still far from the front line? [6]

His steadfastness in subsequent engagements is not a result
of the mere accumulation of experience. There is a quality
of dogged self-improvement about his preparation for future
battles:

He managed to train himself, as he had planned, to boldness
and outward calm, to grasp the situation and cope with it
quickly. But this training took time; like everyone else, he had
to go the way that leads from open confusion and cowardice to
befitting behavior in the presence of the enemy.[7]

He succeeds in rationalizing other disturbing experiences.
On the day he signs his first execution order,

Klychkov was agitated and upset the whole day. He did not
smile and joke, spoke little and unwillingly, and tried to keep
by himself most of the time. But that state of mind did not
survive the day; when he woke up next morning, no trace of it
remained. This was natural. It would have been abnormal to let
such a thing dwell for long on one's mind at the front, when,
daily, hourly, heartrending, gruesome pictures followed one
after the other, and the victims were not isolated, but numbered
tens, hundreds, and thousands.[8]

Later he discussed the matter with his fighting companions.
They agreed "that to cut down a human being . . . to have
him shot, or shoot him with one's own hand is a hard job at
first for anyone, however strong his nerves and however hard
his heart; it always makes him feel confused, ashamed, and
remorseful." [9] But one "gets used to it," the sensibility is
"blunted," and Klychkov reaches the comforting conclusion

[6] *Ibid.*, p. 124.   [7] *Ibid.*, p. 127.   [8] *Ibid.*, p. 281.
[9] *Ibid.*, p. 283.

that "the destruction of an enemy, in whatever way it is done, becomes something almost mechanical." [10]

In the same way that he has conquered cowardice and squeamishness, he curbs his tendency to be swept away by the powerful, inchoate emotions of front-line comradeship. Under the influence of the egalitarian spirit, which sometimes persuaded front-line units to refuse individual decorations and to blur all distinctions of rank, Klychkov wrote a letter on impulse to his superiors to protest raises in pay for political workers in the Red Army. The impulse was an "incorrect" one—as indeed are most impulses in this austere political world—and his own comment on his indiscretion established the scale of values governing his behavior. His letter, he remarked drily, "displays more warmth of heart than reason." [11]

These incidents hardly yield a full-length portrait of the man, but they introduce patterns of behavior that are integral to the stereotype of the Soviet positive hero: the preeminence of conscious self-discipline, awareness of the public consequences of every private act, and a capacity to subordinate every personal emotion to the political program of the Party. Klychkov summarizes his growth after six months of war, and we note that his progress toward maturity has been progress toward austerity, discipline, and toughness:

Looking back upon these last six months, Klychkov, too, found that he could hardly recognize himself—so much had he grown up, acquired moral strength, been steeled by hardships, so simply and unhesitatingly had he come to tackle the solution of all sorts of innumerable problems which would have completely baffled him prior to his experience at the front. Only now did he feel the mighty influence of the hardships of war, the meaning of the front line as a school.[12]

[10] Ibid.   [11] Ibid., p. 330.   [12] Ibid., p. 401.

Klychkov's biggest achievement was the domestication of the "wild horse of the steppes," Chapaev himself. Chapaev was the "born leader" of the peasant masses, "heroic but raw," the expression of their "unlimited bravery, resolution, hardihood, unavoidable cruelty, and stern temper," [13] the voice of "all the irrepressible and spontaneous feelings of rage and protest that have accumulated in the hearts of the peasants." [14] He was fearless, hot-tempered, credulous, illiterate, and an indisputable military genius. Klychkov's job was to tame this elemental force whose appeal to his own kind, the peasant rank and file, was far greater than the bookish commissar's ever could be, to funnel his energies into useful channels, and to preserve at all costs the myth that surrounded him. It was not only difficult, it was dangerous. Wild spirits of the steppes like Chapaev hated intellectuals, officers, and workers, on principle, and were known to have "taken it into their heads to bump off their commissars." [15] Klychkov's job was not alone to direct a single gifted but wayward individual, but through him to harness a force in the revolutionary movement which was often skeptical about avenging its grievances against the Whites under Bolshevik leadership. Klychkov's dangerous and delicate task aimed at a goal that was central to the Bolshevik mission, the establishment of absolute control over all the energies released by October. Klychkov, who, for all the affection he felt for Chapaev, viewed him always from the condescending vantage of his superior education, approached the problem with a cunning sense of tactical manipulation. He had to establish himself as an equal in the exclusive fraternity of fighting

[13] Ibid.   [14] Ibid., p. 86.
[15] Ibid. ". . . not some contemptible . . . cowardly commissar but first-rate revolutionaries," Furmanov adds, "or they have suddenly gone over to the Whites with their whole 'spontaneous' detachments at their heels."

men that surrounded Chapaev, and probe for the weaknesses
in the leader himself. Before he had met him he had devised
a plan that would guarantee him a superior vantage in all
their dealings:

At first he would avoid conversations on military topics, in order not to show that he was a mere layman in these matters. He
would turn the conversation to politics, because then all the advantages would be on his side. He would gain Chapaev's con-
fidence, encourage him to speak quite frankly on all subjects,
including intimate, personal peculiarities and minor details. He,
Fedor, would speak mostly about science, culture, general education—and here again Chapaev would be reduced to the role
of listener. And later—later Fedor would reveal himself as a
brave fighter.[16]

To establish this version of himself and to avoid appearing
sycophantic before the hero, Klychkov determined to set a
tone of Bolshevik crispness: "He must at once establish
simple and cordial relations, with a touch of the necessary
rudeness." [17]

Long after he had undertaken his duties, Fedor stuck to
his plan to bully Chapaev with book-learning. "Spiritual
domination over Chapaev would surely 'curb' him, before
setting him on the path of conscious struggle—not that of
blind instinctive heroism, however colorful, riotous, and
splendid that might be." [18] In that case Fedor would "hold
all the cards and would draw him away from anarchy and
incoherent thinking." [19] But then Fedor was overcome by
one of those engaging lapses of discipline that give his diary
a certain freshness even as he manages a moment later to
stifle it with his sense of Bolshevik duty. In a wildly poetic
moment it occurs to him that the "breaking" of Chapaev,
might, in itself, represent a loss to humanity:

[16] *Ibid.*, p. 84.   [17] *Ibid.*, p. 85.   [18] *Ibid.*, p. 152.
[19] *Ibid.*

Chapaev was a remarkable man, head and shoulders above the crowd—that was true; it would be as difficult to gain control over him as to break in a wild horse of the steppe—difficult but not impossible. But was it worthwhile, Fedor suddenly asked himself. Would it not be wiser to abandon the beautiful, original, and vital character to the will of destiny and leave it untouched? Let Chapaev sparkle with irridescent fire like a precious stone, let him brag and boast and play the bravo! [20]

Why not? Klychkov's Bolshevik conscience gives him a curt answer: "The great struggle that was in progress did not admit of such frivolity." [21] Sternly, then, with programmatic earnestness, Klychkov embarked on his plan of conquest. The books given to Chapaev sapped his self-assurance by opening "new ways unknown to him, new explanations to everything." [22] But when this approach was not enough, when his role as teacher was not effective, Klychkov argued bitterly, resourcefully, and unfairly to curb Chapaev's "anarchist" tendencies. His personal triumph over the hero of the folk is, in the end, complete. The hero has become "wax in his hands." In the midst of a Chapaev tantrum, "Fedor saw that things were getting beyond a joke and decided to triumph over Chapaev as he always did by keeping a cool head." [23] These were the personal terms between them in the final stages of their relationship. It was a partnership, Furmanov insists, in which each handled his specialty: Chapaev, the essential military business, and Klychkov, the control of policy and morale. But the partnership, for all the personal affection between them, conceals a hidden inequality, by the terms of which the Bolsheviks became custodians and manipulators of the Chapaev legend. They could not deflate it if they wanted to, because it exerted a personal appeal on the troops no slogans could match:

[20] Ibid.   [21] Ibid.   [22] Ibid., p. 175.
[23] Ibid., p. 374.

Chapaev's fame was wide, and this fame, it is true, was better de-
served than that of any other man. Chapaev's division knew no
defeat, and for this he was himself largely responsible. To infuse
the whole division with one impulse, to make it believe in its in-
vincibility, and to bear patiently, even to treat with scorn, the
privations and hardships of campaigning, to choose fitting commanders, harden them, permeate and saturate them with his own
impetuous will, gather them around him, and make them concentrate on a single idea, a single aspiration—the aspiration to
victory, to victory, to victory—this was true heroism! [24]

Yet, for all its temporary usefulness, the Chapaev legend
was a primitive makeshift, "how magnificent all this was but
how wrong, harmful, and dangerous." [25] Certainly it was not
part of the ethos of the workers, and, if the future truly be-
longed to them, both the man and his myth were expendable:

Obviously he was the commander they needed at that time, a
commander born of those peasant masses, incorporating all their
peculiarities. When the masses grow up in wisdom and culture,
the need for men like Chapaev will disappear. Even then for
such troops as, say, the Ivanovo-Vosnesensk Regiment, his appeal was not powerful. His primitive speeches did not inflame
the workers, who put sober reason above reckless bravery; they
preferred discussions and meetings . . . and spoke with Chapaev as equals instead of gazing at him with adoration and grin-
ning from ear to ear.[26]

For that matter, the very basis of his reputation was open to
challenge: "Not a few men were braver, better qualified to
lead troops, politically maturer, but their names are forgotten." [27] It was the special hold he had on the imagination
of his own kind that constituted his great value. His "personal bravery, gallantry, daring, and resolution" [28] expressed
the quality of the peasants' heroism and were, because of
their lack of "political maturity," doomed to extinction, as

[24] *Ibid.*, pp. 399–400.   [25] *Ibid.*, p. 202.   [26] *Ibid.*, p. 263.
[27] *Ibid.*   [28] *Ibid.*

the solemn, pamphlet-inspired uplift of the Bolshevik workers became the governing morality of the land.

Furmanov's personal attachment to Chapaev, and his sense of the human differences between worker and peasant, between himself and the living legend he kept watch over, illuminate value conflicts that are later to be resolved unquestioningly in favor of the commissar's own arid kind of virtue. Chapaev's instinctive likes and dislikes, his genuine courage, and his scornful energy represent inchoate aspirations which expressed the real, uninstructed, perhaps unrealizable, needs of the Russian peasant mass. It is not just the difference between worker and peasant, nor between the latter's illiteracy and the "culture" of Bolshevik pamphlets, that is at stake, but the tensions between the authentic grievances of the average Russian (statistically, a peasant) and the dogmatic, strategic solutions the Bolsheviks imposed upon them. Furmanov's exploration of these two "moments" of revolution (grievance and solution), despite its tendency toward the cut-and-dried Bolshevik answer, discloses a permanent and tragic problem in Soviet life.

At the end of the book Furmanov, in his matter-of-fact way, is quite skeptical about the myth he manipulated. He distrusted the extravagant emotion which surrounded Chapaev and saw the real hero of the future in his own dry image. Chapaev was the child, and he the parent. Although he had found great sustenance in the massive emotions of the civil war, and had admired Chapaev greatly, he found assurance in the fact that "our heroic days will pass, and people will call this mere romancing."

Yet the popularity of the Chapaev myth itself indicates that Chapaev was very much to the popular taste. A passage in a much later play, Afinogenov's *Far Taiga*, indicates the kind of currency the myth had, and raises, at the same time, interesting questions about the primitive expectations of the Soviet audience. A peasant girl in the play remarks to her sophisticated Communist visitor, Vera:

Glasha: I read about Chapaev once. That was exciting. But the ending was wrong. He's a hero, then suddenly he drowns. Why should a hero drown?

Vera: That's how it happened in real life.

Glasha: No, that's wrong. As I see it, he only pretended to drown. He went down to the bottom, then crawled quick over the bed, and got out on the other side of the river. . . . That's the ending I've thought of.

Vera: No, Glasha dear, one has to die for victory too.

Glasha: Let the Whites die. Our Red Commanders must live on! [29]

Concessions to folk expectations have contributed to the creation of a special literary formula. The extraordinary event, taken from life, and too improbable to be contained in a conventional novel or story, is recorded in literal detail. As a result, a kind of journalistic mythology replaces fiction. Boris Polevoi's *The Story of a Real Man* (1946), the account of a legless Soviet fighter-pilot in World War II, and Nikolai Ostrovsky's *The Making of a Hero* (1932-34), the disorderly memoirs of a Party primitive, are outstanding later examples of this Soviet genre. Although these best-sellers serve the interests of Party and state, it is hard to believe that official promotion alone could account for their phenomenal success. Bespalov reports, in his article on Gorky in the *Literary Encyclopedia*, that in spite of the novel's serious flaws, *Mother* has always been extremely popular with the workers themselves.[30] Too little can be known of the factor of public taste

[29] Alexander Afinogenov, *Far Taiga*, in *Soviet Scene; Six Plays of Russian Life*, trans. Alexander Bakshy (New Haven, 1946), p. 227. Yuri Sokolov, the Soviet folklorist, describes many oral variants of the "Chapai" legend, with a variety of magical solutions similar to Glasha's above. See Yu. M. Sokolov, *Russki folklor* (Moscow, 1938), pp. 494-97.

[30] *Literaturnaya entsiklopediya*, II (1929), 645-66.

in shaping Soviet fiction for us to speculate further here. Its
existence must be assumed, nevertheless, and kept in mind as
an important, if uncertain, point of reference, in the formation of heroic images.

III

Although it uses few of the resources of fiction, Furmanov's *Chapaev* brings to light most of the dramatic constants
in the major, heroic strain of Soviet writing. There is the
political hero—tough, dedicated, self-controlled; there is the
enemy—faceless, heartless, beyond the reach of pity or understanding; there are the masses—powerful, blind, long-
suffering, requiring leadership, protection, and indoctrination; and there is the central dramatic design—the sorely
tried leader, hemmed in by the demands of public policy,
by personal privation, and set off by the solitude of leadership, summoning the resources in himself and in others to
accomplish the task he believes history has set for him.

In Alexander Fadeev's *The Nineteen* (1927) these elements are organized into a coherent literary pattern. It does
not differ in kind from dozens of later Soviet novels, but
achieves a certain plausibility by muting the note of political
evangelism. The human material is thin, and the situations
are severely limited as means of exposing character. But
Fadeev has concentrated on this dimension to the nearly
complete exclusion of political matters, and further has tried
hard to remain true to it.

The wanderings of a doomed company of mounted guer-
rillas in the back country of the Far Eastern Maritime Prov-
inces provides a setting remote from the main revolutionary
struggle. The novel is organized around two human situations: the first is a political-sexual triangle in which a shop-
worn but kindhearted camp-follower and nurse, Varya, moves

between two men, her "husband," Morozka, a confused coal miner, and Metchik, an oversensitive, self-pitying intellectual. Varya's final reunion with Morozka, whose attitudes have been clarified by the influence of the more steadfast of his fellow miners, is intended to make a political point. Metchik is never able to become a part of the unit, never perceives its inner human "mechanism," and expresses his intellectual's selfishness in a final moment of cowardice that destroys the entire company. Varya's return to Morozka is a return at the same time to the selfless fraternity of her own kind, in response to a *mystique* of class solidarity.

The second situation, less schematic than the first, deals with the inner drama of the company's leader, the hunched, "gnome-like" Jewish Communist, Levinson. He struggles to retain "control" over men, over events, and over himself, and, what is genuinely refreshing, loses out in a certain sense on all these scores. We cannot know Fadeev's intention in this matter, but there is a suggestion, at least, that Levinson's "inappropriateness," because he is a Jew, and is physically deformed, implies that the leader is an isolated, special kind of being, who is crippled in more than a physical sense. Levinson's solitude is established as a primary condition of his existence. He is entirely cut off from his family. At one moment of great fatigue he notes that one of his troopers has the same beautifully rounded head as his son, but a moment later the impression vanishes. The very fact that it occurs to him represents a lapse in control, because of his delirious state of fatigue.

Earlier, long before the crisis that ends in the unit's defeat, a letter from his wife, containing nothing but bad news, provokes Levinson to write a reply:

At first he was reluctant to break the circle of thought enclosing this side of his life, but little by little he penetrated it, his face softening; he covered two sheets with his small, scarcely legible handwriting, and in them were many words which few people who knew him would have expected from him.[31]

Then the "circle" is closed as Levinson gallops off to inspect the sentries, and is not opened again. He is cut off, too, by the nature of his detached guerrilla command from whatever spiritual nourishment he might derive from association with his political brotherhood. He is cut off, too, from his past. The only reference he makes to his childhood concerns the illusions which clouded his view of the world. There is a glimpse of the big-eyed Jewish boy, waiting in vain for the photographer's "pretty little bird" to fly out of the camera, and then mastering his disappointment, as he was to do on countless later occasions, when he had been deceived by false promises and attractive illusions. He had finally learned to distrust them all:

And when he was really convinced he understood what dangers and evils befall men because of these lying tales about pretty little birds . . . and he realized how many of them spend their lives in fruitless expectation. . . . No, he had no further need of those birds! He had relentlessly suppressed all sweet and vain regrets for them; he had crushed in himself everything that he had inherited from past generations brought up on these lying tales of pretty little birds.[32]

The most significant measure of his solitude is the distance separating him from his men. Levinson feels that an inscrutable façade and a cultivated air of certainty about all decisions, even when they are wild guesses, are indispensable

[31] Alexander Fadeev, *The Nineteen*, in *Russian Literature since the Revolution*, ed. Joshua Kunitz (New York, 1948), p. 120. The suggestion that the Communist hero has a hidden family life in his off-duty hours has become a cliché of Soviet writing. There is a second and, one suspects, more accurate cliché to the effect that the married lives of Communists are very meager, indeed. Though it is always a secondary theme, it persists monotonously through subsequent Soviet writing.

[32] *Ibid.*, pp. 194–95.

for maintaining command over his volunteer crew. He needed to struggle remorselessly with his own weaknesses, but those he could not overcome had to be hidden:

From the hour that Levinson had been elected commandant, nobody could think of him in any other capacity. It seemed to each one of them that the distinctive thing about Levinson was that he was made to command the company. If he had told them how, in his childhood, he had helped his father in a second-hand furniture business, how his father all his life had dreamed of becoming rich, but was afraid of mice and played the violin very badly—all of them would have thought it a bad joke. Levinson never spoke of such things. Not that he deliberately avoided them, but he knew that everybody looked on him as an exceptional type of person. He realized his own weaknesses and the weaknesses of others; and he thought that, if one was to lead other people, one must above all make them aware of their weaknesses whilst suppressing and hiding one's own.[33]

This glimpse behind the hero's façade, of course, is never permitted his men. When the military situation is confused, Levinson's

whole attitude . . . was calculated to convey the impression that he understood perfectly how these things had come about, that he knew where they were heading, that there was nothing unusual or terrifying about them, and that he, Levinson, had long ago decided upon a safe, infallible plan for their salvation.[34]

Actually the exact opposite is the case: "In point of fact, not only had he no such plan, but he was completely lost, as perplexed as a schoolboy." [35]

The necessary deceptions of leadership, certainly not unique to Bolshevik guerrilla leaders, impose certain extra burdens on Levinson. The men of this detachment, with its nucleus of class-conscious miners, are not disposed to question their cause, but neither are they likely to consult it very

[33] Ibid., pp. 114–15.   [34] Ibid., p. 116.   [35] Ibid.

often to find reasons for endurance. Levinson is made the
custodian of their collective conscience, longings, and anxieties. But he does not doubt their steadfastness. It was
rooted in an "instinct" as strong as self-preservation:

Because of this instinct every thing they had to suffer, even death,
was justified by the ultimate cause, and without it not one of
them, he knew, would have voluntarily chosen to die in the
Ulahinsk *taiga*. But he also knew that this profound instinct
dwelt in men under a thick covering of the commonplace, of the
trivial necessities of daily life, and of all the cares and anxieties
for one's own insignificant but vital being; they had all to eat and
sleep, and the flesh was weak.[36]

Levinson and his lieutenants took on all these burdens,
looking after the physical comforts, as well, of these simple
partisans, "all of them conscious of their own weakness," as
importunate as children. The parental responsibilities Levinson assumes have a sanction, Fadeev tells us, in the needs of
"the children," who collaborate willingly in the manufacture
of the myth of Levinson's infallibility. Under the pressure of
events, however, his mask of mocking self-assurance is no
longer adequate. An act of open defiance by one of his men
is met by Levinson with his Mauser in his hand. They are
volunteers, after all, in history's cause, bound to it by an
instinct as strong as self-preservation. Strong measures are
necessary to remind the errant one of his obligation. But
such measures are costly:

When Levinson looked round at his men they were all staring
at him in fear and with respect, but that was all. There was no
sympathy in their eyes. At that moment he felt that he was a
hostile force raised above the company. But he was ready to go on;
he was convinced that this force was right.[37]

Defeat was in the air, morale had declined, Levinson had
become harsher: "Every day unseen ties—ties which linked

[36] *Ibid.*, p. 161.   [37] *Ibid.*, p. 163.

him to the heart of the company—snapped." [38] His authority came to depend more and more on the force of his will. As his words lost their effect, the premium on the toughness and rectitude of his personal example increased. He was in the forefront of all the fighting; he dreaded compromising the image of himself at the head of the column by dozing and slumping in the saddle. As the company moves blindly toward annihilation, the final contest begins between Levinson's "control" over himself and the weakness of his flesh, as his body disintegrates under the nervous and physical strain.

Levinson's is not the simple drive of class instinct. The combination of knowledge, doctrine, and emotion which power every Marxian activist has an interesting configuration in him. Almost nothing is said of doctrine; there is very little in his behavior that is tactically motivated. On the one occasion when orders come from higher authority, Levinson rejects four of the five paragraphs as nonsensical, and proceeds to carry out the one he agrees with. There is no "political work" in his detachment, no agitation, pamphlets, commissars, or amateur theatricals. The morale problem of the men is solved, as we have seen, by Levinson's custodianship of their unarticulated aspirations and by the rigorous example of his own conduct. The source of his own strength is to be found in a creed which has echoes in it of classical Marxian humanism, of the Leninist revision of that ethos, and of Chernyshevsky's—and many other Russians'—belief in the eventual appearance of a new kind of man.

A conversation with the self-centered Metchik provokes the central moment of speculation in the novel:

Only with us . . . could such lazy and spineless creatures, so futile and worthless, be found; only in our own country, where

[38] *Ibid.*, p. 162.

millions of people have lived for centuries under an indolent
sun, in dirt and poverty, ploughing with primitive tools, believing
in a vindictive and foolish God—only in such a country, where
there is so little store of wisdom, could they exist.[39]

Levinson is here echoing the ancient complaint of Russian
men of conscience: Russia's tragic backwardness, above all
her *human* backwardness, is the truest measure of her degradation. Belinsky's letter to Gogol in 1848 is as much the
source of these thoughts as Marx's essays on the factory system. Levinson's goals and his deepest beliefs display the same
double origin, recalling the dreams of the radical democrats
a good deal more vividly, perhaps, than Marx's vision of the
human creature restored to wholeness. We are close now to
the heart of his credo:

And Levinson was moved, because these were his deepest and
most intimate beliefs; because the inner meaning of his life lay
in overcoming this poverty and ignorance; because otherwise
he would not be Levinson at all, but someone else; because he
was urged by an overpowering desire, stronger than any other of
his desires, to help create a new, fine, vigorous man. But how
could one talk of a new, fine man when numberless millions of
people still lived such wretched, poverty-stricken, primitive
lives? [40]

For the interim man there is Engels's freedom and Lenin's
activist ethic:

"To see everything as it is, in order to change everything that
is, to control everything there is"—Levinson had achieved this
wisdom, the simplest and the most difficult a man can achieve.[41]

To overcome all enemies, to dispel all illusions, to surmount
all obstacles, he has built his life around a core of revolutionary virtues: clarity of vision and inflexibility of will. If
we recall the critique of the radical personality in the nineteenth century, these virtues are sources as well of his crip-

[39] *Ibid.*, p. 194.   [40] *Ibid.*   [41] *Ibid.*, p. 195.

pling alienation from his fellows. From time to time, like his predecessor, he needs to consult his vision of the future to find the strength to bear the unpromising and intolerable present:

He went on without caring where; the cold, dewy branches freshened his face; he felt a rush of unusual strength, which seemed to carry him high above the actual moment (might it not be toward the new man of whom he dreamt with all the strength of his soul?) and from this vast height, earthly and human, he mastered his enemy, his own weak flesh.[42]

Levinson is not the "new man" himself, as he clearly understands, but he sometimes senses his kinship with him. In preserving the mold of the leader, and passing it on to hand-picked successors, he feels that he is keeping alive the strain that will ultimately issue in the higher human type he dreams of. He carefully refrains from discouraging his assistant Baklanov, who imitates his every act, intonation, and gesture—even the physical movements that result from Levinson's bodily deformation. Baklanov will learn in his own time about the deception of leadership. It is more important to preserve the chain of virtuous being:

As a young man, Levinson had also copied those who instructed him, and they had seemed to him as admirable and right-minded as he apparently seemed to Baklanov. When he was older he understood that his teachers were not what he had supposed them, and he was none the less grateful to them. After all, Baklanov not only copied his mannerisms, but drew on his whole experience of life—his methods of fighting, of working, of living. And Levinson knew that the mannerisms would pass with the years, while the other things, enriched by his own experience, would pass on to new Levinsons and Baklanovs; and that, he felt, was important, that was as it should be.[43]

Levinson's "control," which depends on his own recognition and definition of necessity, is put to a number of minor

[42] *Ibid.*   [43] *Ibid.*, p. 115.

tests. When it becomes "necessary" to poison a fatally
wounded partisan, Metchik, indifferent to the "necessity," is
horrified. Not Levinson, who, though troubled by the decision, falls back on his basic standard of virtue: "If it's
necessary, it can't be helped . . . can it?" [44] This answer is
made easier by the victim's concurrence in his own death.
His men look away while an impoverished Korean peasant
weeps at Levinson's feet, pleading to be allowed to keep his
last pig. Levinson is affected, but necessity's answer is all he
heeds. His men are starving.

These decisions have no after effects because history, after
all, justifies them. But when his control is threatened by a
set of overwhelming circumstances, Levinson is thrown into
the ultimate conflict of the Bolshevik saint: his body and his
nervous system are subject to relentless pressure, increasing
until the breaking point is reached. What is engaging in
Levinson's drama is the fact that he *does* break.

After a hideous night of pursuit through a forest bog, the
battered column of partisans emerges with the daylight on
a peaceful forest road, sparkling with autumn frost. Levinson's brain is reeling with fatigue (it is at this moment that
the image of his son's head appears to him). He is conscious
of a strong feeling of affection for his men but his control
has finally deserted him:

He no longer led them, and it was only they themselves who
were unaware of his powerlessness, and continued to follow him
like a herd accustomed to its leader. And it was precisely this
terrible thing that he had feared most of all in the early morning
hours.[45]

When the Cossack ambush is announced by shots down the
road, Levinson betrays his helplessness by two physical
movements which pass unobserved:

[44] *Ibid.*, p. 168.   [45] *Ibid.*, p. 235.

He looked back helplessly, searching for the first time for support from others; but in the partisans' despairing, dumbly pleading faces, which seemed to melt under his gaze into a single face,
pale, white, questioning, he read only helplessness and fear. . . .
"Here it is, here's what I feared," Levinson thought, and he flung
out a hand as though he sought something to hold on to.[46]

A glance at the simple, resolute face of his lieutenant inspires
a last act of will and he leads his company deliriously to its
doom.

At this moment Fadeev might have ended his epic, with
Bolshevik virtue convincingly intact, and with a sense of
men having died not badly for aspirations which, for all their
incoherence, did them no dishonor. A handful, however,
nineteen in all, survived, and through them Fadeev contrives
a swift moment of catharsis, ending with the obligatory note
of uplift. For a while, Levinson automatically enacts his role
as leader before the surviving handful:

Levinson rode a little in front of the others, thoughtful, his
head drooping. Sometimes he looked back helplessly, as if he
wanted to ask something and could not remember what; he
looked at them all with a prolonged unseeing stare, his glance
strange and suffering.[47]

At last understanding dawns on him and with it the last
shred of his Bolshevik control departs:

Levinson's eyes remained fixed for several seconds on the men.
Then all at once he somehow collapsed and shrank, and everybody at once noticed that he had become weaker and much older.
He was no longer ashamed of his weakness and he no longer
tried to hide it; he sat huddled up in his saddle, slowly blinking
his long wet lashes, and the tears ran down his beard. . . . The
men turned aside in fear that they might lose control of themselves.[48]

Here again Fadeev might have ended his tale with the
pathos of loss still uppermost, with Levinson reduced at last

[46] *Ibid.*, p. 238.   [47] *Ibid.*, p. 242.   [48] *Ibid.*, p. 243.

to his human dimensions, but more plausible because of it. But this unpretentious novel, not distinguished for its depth of insight or richness of character, yet sound enough up to this moment because of its response to the inner logic of its elements, must now proceed to its directed conclusion. This characteristic moment of the Soviet novel deserves a careful look. The standard mechanism is the verbal coda, presented most often in the form of a flat declaration of faith or belief. Fadeev relies rather on the transfiguring effect of a natural landscape, and thus approaches by indirection his final statement of affirmation.

Levinson is weeping uncontrollably, the others are silent when they finally ride out of the forest:

The forest came to an end in front of them quite unexpectedly, merging into the vastness of the high blue sky and the bright russet-colored earth bathed in the sunshine; the harvested fields spread out on either side.[49]

The valley is full of the voices and the movements of people, "resounding with a joyful, busy life of their own." [50] In the final poetic lunge, Fadeev reaches for the transfiguring note:

Behind the river, propping up the sky, rose the blue mountains, and from their sharp peaks, which seemed to grow out of the sky, a transparent foam of pinkish-white cloud, salted by the sea, poured into the valley, foaming and speckled like new milk.[51]

Levinson is delivered from his lapse into the human, as if by magic, and returned to his political matrix, and to his master image of control:

Levinson looked silently, with eyes which were still wet, at this vastness of earth and sky, promising bread and rest, at these distant people on the threshing-ground whom he would soon have to make his own—as near to him as were the eighteen men who followed him in silence. He ceased crying; it was necessary to live and a man had to do his duty.[52]

[49] Ibid.   [50] Ibid.   [51] Ibid.   [52] Ibid., pp. 243–44.

It requires care to decide what the grounds are for questioning this resolution. It is possible, of course, that this final paragraph is not a response to the formula but was intended simply as a conventional and rather noncommittal contrasting of a vulnerable character with the "eternal" aspects of life, in order to give Levinson a final poignancy. If this is so, the effect is certainly too abrupt—not deep enough (or relevant to what we know of Levinson) to be a religious experience—and not pointed enough to be ironic. We have not, after all, known Levinson very well. But that is the novelist's fault, in the end. And there are grounds within the novel for pronouncing its ending false. Levinson's abrupt recovery may be taken as a possible response of the politically obsessed personality, or it may be explained simply as a shallowness of affect on Levinson's part. But this is unkind to the image we already have of him. We have seen him stretched to the limit of his endurance, and have not the evidence to term him any more than an ordinarily limited man, with ties to the nourishing commonplaces of human experience that have not yet been snapped. The "fault" and the violation of the material's logic are Fadeev's in the end. To suggest that "life" for Levinson involves a simple return to the political image of himself, or to imply that the prolonged suffering he has undergone can be assimilated through the restorative effects of nature, is to betray the integrity of his image. To ignore entirely the inference that if "life" means the repetition of what Levinson has just gone through, it forecasts a downward progress toward aridity, exhaustion, and death, is simply to write badly. Or it is to impose on the reader the dictum that the cause matters above all things and its casualties will be forgotten.

IV

The basic design of *Chapaev* and *The Nineteen* has remained a standard one. Scores of Soviet novels may be classified as variations of this archetypal pattern. The degree of fallibility permitted the hero, or the amount of suffering inflicted on him, or the complexity of his dilemma may vary, but certain limits are never overstepped. All the writing in this vein is distinguished by the writer's identification with his protagonist and with his cause. Other attitudes toward the dominant political power are evident, however, in these early years. The writer who is not a committed partisan may fall under two other general headings: that of the detached but sympathetic observer, or that of the regretful agnostic. A fourth approach, that of open hostility, was proscribed even in those relatively unregulated years.

The other two approaches, rich at times in irony and ambiguity, naturally give rise to greater variety of character, and a richer choice of destinies. Interesting in this connection is Konstantin Fedin's *Cities and Years* (1926) which records the disintegration of an artist under the stresses of civil war, after a lengthy account of his private emotional life as a prisoner of war in Germany. Fedin's sympathy for his hero is evident in the long treatment of his adventures abroad. But the note of reproach in his final comment indirectly expresses Fedin's acceptance of the new regime:

And now we finish the story of the man who waited in anguish to be accepted by life. We contemplate the road along which he followed love's cruelty, the bloody and flowered road. He traversed it without once being splattered, without crushing a flower. . . . Oh, if he had been spotted once by blood, or had crushed a single flower. Then, perhaps our pity for him would turn into tenderness, and we would not have allowed him to die so frightfully. . . . But until the very end he could not act, not a single time. He only waited for the wind that would push him toward the shore he wanted to reach. That is why we can change nothing about his destiny.[53]

Unable to act, eaten away by his morbid sensitivity, one of the last of the superfluous men, he falls to pieces before the brutal choices of civil war. Fedin's independence as a writer is evident in the dramatic design he has allowed himself: the revolution is in no sense glorified, but it has the rightness of its inevitabilty, and the man who cannot accommodate to its rigors, when he falls before it is neither honorable nor dishonorable, but a pitiable victim of it. This is a viable formula, it would seem, avoiding overt political statement, yet opening a certain area for the exploration of character. It was never to become a dominant pattern in Soviet writing, but it was to provoke an uproar, as we shall see, when it turned up as the central dramatic design of Sholokhov's *The Silent Don.*

Isaac Babel's *Red Cavalry* (1926) displays none of the qualities of the official heroic strain, and if the writer's attitude to the cause verges on agnosticism, it is because he is indifferent to political loyalties while he records the savage human truth of Budenny's campaigns in Poland. A detached writer's intelligence, unconcerned with political testament, moving through the maelstrom recorded by Furmanov, turns up a strikingly different version of events. The antiseptic judgments, and the persistent political rationalizing of the solemn commissar, are replaced by artful revelations of the naked experience. The casual, gratuitous brutalities—looting, rape, murder—the curious fusion of revolutionary idealism and Cossack blood lust, of propaganda and obscenity, may contribute in the end to the making of a legend, but it would draw few recruits to the cause of the World Revolution.

[53] Konstantin Fedin, *Goroda i gody* (Moscow, 1926), p. 376.

In the absence of the didactic function, heroes, too, drop
from view. High rank and political virtue confer no distinction in Babel's eyes. Biographies of commanders and common soldiers are set down with the same ironic detachment.
Jews, Cossacks, Poles, priests, soldiers, whores, and agitators
are equal possibilities for literary representation. If virtue is
resident in men (and there is relatively little), it is not distrib-
uted according to men's external allegiances. The treatment
of the conventional hero-types in other kinds of novels is
directly challenged. The ex-herdsman, Pavlichenko, now a
ranking Red commander, tells his story to Babel, and does
not omit the account of the conscientious revenge he takes
on his former landlord:

Then I stamped on my *barin* Nikitinsky. I trampled him for an
hour or more. And in that time I got to know life through and
through. With shooting—I'll put it this way—with shooting you
only get rid of a man. With shooting you are letting him off,
and it's too damned easy on yourself. With shooting you'll never
get at the soul, to where it is in a fellow and the way is shows
itself. But I don't spare myself, and I've more than once
trampled an enemy for an hour or more. You see, I want to find
out what life really is.[54]

It is unlikely that Babel intends "a slander" on Budenny's
"glorious falcons." It may be said that he is a trifle too concerned with self-conscious literary effects—the tone of solemn
philosophic inquiry, for example, with which Pavlichenko
stamps the life out of his enemy. But the striking element in
this and other episodes is the incomparable savagery toward
the human person, part of the Cossack ethos as Babel,
Sholokhov, and others testify. Perhaps a fourth of the book
is concerned with similar studies in cold-blooded murder,
often presented, for ironic effect, in the naively rationalized
language of the murderer himself.

[54] I. Babel, *Konarmiya* (Moscow-Leningrad, 1926), p. 75.

The division commanders, all of them comparable in status, if not in ability, to Chapaev, present themselves to Babel in a very different light. When a new, young commander returns to his bivouac, blooded by his first successful cavalry charge, his naked thirst for glory has found an almost sexual fulfillment:

I happened to see Kolesnikov that same evening, an hour after the Poles were wiped out. He was riding at the head of his brigade—alone and dreaming—on a chestnut stallion of great beauty. His right arm hung in a sling. Ten paces from him a Cossack cavalryman carried the unfurled banner. The leading squadron began lazily to sing obscene verses. The brigade stretched out dusty and endless, like peasant carts on their way to the fair. At the tail end of the column weary musicians were wheezing.

That evening, in Kolesnikov's quarters, I saw the masterful indifference of a Tartar Khan.[55]

The only Communist identified as such is the "Ryazan Jesus," Galin, an editor of the First Cavalry Army's newspaper. In the course of the story he talks significantly to the self-pitying "I" of the story (presumably Babel himself) about the situation of the Party and the writer:

You're a driveler . . . and we're condemned to put up with you drivelers. . . . The whole Party goes around in aprons smeared with blood and excrement. We are shelling the nut for you. Some time will pass. You'll see the shelled nut. You'll take your finger out of your nose then, and you'll sing of the new life in no ordinary prose. Meanwhile, sit still, driveler, and don't whimper.[56]

Besides suggesting Babel's own relations with the Party, the contempt in these words contains prophetic overtones about his own tragic fate.[57] But the exposure of this friction

---

[55] Ibid., pp. 60–61.   [56] Ibid., p. 99.
[57] Babel disappeared several years after his speech at the Writers' Conference in 1934, a victim, presumably, of the political purges. It is believed that he died in a concentration camp in 1939 or 1940.

is not the point of the sketch. While Galin talks the night through, the unit's washerwoman, whom he covets, is bewildered by his eloquence, and disappears with the cook. Babel's real concern is to expose with precision and indirectness the sexual alienation of the Communist:

And Galin talked on about political instincts in the First Cavalry Army. He talked for a long time, in a dead voice, but perfectly clearly. His eyelid fluttered over his wall-eye, and blood flowed from the lacerated palms of his hands.[58]

Doctrine is nowhere presented in its barefaced literal meanings. Babel, rather, uses it for ironic effects. The men repeatedly use their skin-deep indoctrination to justify their private Cossack tantrums. The platoon leader, who throws a woman smuggler off a troop train and then shoots her, describes it in a letter to the press: "So I took my faithful rifle off the wall and washed away that stain from the face of the toilers' land and the republic." [59]

A bitter wrangle over the ownership of a white stallion between two ranking officers ends with this letter of reconciliation, which resembles the work of the gifted Soviet humorist, Mikhail Zoshchenko, in its agile mockery of official jargon:

And I cannot be angry at Budenny's army any more. I understand my suffering in that army and I keep it in my heart cleaner than holy things. And to you, Comrade Savitsky, as a world-wide hero, the toiling masses of Vitebshchina where I am chairman of the revolutionary committee send you proletarian greetings—"On with the World Revolution!"—and hope that the white stallion will carry you for many years along soft paths for the good of

[58] Babel, *Konarmiya*, p. 100. It is worth noting that in later editions of this work the final phrase (". . . and blood flowed from the lacerated palms of his hands") has been deleted. Whether it was Babel or anonymous political editors who did it we do not know. Much of the sting of the story is removed.

[59] *Ibid.*. p. 96.

the freedom we all love and the fraternal republics, on which we must keep a sharp eye in local government and on district units concerning all administrative matters.[60]

Nor is this a "slander." It is, rather, a device Babel frequently uses to effect those human exposures that are his main concern. It is the technique of the slow disclosure of a situation through the naive view of a participant who comprehends dimly (if at all) the consequences or meanings of what he is describing. The method, in the end, serves one of the most searching and tragic comments he hoped to make: that no one understood the events that were shaping or ruining their lives.

Only once does Babel venture close to a personal statement. In one sketch, the wise old Jew, Gedali, discusses the revolution's violence:

But the Pole shot . . . because he was the counterrevolution. You shoot because you are the revolution. But the revolution means happiness. And happiness doesn't like orphans in the house. Good men do good deeds. The revolution is the good deed of good men. But good men don't kill. It means bad people are making the revolution. But the Poles are not bad people. Who will tell Gedali where the revolution is and where the counter-revolution is? [61]

The stubborn, impractical simplicity of these remarks does not express Babel's "position" toward the revolution as much as it reflects his misgivings about the gratuitous sufferings he records elsewhere without comment. This book may be taken as representative of that tendency in Soviet literature which is opposite to Furmanov's and Fadeev's. Many of the situations it treats have been made familiar in the work of the Communist writers. But the final result is quite different. The freely judging sensibility has remained true to its traditional concerns, and the final result rings true to the classical

[60] *Ibid.*, p. 133.   [61] *Ibid.*, p. 47.

inheritance in the most important sense: human truth eclipses and contains the political truth.

V

In a certain sense there is not a distinctive literature of the NEP period that can be set apart from the civil war writing we have been examining. There is, rather, the literature of the twenties, dealing with the present or with the immediate past, reflecting, in both cases, the relatively tolerant, pluralist solution to the literary "problem" that events had dictated and the Party had accepted.

There is, of course, a literature *about* the NEP, though even here distinctions are blurred. A novel like Leonid Leonov's *The Thief* (1927) is typical. The hero wanders through the thieves' underworld of the newly restored commercialism, driven by the need to expiate a Dostoevskyan sense of guilt. But the act itself, the murder of a White officer in a row over a horse,[62] occurred during the civil war. Problems of readjustment, of war neurosis, of guilt and nostalgia, all imply that the civil war is the dominant experience, even as it receded somewhat into the background. When the NEP ended in 1929, its particular flavor disappeared entirely from fiction, while the civil war remained a permanent point of reference for the literary imagination.

One novel, Fedor Gladkov's *Cement* (1924), reflects the prescriptive tradition in all respects, and at the same time moves it forward by adjusting it to the new social situation as it was defined by the problems of industrialization. The compliant literary imagination was now presented with a new set of conditions to work with: problems of factory administra-

[62] A study would show, I am sure, that horses were valued more highly than men.

tion, of construction, and of production. It is not surprising that in the majority of cases these conditions have, by their intrinsic dullness, defied the already inhibited imaginations of Party-oriented writers. But the mimeograph machine and the blueprint had replaced the machine gun and the cavalry saber as the instruments of social progress, and this fact took precedence over all others. In human terms, the literature of the time testifies repeatedly to the emotional wrench that the sudden transition from war to peace meant for "incorrectly" oriented believers in the revolution. The man who survived the shift and acquired the new virtues was the obvious candidate for heroism.

The return of its hero, the demobilized military commissar, Chumalov, in the first pages of *Cement* suggests a sequel to *Chapaev*. Tired and confused, he is confronted immediately by the challenge of finding his home town demoralized and in ruins. The key breakdown is in the cement factory where Chumalov had worked before the war. The rebuilding of this factory against a sea of troubles—bad morale, lack of materials, sabotage, Party bureaucracy, private emotional crises, and bandit attacks—is the main thread of Gladkov's story. Chumalov, as workers' representative on the Factory Committee, is the prime mover in getting the factory back into production.

The implacable partisanship we have already seen in *Mother* and *Chapaev* underlies the conflict in *Cement*. The shooting war is over but a spirit of mortal combat pervades the book. There is a sense of not too distant menace, with survival itself always at stake. The external evil, however, remains below the horizon, and the immediate conflict in the book is between a secondary evil—all the obstacles human and material that block reconstruction—and the forces, principally human, which overcome the obstacles, solve the problems, and provide leadership for the recalcitrant, the demoralized, and the ignorant.

Cement has a quality of documentary authenticity which interferes at times with its didactic plan, and poses the question of the standards for selecting the hero from a gallery of potentially more interesting characters. Human inadequacy and moral failure appear in a variety of suggestive portraits. Many of these characters are Communists. One of the more arresting figures, Polia, her heart broken by the moral letdown of the NEP period and the ebbing of civil war fervor, utters the oft-quoted words about the heartbreaks of readjusting to the new situation:

> I can't endure it, because I can neither understand nor justify. . . . We have destroyed and we have suffered—a sea of blood—famine. And suddenly—the past arises again with joyful sound. . . . And I don't know where the nightmare is: in those years of blood, misery, sacrifice, or in this bacchanalia of rich shop windows and drunken cafes! What was the good of mountains of corpses? Were they to make the workers' dens, their poverty and their death, more cheerful? Was it that blackguards and vampires should again enjoy all the good things of life and get fat by robbery? I cannot recognize this, and I cannot live with it! We have fought, suffered and died—was it in order that we should be so shamefully crucified? What for? [63]

This outburst exposes for a moment a real human situation, but it is politically harmful, so it is dropped. Polia is accused of "lyricism" (*sic*) and expelled from the Party. It is interesting, too, that Chumalov watches the purge with an attitude that is typical of his response to all human situations, "with the dull gaze of a stunned beast." [64] But his emotional illiteracy, brought out in his incomprehensible

[63] F. Gladkov, *Cement*, trans. A. S. Arthur and C. Ashleigh (New York, 1929), p. 275.
[64] *Ibid.*, p. 276.

estrangement from his wife, never interferes with the solution
of the production problem. His heroic credentials are, therefore, of the highest quality.

There are other glimpses of human interest: Chibis, the
Cheka man, who is carrying an intolerable burden; Badin,
the iron Communist and libertine; Shuk, the raging, inarticulate, and ultimately disruptive worker; Serge, the gentle, dedicated intellectual who is harshly expelled from the Party;
Schramm, the self-seeking bureaucrat; and others. These
people give promise of much greater complexity than the
blunt Chumalov, and their lives would provide richer literary
material than the prosaic matter of getting a cement factory
into production. But they are set aside, or reformed, or forgotten by the novelist. The evidence of their fallibility is at
the same time evidence of their inability to perform the paramount task, or to serve as models of emblematic Bolshevik
behavior. Successful function within the terms of the Party
program is the only criterion of selection. Chumalov is
chosen because he contributes most to the survival of the
new social order.

But, Gladkov suggests, this life of public dedication is not
without its costs. Chumalov's attempts at reconciliation with
his estranged Bolshevik wife show him inept and inarticulate
in matters of private emotion. The idea that dedication to
public matters might be the *cause* of his emotional inadequacies, or that his public life might be a form of sublima-
tion, remains unexplored in the novel. But apparently it is an
unimportant consideration, since private matters are lost
sight of in the triumphant resolution of the social problem.

The socially efficacious solution of personal problems is
illustrated in Chumalov's relations with Kleist, the old-
regime engineer, whom he has ample reason to hate. When
Kleist indicates his willingness to direct the reconstruction

of the factory, Chumalov's forgiveness has a threefold social
significance: it aids in the reconstruction of the factory, it
opens the way for Kleist's redemption through constructive
work, and it marks Chumalov's own abandonment of the
fierce personal emotions of civil war. Confronted with such a
definition of the public interest, Chumalov would have been
guilty of antisocial behavior if he had acted to satisfy his
personal revenge. As he says himself, "Not he, but everything
mattered." [65] His success in safeguarding the collective interest is the test of his moral personality and the source of
his heroism.

The sense of selfless participation, we are led to believe, is
its own reward. The masses for whom Chumalov works share
not only the increased prosperity and stability, but the credit
for achieving it: "If I am a hero," Chumalov tells the assembled workers, "then you are all heroes." [66] Finally, we are
confronted with the same kind of declamatory utterance, the
inspirational coda, which we found in Gorky's *Mother* and
elsewhere. Describing Chumalov's jubilation at the final
triumphant ceremony, Gladkov tries to draw together the
individual and the mass emotions and to suggest at the same
time that private defeats are eclipsed in the public victory:

Unbearable rapture, and his heart was almost bursting from the
flooding blood. The working class, the Republic, the great life
they were constructing! God damn it, we understand how to
suffer, but we also know the grandeur of our struggle, and how
to rejoice.[67]

In conclusion, we are invited to rejoice with the chief architect of the triumph, to share his generalized feeling about
the objects of his own loyalty, and finally to welcome the
future which we are expected to believe is brought nearer
through his achievements. Chumalov's experience is the most

[65] *Ibid.*, p. 278.   [66] *Ibid.*   [67] *Ibid.*, p. 304.

instructive; the failure of others is not treated sympathetically, because it is uninteresting. The nonconformist and the special pleader do not receive sympathy nor deserve pity. To function successfully, whatever problem is set by the Party, is the virtue, Gladkov tells us, that comes before all others. This, in turn, explains the general function of this kind of novel. Representation of a problem successfully solved by human agency, it is assumed, will inspire all who confront similar problems. This is the fundamental aesthetic aim of all official Soviet art.

To the degree that the Soviet novel solves problems, it is analogous to a manual of technology. The hero is central to this aspect of Soviet fiction. He may expect assignment to any task the Party chooses for him. He will be invested with the virtues appropriate to the situation, including the correct *technical* approach to the problem, and his behavior will illustrate their correct application. The engineer, for example, has an engineer's virtues: caution, daring, boldness of vision, and attention to detail. The Polar aviator and the collective farm manager will each have his occupational *vertu*, too. But at the center of their beings will be the same catalogue of politically efficacious moral qualities: loyalty, resourcefulness, steadfastness, vigilance, and, whenever they are called for, ruthlessness and intolerance.

Chumalov's emotional illiteracy calls attention, finally, to Yuri Olesha's novel *Envy* (1927), which discusses with extraordinary frankness the terrible human losses in the postrevolutionary years. Cast partly in the form of a debate, with both sides contained in an all-embracing ambiguity, the idiom sounds strange to the modern ear. The Communist spokesman, Babichev, has the attributes of a bourgeois *en caricature*: he is the smug, well-fed (with a roll of fat on the back of his neck) administrator of a large food trust. In his

self-assured Babbitry this man symbolizes the achievements
of the revolution as well as its losses. The insuperably high
cost of this kind of progress, as Olesha sees it, is the atrophy
of all the traditional human emotions. A spokesman for the
doomed life of the heart, who calls himself "king of the
rabble," outlines his position in a discussion with a barroom
companion:

". . . a whole series of human emotions is about to be eliminated. . . ."

"Which, for example?"

"Compassion, tenderness, pride, zeal, love—in short, almost
all those emotions which constituted the soul of man in the age
which is now dying."

"I see."

"I take it you understand me. Stung by the serpent of jealousy,
the Communist who can feel pity is a prey to persecution. The
buttercup of pity, the lizard of vanity, the serpent of jealousy,—
all this flora and fauna must be eradicated from the heart of the
new man. . . .

". . . we know that the grave of a young Communist who has
committed suicide is alternatively covered with wreathes and the
curses of his colleagues. The man of the new world says: 'Suicide
is the deed of a decadent.' But the man of the old world says:
'He must have committed suicide in order to save his honor.'

"Thus we see that the new man schools himself to scorn
sentiments that are hallowed by poets and by the muse of history
itself."

"So that is what you mean by the conspiracy of the emotions?"

"Yes, that is the conspiracy of emotions of which I am the
leader." [68]

Without the old stock of emotions and cast of characters,
he decides, there can be no heroes of any kind:

". . . history is watching us with its dazzling glance through
the eye slits of its mask. And I want to be able to say: 'This is the

[68] Y. Olesha, Envy, introduction by Gleb Struve (London, 1947),
pp. 88–89.

lover, this the ambitious man, this the traitor, this the intrepid
hero, this the faithful friend, this the prodigal son—these are
the standard-bearers of great emotions now regarded as valueless
and base. . . .' "

". . . it's so hard to find heroes. . . ."

". . . there are no heroes." [69]

[69] *Ibid.*, pp. 90–91.

12
TWO BUREAUCRACIES

When the revolution was abruptly resumed with the initiation of the five-year plans, literary debate came to an end; all but one of the quarreling groups of the twenties were dissolved, and their leaders were either "captured" or hounded into silence. Thus began the unprecedentedly grim hegemony in Soviet literature of the Russian Association of Proletarian Writers (RAPP). It was a time of nightmarish unreality. The complex problems of the written word were reduced to such crude constructions as: "literary shock-workers," "wall-newspapers," "worker-correspondents," and "the dialectical literary historical method." Professor Edward J. Brown in his study of the period cites the following as typical of the slogans that filled the air: "For a Great Art of Bolshevism! Against the Varnishers of Reality! For the Hegemony of Proletarian Literature! Liquidate Backwardness!" [1] The atmosphere of frenzy and bickering, the endless "struggles," conferences, resolutions, and the back-alley warfare of literary politics— all suggest an Orwellian fantasy.

Yet, beneath these surface extravagances, the clash between two contrary theories of art went on, in a pattern the nine-

---

[1] Quoted in Edward J. Brown, *The Proletarian Episode in Russian Literature, 1928–1932* (New York, 1953), p. 171. I would like to acknowledge my debt to this excellent study, and not alone because it confirms my hypothesis of the continuing competition between the two branches of the Russian realist tradition, in its detailed study of a critical moment in that conflict. It also finds coherent patterns in a confused period which my own researches, necessarily less thorough here than Mr. Brown's, might not have yielded.

teenth century has already made familiar. RAPP aesthetic
theory was an unresolved mixture of elements taken from
the arguments of their bitterest opponents, notably Voronsky
and his "cognition" school; and of other, contrary elements
which bespeak an agitational, world-changing view of literature. As Brown indicates, the combination of incompatible
elements was a source of profound confusion in RAPP's
theoretical pronouncements. His analysis of a pivotal statement by the RAPP leadership in October, 1930, leads him
to this interesting conclusion:

The document . . . is admittedly a strange and not entirely
clear one. The reason for this lack of clarity is, I believe, that
the leadership of RAPP is attempting to steer a middle course
between the cultivation of literature as "cognition of life"—
the understanding of art given to them by Voronsky—and the
Party demand that it be cultivated as a handmaiden of the
"class," as a means for "changing the world"—in practical
terms, as propaganda for the Five-Year Plan. Though in its
day-to-day leadership of Soviet literature RAPP was of course
obliged to give weight to enforcing such a literary program, and
therefore was forced to modify its literary theory and devise new
literary slogans of a utilitarian character, yet the subsequent
history of the organization indicates that in steering its compromise course the leadership continued to lean in the direction
of "Voronskyism," and to resist the intrusion of utilitarian ideas
which it could not absolutely reject.[2]

It is surprising to discover that the RAPP leaders emerge
as the true, and very nearly the last, defenders of the classical
Russian tradition. They made substantial concessions to expediency and they vulgarized what they defended, but they
continued to speak for an essential fund of literary values,
which included a notion of apolitical objectivity, an insistence, with qualifications, of course, on the author's right
independently to judge of all he treated, and, what concerns

[2] *Ibid.*

us most, a demand for full human portraiture in fiction.

Characteristically, the RAPP leadership condensed these issues into two slogans: "Tear off the masks!" and "For a living man!" The first injunction is derived from Tolstoy's conception of art's essential work—the "removal" of successive layers of "coverings" which hid essential truths from the casual eye. The conception of art as an especially intense kind of vision was central to Voronsky's "cognition" theory, and had only to be stripped of its intuitive overtones and restated in the homely, violent language of the Bolsheviks (Lenin is credited with the expression "tear off the masks") to become the first principle of the RAPP aesthetic. It is true that the eye of the RAPP writer was directed by certain *a priori* notions that were not to be questioned: he worked in the interests of the proletariat, and the reality he was to explore was their new, confident, and expanding world. But his faith in the stability of that new reality was so great that it was expected to withstand and to profit from the most merciless scrutiny. The principal construction put on the slogan concerned its hostility to falsifying, embellishing—as the critics put it—to "varnishing," reality. Fadeev, who began his career as a literary bureaucrat in the higher echelons of RAPP, indicated the kind of emphasis the slogan should lead to:

The new style of proletarian literature is a stranger to any and all adornment of the truth; it is a stranger to all "illusions which exalt us"; it must and will be a style involving the most resolute, consistent, and merciless removal of all masks.[3]

Whatever *arrière-pensées* lay behind this statement, it bears an obvious relation to the classical cry for "the absolute truth." It may be argued that too many key positions had

[3] Quoted by A. Selivanovski in *Oktyabr*, No. 5 (May, 1929), p. 187. Selivanovski goes on to say that Fadeev's formula is the only one which makes possible the "reflection of reality as it is."

already been surrendered to one-sided political doctrines, or
that the "unadorned truth" turned up by the writers would
be put to too narrow a use—a kind of short-range, editorial
self-criticism—to bear any important resemblance to the
Tolstoyan canon. But, whether or not RAPP theorists had
compromised the position they were defending, they went
down under the assaults of the new "Leninist" activism in
1931 and 1932, as champions of the last patch of free ground
open to the Soviet artist. Their assurance that *within* the
compass of the assumptions he shared with the Party magistrates, nothing was exempt from the writer's skeptical attention, had threatened to "unmask" entire institutions or value
systems, instead of their inadequate or dishonest human
representatives. In 1932 a new set of masks was made and
a new theory of adorned truth was devised which would
guarantee them permanent inviolability. Socialist realism and
its counterpart theory of embellishment, socialist romanticism, were to divert the writer's eye from the faults of the
officially virtuous forever after.

The RAPP theory of character paralleled its approach to
reality in general: it insisted upon absolute accuracy within
the limits of a class-divided universe. It is typical of the
RAPP compromise that it accepted a fundamental moral
distinction between men as defined by the class struggle, and
then insisted that the Communist and the class enemy be
shown in their full "living" reality. Again the RAPP theorists'
impatient emphasis is directed against simplification and
idealization. Man is complex in himself, and is made more so
in the historical process he reflects, they insisted, and proletarian literature defeated its own purposes when it ignored
that fact. A quotation from the resolutions of the First
Congress of Proletarian Writers betrays some of the confusion of their position:

The slogan for the presentation of the "living man" . . . on the one hand correctly orients proletarian literature toward the reflection of contemporaneity, and on the other hand expresses the necessity of struggle with stereotypes, with schematic portrayal, with "bare poster art," and of development in the direction of showing forth the complex human psyche, with all its contradictions, elements of the past and seeds of the future, both conscious and subconscious.[4]

Some of the mysteries of human existence apparently transcended the limits of *class* psychology. But if virtue was still defined in class terms, it is clear that RAPP theorists had put themselves in a dangerously contradictory position. The "unmasking" of a "bad" Communist might indeed be psychologically sound, but the writer who did it always ran the risk of seeming to put the objects of the Communist's allegiances in question at the same time. For this reason it was soon decided with RAPP's overthrow that a "psychology" which did not blur the primary moral (class) distinctions— between good Communists and bad wreckers—would serve the agitational function in literature far better. In general, the "living man" theory sustained the following tendencies in characterization, all of which were to be challenged in the change-over to socialist realism: opposition to idealized, or, as it was to be called soon, "romanticized," portraits of Communist protagonists; [5] a broad standard of selectivity which

---

[4] As quoted in Brown, *The Proletarian Episode in Russian Literature*, p. 78, from *Na literaturnom postu*, No. 8 (April, 1927), p. 8.

[5] It is impossible to fix the line between true and false in this connection, since the most objective RAPP writer had made heavy commitments to the Communist cause. But I should be inclined to name Fadeev's Levinson as an index of the degree of fallibility permitted the "living man" hero. There are more drastic instances of Communist failure (suicide, breakdown, resignation, etc.) but they are extreme rather than typical. Fadeev's comment on the hero of Gladkov's *Cement* is instructive in this regard: "What character types have been represented in our literature? In the first place you all know the . . . iron Communist in a leather jacket with an iron jaw. . . . I believe this

permitted not only Communist failures, but sanctioned a wide range of non-Communist literary protagonists (so long as they were psychologically true to their class-conditioning); and a generally greater responsiveness to human truth as opposed to ideological truth.

The overthrow of RAPP, the Party's chosen instrument in literature, was carried out, of course, by the Party itself. The process of destroying RAPP occurred on two levels. Administrative liquidation by decree of the Central Committee of the Party on April 23, 1932, took care of one phase of the matter with dispatch. But a long period of undermining preceded its demise, and the inner ideological "struggles" that accompanied this process are of great importance in the Party's campaign to capture the literary imagination.

The offensive against Averbakh and other RAPP leaders was carried out by a little-known group known as Litfront, which had formed within the parent body of RAPP. Its leaders were not famous or gifted men but they had the Party's cachet, by all accounts, and, in addition, were equipped with the message of the new "Stalinist" interpretation of Marxism-Leninism, which had first been hammered out in the philosophers' debates at two historic meetings in 1929.[6] All the consequences of this major doctrinal upheaval

---

type reached its highest artistic expression in Gladkov's *Cement*. . . . But the weakness of Gleb Chumalov as a character is in this very quality. He is an incarnation of the mighty will of the working class to build socialism . . . but he is not shown as a real human being: that's the weakness of the book. And now uncounted numbers of prolet-writers grind out their heroes on the model of Gleb Chumalov. And they are all as alike as two drops of water." (A. Fadeev, "Na kakom etape my nakhodimsya," *Na literaturnom postu*, Nos. 11–12 [June, 1927], p. 6.) Perhaps a line can be drawn between Levinson and Chumalov, but the resemblances between them far outweigh the differences, it seems to me. The fact that both are high on the present-day roster of Soviet heroism tends to support my contention.

[6] These credentials were not enough to protect Litfront later from

can only be outlined here, but it is clear that it affects
literature at many points. This redefined Marxism was embodied in the word "Leninism." In general terms this meant
a full and final turn to Marxism's activist, world-changing
role in all spheres of human behavior. In the consequent
devaluing of the determinist strain, all objective analysis of
past phenomena in all intellectual disciplines became subject to "correction" according to Party-defined present and
future needs. In psychological theory all aspects of environ-
mentalism were done away with in favor of the new doctrine
of conscious, willed, goal-oriented behavior.[7] In education,
"training" replaced conditioning, discipline replaced experiment, and indoctrination replaced instruction. In the realm
of morality, the Leninist ethic, which had evolved in the
prerevolutionary underground and, since then, had been
imposed on every Party member, was extended to the entire
population. The final measure of truth, the final touchstone
of value, the final determinant of behavior were all declared
to reside in Lenin's single, all-embracing term, *partiinost*.
The word defies precise translation because its meaning is so
alien to the English-speaking cultures, but the usual rendering, "Party spirit," will do if it is also understood to mean
complete identification with the Party's interests. Derived
from Lenin's theory of knowledge, it rests on the general
proposition that whatever serves the Party is true, valuable,
and legislative for all men. It is all-embracing, minutely intimate, and unlike other, similar codes of allegiance, it solicits
not obedience, or reverence, or acquiescence, but the conscious, wholehearted collaboration of every individual. From
this Leninist-Stalinist complex of ideas there arose an of-

---

the charge of "Trotskyism" which was also leveled at Voronsky, Averbakh, and many others after 1937.
   [7] See Raymond Bauer's *The New Man in Soviet Psychology* (Cambridge, 1952), for the fullest account of this change.

ficial model for men, the New Soviet Man, whose image was expected, after 1932, to dominate imaginative literature.

The new values were not imposed on writers at once or without friction. But the initial attack on RAPP by the Litfront group in 1930 contained most of the key elements of socialist realism. The whole of the controversy was conceived as an opposition between Plekhanovism and Leninism. The RAPP leaders' unqualified commitment to Plekhanov's ideas brought them under fire on this point, and whatever support they had found for a contemplative aesthetic in Plekhanov's passive determinism was brought directly into question. Certain elementary distinctions Plekhanov had made between the properties of literary language and form and those of other kinds of discourse were likewise challenged. Voronsky's cognitive aesthetic, even in the cramped restatement that RAPP had given it, was declared anathema. The aim of art was no longer knowledge about the human mysteries, but guidance and inspiration entirely within the official canon of belief. A call for emblematic literary heroes —"heroes of labor" they were called in those early days— followed automatically from the enunciation of these views, and has remained the central command to Soviet writers ever since.

The Litfront attack was centered on the two ungainly slogans we have already noted: "Tear off the masks!" and "For a living man!" Whose masks were to be torn off, it was asked, and in whose political interest were these indiscriminate exposés to be carried out? This kind of unmasking was a negative, pointless, if not actually dangerous, activity, the criticism ran, and had nothing to do with stimulating the great forward thrusts socialism was making. Preoccupation with "the living men" had led writers to concentrate entirely too much on the psychological problems

of isolated men, and, it was pointed out scornfully, to set
"eternal problems" above the far more important matters of
socialist construction. The burden of these criticisms is summarized in the relatively mild article on RAPP in the
Literary Encyclopedia (1935):

The slogan of the "living man," in favor of a psychological analysis of the heroes depicted, was complemented by another slogan
"for tearing off each and every mask," and with this RAPP's artistic program and its understanding of realism was exhausted. By
concentrating writers' attention on the moods and feelings of the
separate, isolated person, by demanding from writers the exposure
of the conscious and unconscious movements of the soul, the
RAPP theorists at the same time led the writers away from the
paramount tasks of reflecting the objective processes of the socialist revolution.[8]

The writer goes on to explain in more detail what was
wrong with this "psychologism." The slogan of the masks,

demanded of writers that they distrust the external conditions
and actions of men, demanded the discovery in the heroes of contradictions, of duality, and in essence, of a lack of full-valuedness,
from the point of view of certain abstract, moralistically colored
criteria. Given such an interpretation the unmasking slogan was
politically wrong.[9]

This, finally, is the point: the revelation of human complexity is politically harmful.

The administrative dissolution of RAPP was accompanied
by a number of charges that had nothing to do with the
leaders' theoretical "errors."[10] They were accused of a

[8] "RAPP," *Literaturnaya entsiklopediya,* IX, 524.
[9] *Ibid.* RAPP's troubles arose in part from its misuse of the past:
"RAPP was oriented primarily toward the work of L. Tolstoy, Flaubert,
and toward psychological realism in general, and in the critical work
of RAPP-ites an apologetic attitude toward the Tolstoyan method was
expressed."
[10] Problems of literary *administration* are new to students of culture
but they must be recorded with the same solemnity we accord to other

loyalty-test harshness toward fellow-travelers, which cut those writers off from the literary world. The lower-level literary output RAPP supervised, the grotesque world of writers' shock-brigades, literary competitions, worker-correspondents, and wall-newspapers had proved, it was generally agreed, a complete failure. As administrators, then, the RAPP leaders had failed to fulfill the production plan, had mis-allocated their resources, and had produced work which served no agitational purpose—that is, goods of low quality. Yet these strangely confused men who had persecuted fellow-traveling writers of dubious loyalty had, at the same time, defended with mysterious stubbornness all that was left of the aesthetic those same writers expressed. The reformers of the literary line were to make the most of the situation: turn-ing to all who had bcome disaffected by RAPP, the socialist realists offered them forgiveness and full restoration of status. At the same time they came forward with a scheme for an administrative apparatus that would enfold them forever in organizational and doctrinal commitments.

RAPP's final obituary was not written in the administrative decrees that dissolved it as an organization. Personal charges of "Trotskyism" were brought against many of its leaders five years later, and the history of RAPP has since been rewritten to prove that Averbakh and others were conducting a gi-gantic wrecking operation all the time. Voronsky, before this, had disappeared under the same charges, and it is odd to record that of all the traditions and values that went down with the purge trials, the last remnants of humanist realism, and the view of human complexity that accompanied it, were among the greatest casualties.

---

matters marginal to the literary process. The real point, I suppose, is that in the USSR they are not marginal at all.

II

In the literary output between 1929 and 1932 the mood of dogmatic, sloganized arguments was not so insistently present as it was in criticism. Despite persistent efforts to lay hands on the imaginative product, the works of any value at all show no more than a partial response to the pressures that were exerted on them. Nearly all the novelists accepted the unpromising theme of industrial construction or agricultural collectivization (we may assume that this was a first condition of publication).[11] But the elements they worked with had not changed since the twenties, and when the works failed, as they often did, it was because the writers were unable to devise any more than clichéd solutions to timeworn situations. The constants were: the fundamentalist for-or-against morality of civil war days; and the narrowly rigid and unchanging human situation of the virtuous Communist. The writer's relative freedom to explore could not withstand these negative pressures. None of this writing may be called a contribution to world literature; comparatively little of it acquired a lasting reputation even in the USSR. But it has great documentary interest at times, and there are moments of poignant revelation, and an occasional sense that the writer has touched on a rewarding human situation, even if he backs away from it, or imposes a finally spurious political resolution on it.

RAPP orthodoxy was never completely effective, nor was it completely binding on those who accepted it, nor did it automatically depress literary standards. Few of the works which have received favorable mention in foreign histories of Soviet literature were produced by writers who were members

[11] Though some RAPP critics, as Brown has shown, maintained that this was not so.

of RAPP,[12] yet Mikhail Sholokhov, perhaps the greatest Soviet writer, was a full-fledged member. The most controversial and least orthodox book of the 1929–32 period, Libedinsky's *The Birth of a Hero* (1930), was written by one of RAPP's most devout communicants. One may conclude that the literary process went on somehow, under the impetus of its own inner vitality. It was increasingly harassed, to be sure, but behind the political clamor that passed for criticism there still existed that *relatively* tolerant standard of aesthetic judgment, inherited from Voronsky and, more remotely, from Tolstoy and the classical past. In this one particular the RAPP era differs sharply from the present. It is the implacable central intolerance of the recent Zhdanov position that has reduced Soviet literature to its post-1946 condition of *rigor mortis*.

A glance at a cross-section of the writing reveals ingenuity at least in the writers' struggles with the stereotypes. Valentin Kataev in *Time, Forward!* avoided the heavy melodrama of black-hearted wreckers and pure-hearted Communists by pitching his novel in a key of amiable satire. His hero, the Jewish engineer, Margulies, has exactly the right combination of temperamental qualities for his profession—caution, curiosity, and a calculated daring. As basic character traits they offer little to work with, but Kataev attempts to make these prosaic virtues palatable by investing Margulies with an engaging air of slovenliness and absent-mindedness. This does not represent invention on a high level, but few of the technican-heroes of the Five-Year Plan literature are granted even this degree of "embellishment." Polonsky's description of the dry, grim, effective, practical Communist is much closer to the image most writers worked with:

[12] See Brown, *The Proletarian Episode in Russian Literature*, p. 281.

He runs the lathe, he carries a rifle, he directs the government, he does big deeds and engages in a work that may remain unnoticed. He builds plants and collectives, railways and blast furnaces. He destroys illiteracy, eradicates religion, banishes the dirt of ages, and uproots the advocates of private property. He loves work. He hates phrases. He is a soldier of the revolution. . . . He identifies himself with society. His aim is to understand the world in order to remold it. His personal responses are secondary. Social interests dominate over the egotistic. Indeed, his social and individual interests coincide. His life is broad and embraces a universe. . . .

The hero of our day . . . does not engage in sentimentality. He is a bit dry, somewhat hard, likes to stick to concrete facts. He is a realist. The unearthly, the unmaterial does not exist for him. He abhors idealism, mysticism and religion. He prefers dialectic materialism to metaphysics. He thirsts for knowledge so that he may destroy and create efficiently, and, of course, he lives a full, healthy personal life just because it is not the end of his existence.[13]

The writer confronted with this set of qualities may have recourse only to heavy melodrama.

In two notable instances the dehumanized world of the new industrialism was challenged to account for the casualties it was producing. Libedinsky's *Birth of a Hero* presents the value conflict between an older generation whose humane, questing radicalism is shown to be in direct collision with the schematic, shallow opportunism of the new generation, "the arrogant, superficially correct, self-assertive brittleness which gives way before everything obscure or elemental." [14] Ilya Ehrenburg, in *Out of Chaos*, sketched a similar opposition in the conflict between a young, self-educated humanist and the mindless, semiliterate technicians he is forced to live with, and defer to. It is Volodya's misfortune that he has

[13] Quoted in Louis Fischer, *Machines and Men in Russia* (New York, 1932), pp. 262–63.
[14] Yurii Libedinsky, *Rozhdenie geroya* (Leningrad, 1930), pp. 183–84.

discovered great literature and made a fatal commitment to it. The questions it put in his head gave rise to a mysterious estrangement from the status quo:

He was not an Onegin, or a Pechorin or a Bolkonsky. He was twenty-two. He did not remember the old life, nor did he long for its return. He studied in the department of mathematics. He could have been laughing as gaily as his fellow-students. What then prevented him? What spore was developing in him? Where lay the explanation of his tormenting irony—in historical materialism or the migration of souls? [15]

The "spore," Ehrenburg indicates, is an ineradicable knowledge of the cultural past and of the complexity of existence:

He did not explain Dr. Faust's boredom by the peculiarities of the period of initial accumulation of capital. When spring was in the courtyard and lilacs blossomed in the old gardens of Tomsk, he did not quote Marx. He knew that lilacs were more ancient than Marx. He knew that spring had come even in the days before the revolution. Ergo, he knew nothing. He was dense and illiterate.[16]

Volodya's sickness is incurable. But Ehrenburg blurs the conflict, conducts his maladjusted spokesman to a pointless suicide,[17] and shifts his own attention, in a typical gesture of accommodation, to the successful construction project. The novel ends in a rousing political speech.

Routine melodrama is the order of the day, however, despite these wayward examples and despite the embellishments disorderly writers like Pilnyak (*The Volga Flows Down*

[15] Ilya Ehrenburg, *Out of Chaos*, trans. A. Bakshy (New York, 1934), pp. 68–69.

[16] *Ibid.*, p. 66.

[17] If Ehrenburg were more than an agile journalist, he might have intended genuine irony in the reason he gives for the suicide: Volodya has spoken passionately in favor of Dostoevsky, and a young malcontent who heard him went out to the construction project and committed an act of sabotage. In the absence of a serious ironic intention, Volodya's guilt on this score is simply ludicrous.

to the Caspian) and gifted writers like Leonov (*Sot*) attempted to impose on the given stereotype.

III

One novel of the period deserves a lengthier examination. Sholokhov is a writer of genuine attainments, and his study of the grim battle for collectivization, *Virgin Soil Upturned*, represents a maximum effort to write well, yet entirely within the official canon. The novel has become a permanent bestseller, and a textbook in the schools. Under the surface the essential dramatic situation reflects the same pattern that has been discovered in every other conformist Soviet novel. Davidov, the leathery worker from Leningrad, "a dry, hard chap," has accepted the Bolshevik mission of leading the unready and unwilling to a better life. Like all his kin, he has added to the role of the solicitous instructor—Lenin's "patiently to explain"—the capacity to pry, to goad, to deceive, and to punish. When he enters the Cossack village he has been ordered to collectivize, he directs his attention first to the hostile strangers he must manipulate in the name of their best interests:

He had been by no means a naive town dweller before he went to work in the country, but he had not realized all the complexities of the class struggle, its tangled knots and frequently secret courses, until he arrived in Gremyachy. He could not understand the stubborn reluctance of the majority of the middling peasants to join the collective farm despite the tremendous advantages of collective agriculture. He could not find the right key to an understanding of many of the people and their inter-relationships. . . . All the inhabitants of Gremyachy passed before Davidov's mental vision. And there was much in them that was incomprehensible to him, that was hidden behind a kind of impalpable curtain. The village was like a new type of complicated motor, and Davidov studies it intently and tensely, trying to understand its mechanism, to see clearly every detail, to note every interruption in the daily, incessant throbbing of this involved machine.[18]

He must persuade the unwilling Cossacks to act against tradition, belief, and instinct, in the name of a drastic redefinition of their own and of the nation's interest which has been decreed in distant Moscow. Acting out of his core of Communist virtue, he improvises the local virtues and techniques appropriate to the task, but it is the core itself, the combination of personal qualities and ideas, which enables this severely functional hero to gain mastery over any situation he confronts.

The doctrinal component of his sense of Party duty, apart from the general fund of Marxist-Leninist ideas, is contained in the directives he carries in his pocket. He quarrels with the district leaders on the correct interpretation to be placed upon them, but never questions their claims on his loyalty and energy. Doctrine provides the rational framework for every decision he makes, sometimes affecting the most minute details. When it has led Davidov's villagers to the point of revolt, his situation is miraculously resolved by the arrival of Stalin's new policy statement, "Dizzy with Success," which includes the magically successful order to decollectivize chickens. Davidov is saved in the nick of time from the defeat of his plans, or from the unthinkable alternative of having to go against handed-down orders. The entire grotesque episode suggests that Davidov is the instrument of an all-seeing, infallible power, and that his faith in its policies will never betray him.

But Davidov is not merely the blind executor of policies drawn up by others, nor is he simply a technician or admin-

[18] Mikhail Sholokhov, *Virgin Soil Upturned*, trans. Stephen Garry (London, 1948), pp. 136–37. The novel was first published in 1932 and has served as a primary exhibit of the new literature of positive heroes through the thirties to the present.

istrator. He is a leader, imposed from without on the men he is to lead, and in the forceful and flexible application of policy to the local scene he is forced to act in a number of painful and difficult human situations. In these decisions there is revealed in Davidov that perfect fusion of conviction with emotion that the nineteenth-century radicals had sought in their champion. In contrast to Davidov, both of his local Communist assistants come unstuck at the very point where the two elements are joined. Nagulnov, the overzealous "leftist," is carried away by the frenzied emotions he had acquired in the civil war and makes half-cracked decisions which threaten the success of the entire program. Such display of emotion is viewed as a kind of self-indulgence, and neither his years of loyalty to the cause nor the evident sincerity of his intentions are permitted to interfere with the punishment that is visited upon him. Davidov's rigid control over himself makes this kind of irresponsible outburst impossible in his case. But the furious emotion is in him, too, in the form of an inexhaustible fund of hatred for the old regime, the extermination of which he conceives as his world-historical mission. When Razmiotnov, his other assistant, breaks down and announces that he refuses to go on dispossessing kulaks and their families because it is no part of his work to wage war on children, Davidov erupts in a fury. "Did they ever weep over the orphans of those they killed?" he shouts at Razmiotnov, and exposes the deepest source of his energy in an account of the bitter suffering the old society inflicted on him in his childhood.[19] The emotion is there but it has been harnessed and put at the service of doctrine. When duty demands inhuman acts, Davidov's experience, generalized into the sufferings of his class, enables him to administer the awful individual injustices implicit in

[19] *Ibid.*, p. 84.

"class justice," without apparent damage to his own conscience.

The same subordination of personal emotion to the public interest, as he conceives it, determines his behavior in the novel's crisis. At its height, Davidov is attacked by furious women and beaten through the streets of the village while the men plunder the grain from the collective seed fund. One woman beats him with her fists in tearful, impotent rage, not because he is wicked, but because he is so inevitably and unshakably correct. When order has been restored, Davidov's speech is a model of Communist leadership. He instantly overlooks his personal humiliation, but exploits the Cossacks' guilt by telling them that the only expiation open to them is through support of the collective farm. An act of Communist forgiveness, like any other act, serves as a goad toward the desired social resolution.

Finally the question arises: What are the rewards and what are the costs implicit in Davidov's design for living? As always, in Soviet writing, the answer is less than adequate. We are never to find the full human exposure we might expect from the nineteenth-century writers. But enough hints are to be found that suggest that the negative features of the new man of the 1860s—the aridity, the one-sidedness, the blunted moral sensibility—have been duplicated in his Soviet counterpart. The calculus of his personal happiness and the means he uses to justify his life to himself must be set in this context of damage and deprivation.

The rewards are few enough. The uncertain pleasure of serving as history's instrument finds its expression in an occasional vision of the future. In a rare moment of introspection, Davidov discloses how bare and prosaic, yet how intensely felt, that vision is. A talk with a child has prompted him to speculate about what is to come:

We'll build a good life for them. Fact! . . . In twenty years
time he'll [the little boy] probably be plowing up this very earth
with an electric plow. . . . Machinery will do all the heavy
work for man. The people of those days will have forgotten the
smell of sweat, I suppose. I'd like to live till then, by all the
devils. If only to see what it was like. . . . You'll die . . .
brother Davidov, as sure as you're alive! Instead of descendants
you'll leave behind the Gremyachy collective farm. The farm
will become a commune, and then you'll see, they'll call it by the
name of the Putilov locksmith, Semion Davidov.[20]

Davidov lives in great solitude. It is not the terrible metaphysical aloneness that Dostoevsky has inflicted on his rebels,
but it is nonetheless complete and unrelieved. The instance
of the woman who beats him because he is so infallible reminds us as much of his isolation as of his rectitude. He
is unmarried. His shirt is dirty—so dirty that, as Razmiotnov
points out, he "couldn't cut it with a sword." [21] But Davidov
insists he will take care of it; an ex-sailor, he has learned to
wash and mend his own clothes. His most outspoken display
of personal emotion, which follows the receipt of a modest
gift-box from his comrades in the Putilov Works in Leningrad, merely accents the austerity of his private life.[22] That
the Soviet Communist's life is very often loveless is a cliché
of pre-World War II literature. Sholokhov has given the
cliché a special emphasis by exposing Davidov to a beautiful
temptress, the wife of a Party colleague. Davidov is, indeed,
tempted; he asks himself, "Am I a monk, or what?" [23] But,
as always, public concerns crowd in on him. "Though he
was attracted to Lukeria, he had feared that his association
with her would undermine his authority." [24] His final, grudging acceptance of her favors gives rise not to a feeling of
release but to new anxieties. Nor does it promise any kind

---

[20] *Ibid.*, pp. 345–46.   [21] *Ibid.*, p. 162.
[22] *Ibid.*, p. 161. Davidov's comment: "A touching fact."
[23] *Ibid.*, p. 476.   [24] *Ibid.*, pp. 479–80.

of communion with the people he has been manipulating by involving him in the emotional substance of their daily lives.

The costs of his rigidly exemplary life are not counted out in full. There is no suggestion, for example, that his burden of duty is in any way increased by guilts arising from the injuries he has done to others in the name of that duty. We are left with the impression that his conscience is entirely contained within his concept of Party obligations. But it takes a small adjustment of the lens to see Davidov as his enemies might have done: ruthless, fanatical, limited, and remote, insulated against all the ordinary human weaknesses, yet protected against a true knowledge of his condition by the narrowness of his own vision.

IV

The shift of power from one literary bureaucracy to another required more than two years—from RAPP's dissolution in 1932 to the grand inaugural fete of socialist realism, the First Soviet Writers' Congress, held in August, 1934. The second event marked the end of a thorough process of overhaul, which resulted in complex readjustments in theory and practice. In all these decisions there is a consistent pattern of simultaneous release and constriction. Thus RAPP's harshness toward fellow-traveling writers was countered by the elaborate welcome extended to Babel, Olesha, and others whose cranky, individual approach had led them into estrangement and silence under RAPP. At the same time the foundation was laid in the protocols of the new Union of Soviet Writers for the most thorough administrative control (through a Party "fraction" and other devices) over writers yet attempted. On the level of doctrine there was a heady sense of release from the inanities of RAPP's agitprop activities. Yet the elaborate formulations of the new socialist realism concealed a theory of literature that was potentially far more restrictive than RAPP's assumption that art was a kind of passive cognition. In general, a sense of liberation and advance dominated the proceedings of the Congress and the succeeding years, at least until the purge trials sent new constrictive spasms through the entire social organism.

The fact that the controls were largely held in reserve in the early years may be attributed in part to the requirements of literary "foreign policy." RAPP's efforts in this direction had been concerned largely with enlisting pledges from foreign writers to sabotage their own armed forces in any impending attack against the USSR. An entirely new approach was inaugurated with the Popular Front strategy of the thirties. An air of tolerance toward the West and toward the past was designed to enlist the affiliation of foreign writers in terms far less bloodthirsty than RAPP's. Long, scholarly articles in the literary journals on Aristotle, Lessing, Hegel, and others affected to explore the aesthetic heritage for its possible relevance to socialist realism; Proust, Joyce, and Dos Passos became fixtures on the agenda of literary meetings. A minority of critics raised the disturbing question of the possibility of a tragic art within the framework of socialist realism. But these potentially liberating efforts had no lasting effect on the official doctrine because the doctrine's "purity" was in the custody of men entirely unconcerned in the end with literary values. The real legislators of socialist realism at the Writers' Congress were Radek and Zhdanov, and not Gorky, who simply managed, by a peculiarly tortured reading of the literary past, to find confirmation for the propositions laid down by the political magistrates.

Socialist realism does not require a lengthy exposition here. That has been done often enough in the West, both well and badly.[25] The juxtaposition of half a dozen authoritative utterances will show us all the central notions—service, optimism, selectivity, "romanticism" (orientation toward the future)—that result in the total politicalization of art.

Zhdanov defines the function of art in these familiar terms:

Our literature is impregnated with enthusiasm and heroism. It is optimistic, but not optimistic according to any kind of zoological, "interior" sensation. It is optimistic essentially because it is the literature of the rising class, of the proletariat, of the only progressive and advanced class. Our Soviet literature is strong because it serves a new cause—the cause of socialist construction.[26]

Here is the grim optimism of Hegelian history, and the related assurance that a literature which reflects history's unfolding will be a great one because it *serves* that process by publicizing it. In performing that service it cannot fail to be "tendentious because there cannot be in an epoch of class struggle a literature which is nonclass, nontendentious . . . apolitical." [27] Here Zhdanov goes beyond the radical democrats in demanding that literature propagate not merely "healthy ideas," but specific political values. But the difference is merely in degree, not in kind, as far as the *fact* of

[25] A good analysis is Herbert Read's brief essay in *Art and Society*. His conclusions are worth quoting: "In effect, then, socialist realism is but one more attempt to impose an intellectual or dogmatic purpose on art. It may be that the actual circumstances of the moment—the revolutionary urgencies to which most intellectuals and artists subscribe —demand a temporary supersession of the primary conditions of a great art: that art, like much else, must be sacrificed to the common good. If this is so, let it be clearly recognized, and do not let us deceive ourselves into imagining that a great art can be created under conditions which both the history of art and the psychology of the artist prove to be impossible." (Herbert Read, *Art and Society* [London, 1945], p. 133.)
[26] *Pervyi vsesoyuznyi s'ezd sovetskikh pisatelei, 1934; stenograficheski otchet* (Moscow, 1934), p. 4.
[27] *Ibid.*

commitment is concerned. Finally, literature departs from reality, involves itself in the future, and as the logical consequence of this (and all else we have noted), assumes its ultimate role as a vehicle for heroic "romanticism":

Socialist realism is the basic method of Soviet literature and literary criticism but this assumes that revolutionary romanticism must enter into literary creation as a constituent part, because the whole life of our Party, the whole life of the working class and its struggle consists of the combination of the grimmest . . . practical work with the greatest heroism and most magnificent perspectives. Our Party has always been strong because it is united and combines . . . practicality with a broad perspective, with a constant striving forward in the struggle for the construction of a Communist society. *Soviet literature must be able to show our heroes, be able to look into the future. It will not be a Utopia, for our tomorrow is being prepared by planned, conscious work today.*[28]

When we note that the only officially authorized views of the future are contained in the blueprints of the five-year plans, all area of creative maneuver is shut off on this point too. There can be only *one* kind of hero, performing *one* kind of work, with *one* kind of outcome: the politicalized technicians—from skilled worker to plant manager [29]—will work within the framework of the plan, and will fulfill its directives through the exercise of courage, initiative, self-denial, and the rest of the copybook virtues. The hero will perform a threefold function for the reader: he will inspire him to emulation, he will earn his respect as an admirable representative of political virtue, and he will, by linking the present with the future, provide magic assurance that the

[28] *Ibid.*, pp. 4–5.
[29] Zhdanov defines the true heroes thus: "In our country the principal heroes of literature are the active builders of the new life: workers . . . collective farmers, Party members, managers, engineers, Komsomols, Pioneers. Here are the basic types and the basic heroes of our Soviet literature." (*Ibid.*, p. 4.)

job can be done. Chernyshevsky's heroes were intended to have precisely these effects on the reader. The merging of the Leninist ethic with the Russian utilitarian aesthetic is publicly consummated at this moment. The elevation of the radical stereotype to the level of a nation-wide doctrine, binding on all writers, represents at the same time the "world-historical downfall" of the Russian classical aesthetic, at least on its native grounds.

The Writers' Congress went on to endless discussions *within* the limits of Zhdanov's introductory remarks. Bukharin, for example, developed an original thesis on the differences between the kinds of knowledge art and science provide, and then abandoned his distinctions and rushed to the same conclusions Zhdanov had come to. The most critical remarks were uttered by André Malraux, who spoke briefly as a visiting dignitary. Behind a façade of compliments, he complained that the world had yet to learn of the true inner nature of the Soviet hero because the literature had failed to disclose it.[30] Then he outlined the principles that underlay his own work, including, presumably, his revolutionary novels. Primarily, art helps men live, he told the delegates. It is at once an act of "discovery," "invention," and "conquest" (above all of the unconscious), and he cited Prince Andrei's revelation at Austerlitz in *War and Peace* as an instance of all these functions. Art must be more than a photographic documentation of external events. The challenge to Zhdanov's doctrine contained in these brief remarks was met only tangentially by later speakers, although the irritation Malraux provoked is unmistakable in several of their comments. Certainly Malraux did nothing to arrest the underlying movement toward agreement.

The principle of selectivity, the connecting rod between

[30] *Ibid.*, p. 286.

political principles and their artistic representation, was discussed at length by Radek. On the basis of standards of selection, controlled from outside the creative process, the all-important definitions of "the typical," "the significant," "the essential," "the true," "the correct," and "the incorrect" are derived. Radek's remark is perhaps intended as an answer to Malraux's charge of "photography." It does not meet the substance of the charge, actually, and in its total effect moves art still further away from Malraux's sense of its necessarily autonomous functions. Radek's ideas, like Zhdanov's, are strongly reminiscent of the Russian ideologies of the nineteenth century:

We do not photograph life. In the totality of phenomena we seek out the main phenomenon. Presenting everything without discrimination is not realism. We should select phenomena. Realism means that we make a selection from the point of view of what is essential, from the point of view of guiding principles. And as for what is essential—the very name of socialism tells us. . . . Select all phenomena which show how the system of capitalism is being destroyed, how socialism is growing, not embellishing socialism but showing that it is growing in battle, in hard work, in sweat. Show how it is growing in deeds, in human beings.[31]

What the critics in the nineteenth century could only propose, an all-powerful state could now dispose. This apparatus of manipulation could lie dormant or could be applied to the literary imagination with any variation of pressures the magistrates felt to be necessary. Theme, character, scene, action, or resolution were all at the mercy of the policy makers. Thus Zhdanov's 1946 "Report" represents a particularly abrupt and severe tightening of the screws that have been there to turn since 1934. And it is the same man, of course, who is manipulating the controls on both occasions.

[31] *Ibid.*, p. 373.

Gorky's journey through world literature was intended to prove that socialist realism is a culminating point in the history of art. As he traced its ancestry back through the nineteenth century, and the Renaissance, to its origins in folklore, Gorky injected his own moral standards into his curious literary judgments. Labor, to Gorky, is the fundamental condition of dignified human existence. Soviet society has made it the most honored function of human beings, hence the first source of heroism and dignity:

As the fundamental hero of our books we must choose labor, that is, man organized by the labor-process, which is armed here with the full power of technology, man in his turn making labor easier, more productive, raising it to the level of art. We must learn to understand labor as creativity.[32]

Folklore, which Gorky considered the most vital of all literary forms, he analyses as principally concerned with the celebration of great feats of labor or craftsmanship. In an indictment as sweeping as Tolstoy's, he traces the slow disappearance of heroic feats of labor from literature and equates it with an overall decline in literary quality. The steepest descent he dates from Shakespeare and ascribes it to the growth of capitalism which destroyed the creative relationship between man and his work, and brought about, thereby, a fatal degeneration of personality. The "superfluous" heroes of Russia's nineteenth century are some of the brightest images in the long record of decay, according to Gorky, but they provide at the same time the best illustration of the fatal results of ruling-class idleness. Soviet society has restored the creative relationship between men and labor which existed in pre-state society, has ended the sickness of individual-

[32] *Ibid.*, p. 13. Gorky's feeling about the virtues of labor resembles the Five-Year Plan *mystique*, but he held it long before the revolution. It is one of the points of his personal accommodation with the Bolshevik regime.

ism, and has created the basic condition for the heroic personalities which are to be recorded in the new era of world
literature to be known as socialist realism.

Gorky's celebration of labor in 1934 as a source of virtue
and dignity is not new in Soviet life. What is new is his
emphasis on what might be called "mythic realism." His
remarks are the first authoritative recognition of the legend-
ary quality in Soviet fiction we have already noted in the
primitive response to the story of Chapaev. Gorky's advocacy
of a hero image which is larger than life, on the scale of the
folk hero, was reflected in very little of the critical writing
which followed the Writers' Conference. It seems to contradict the widespread insistence on the averageness in the
"typical character in typical circumstances" as it was applied
to the standard Soviet hero. Gorky's models may voice the
aspirations of the mass, but they are hardly typical characters,
in any kind of circumstances.

I again direct your attention, comrades, to the fact that the deepest and brightest, the most artistically perfect types of heroes
were created by folklore, the oral creation of the working mass.
The perfection of such images as Hercules, Prometheus, Mikula
Selyaninovich, Svyatogor . . . Doctor Faust . . . Ivan-durak,
and finally Petrushka who overcomes the priest, the policeman,
the devil, and even death . . . all these are images in the creation of which reason and intuitive feeling and thought are har-
moniously combined.[33]

In calling for a return to the hyperbole and fantasy of folk
literature, it may be that Gorky is reminding the makers of
ideology of the survival of the folk imagination among large
sections of the reading public. In any case, Gorky is clear
about the manipulative value his "mythic" folklore-derived
literature has for the ideologists:

[33] *Ibid.*, p. 8.

Myth is an invention. To invent means to extract from a sum of real data its basic significance and to embody it in an image—in this way realism is achieved. But if we add to the significance of what is extracted from the real data . . . the desired, the possible and with these we complete the image we achieve that romanticism which is at the basis of myth and is extremely useful in that it contributes to the awakening of a revolutionary attitude toward reality, an attitude which in a practical sense changes the world.[34]

It is folklore, according to Gorky, that offers the most convincing example of that amalgam of present and future, of *is* and *should be*, which is at the heart of the new Soviet art. The lack of public response to Gorky's ideas at the Congress and later does not mean that the mythic component is absent from later Soviet writing. It is, on the contrary, very much present, but is deliberately concealed behind a prosaic, "realistic" surface. The Soviet reader is expected to recognize some part of his own life in his fiction, and to respond in terms of personal action. The oversized figures of folklore might encourage complacency about the capacities of his champion. The fabricated myths of Soviet literature are functional in intention, designed to propel the reader into action, not to give him objects for remote veneration or passive identification.

[34] *Ibid.*, p. 10.

13
IN CONCLUSION
Four Novels

Four novels that appeared in completed form in the years between the overthrow of RAPP and the beginning of World War II, Mikhail Sholokhov's *The Silent Don*, Alexei Tolstoy's *Road to Calvary*, Leonid Leonov's *Road to the Ocean*, and Nikolai Ostrovsky's *The Making of a Hero*, represent a cross-section of the writing in these years, and demonstrate the full range of possibility in Soviet literature. One of the novels, Sholokhov's, quite clearly goes back to the classical Russian tradition itself. Two of the novels, Tolstoy's and Sholokhov's, resist strict classification under the heading "socialist realism" because they were conceived and their early sections were published in the twenties. Leonov's and Ostrovsky's novels are authentic products of the era of socialist realism although they differ radically in form, in approach, and in artistic worth.

These novels will be considered in a descending scale of literary value, since that has been the unmistakable direction of the historical trend. By this standard Sholokhov's novel must come first. Publication of its concluding sections in 1940 (the first chapters were published in 1928) raised a number of instructive issues because, although it was not generally admitted, Sholokhov had challenged every tenet of socialist realism in the tragic fate he devised for his hero. The most important aspects of the discussion of the novel in the USSR centered on the question: does the Soviet Union have "a right" to a tragic literature? The question is very much in point. Although they exist in attenuated and incomplete form, there are the elements of an Aristotelian design in *The Silent Don*. The novel's hero, the gifted, humane, passionate Cossack, Gregor Melekhov, is a man of more than average human stature who is destroyed by superhuman forces he can neither comprehend nor control. His intellectual inability to understand history's movement cannot in itself be considered a tragic "flaw," though it does contribute to the blind sins of political affiliation with the Whites that is the external cause of his downfall.

But the basic terms of his collision with reality are moral. He prepares the way for his own destruction by a habit of impulsive decision which results in a sequence of temporary enlistments with both factions in the civil war. If this zigzag pattern of commitment were the product only of bewilderment, Gregor's destruction between implacable hostile forces would be productive only of a remote kind of pathos. But he is an assertive moral being, and beneath the inarticulated tangle of motives which produce his impulsive actions, there is a plain code of human decency and tolerance. A respect for the human person and a distaste for gratuitous acts of cruelty always underlie the other considerations—self-preservation, Cossack self-interest, love of the land—which motivate him. Acts of rape, looting, murder, or torture—committed by either side—are the determinants of his judgments.

He remains in a state of bewilderment to the end of his "strange and incoherent life," [1] but at one moment he ventures close to an understanding of his dilemma. He had sought "one truth," he notes, which would embody his per-

---

[1] Mikhail Sholokhov, *The Silent Don*, trans. Stephen Garry (New York, 1946), p. 552.

sonal code and aspirations in political terms. But the world
offered him "two truths," and neither fully comprehended
the demands he made on life. A further step (which he cannot make) might have led him to reformulate the notion of
truth's duality into the deeper division between human truth
and political truth or between man in nature and man in
history. Though Gregor is never permitted to know this,
Sholokhov appears here to be suggesting that private moral
judgment is sometimes irrelevant to the higher struggles of
historical forces, and that in this fact there is genuine human
tragedy.

Perhaps this is not Sholokhov's intention—and for it to be
so the writer would have to betray the Communist in himself—but it is a defensible reading of the novel and it is
possible to speculate about its function in Soviet society.
Despite the absence of positive affirmation at the novel's end,
when Gregor returns home for a brief reunion with his son,
stripped of hope and aspiration, and prepared to meet his
fate at the hands of the Cheka, there is a strong sense of his
final reconciliation with a remote historical destiny, hence,
with the new revolutionary status quo itself. It might be
imagined that this effect could have a strict practical utility
for the rulers of Soviet society, as a solvent of doubt, unruli-
ness, and grievance in their own population. If this were accepted as minimum compliance with the "social command,"
the world might be entitled to expect the continued survival,
at least, of the Russian tradition. But such "negative" effects
are not officially countenanced, and we must assume that the
book's publication and great success are the results of a partial accident which has been accepted because of Sholokhov's
enormous popularity and his unquestioned talent.[2]

[2] Serial publication accounts in part for the bombshell effect the
novel had. Apparently there was a widespread expectation that Gregor

Sholokhov's novel does not deserve the designation "Tolstoyan" which is often attached to it because it lacks the
human density of his predecessor's work. The very inarticu-
lateness of Sholokhov's characters, and the unmitigated violence which engulfs all assertions of moral worth, automatically deny it such depth of insight. But its connections with
the past call attention to one general question that spans the
century we have been concerned with. Ever since Chernyshevsky's clumsy attack on tragedy, there has been an obvious
opposition between the affirmative and the tragic vision of
experience. There are not many explicit discussions of the
matter in the Soviet era but the problem is never absent, and
occasionally it found its way into print. Lunacharsky, himself a would-be playwright, raised the question in an article
in the early twenties which discusses the tragic formula Marx
and Engels sketched in the correspondence with Lassalle,[3]
the situation of the premature revolutionary whose tragedy
resides in his historical "inopportuneness." Trotsky, who felt
that the task of the "cultural revolution" was not the building of "proletarian" art but the creative repossession of the
artistic heritage, remarked in *Literature and Revolution* that
he considered dramatic tragedy the highest form art had ever
achieved.[4] Gorky noted in his concluding remarks at the

---

would be "converted," or at least brought to a positive acceptance of
the new regime. Such a resolution, of course, would violate all that had
gone before. The somewhat grudging Soviet acceptance of the novel has
taken two forms: first, that socialist realism is broad enough to encom-
pass all the complexities of social struggle even when the outcome is
tragic for individuals engaged in it; second, that Gregor's tragedy is that
of a willful individualist who "has cut himself off from the people," and
therefore must die (L. I. Timofeev, *Sovremennaya literatura* [Moscow,
1947], p. 311).
    [3] A. Lunacharsky, "Mysli o kommunisticheskoi dramaturgii," *Pechat
i revolyutsiya*, No. 2 (1921).
    [4] See Leon Trotsky, *Literature and Revolution*, trans. Rose Strunsky
(London, 1925), pp. 240–45, for his discussion of tragedy.

Writers' Congress that the impending anti-Soviet war should provide writers with material for great tragic works of art.[5] The problem of tragic resolutions was implicit in the approach of some writers of the declining trend in the twenties, and there had been a spate of articles in the mid-thirties on the question of "a Soviet tragedy." The matter came to a climax after the whole of Sholokhov's novel had appeared, but the final resolution of the question did not coincide with Sholokhov's formula. The full answer, as it is now formulated,[6] is to be found in two earlier articles. One of these, entitled "Prometheus Liberated" (Marxism has set him free!), declares that there can be no tragedy in the USSR because man is now master of his own fate, is no longer at odds with his society, and fulfills himself through the collective's achievements.[7] The second article, "The Dramaturgical Principles of Aristotle," reviews Hegel's and Aristotle's theories of tragedy with some sympathy and understanding, and then attempts to readjust them to fit Soviet conditions.[8] The author focuses his attention on the catharsis, as the critical moment at which new truths are apprehended, and tinkers with its mechanism so that it yields the spectator not tragic reconciliation (through pity and terror), but political inspiration (through pity and respect). The politically motivated hero thus may die (without inner defeat, of course) and the spectator will emerge from the drama determined to fuse his will with the collective's as the hero had done up to the moment of his death. This is not to be taken seriously as a tragic formula since there is no real torment, doubt, or

[5] *Pervyi vsesoyuznyi s'ezd sovetskikh pisatelei, 1934; stenograficheski otchet* (Moscow, 1934), p. 680.

[6] See Appendix, pp. 333–34.

[7] Yu. Yuzovsky, "Osvobozhdennyi Prometei," *Literaturny kritik*, No. 10 (October, 1934), pp. 113–39.

[8] I. Altman, "Dramaturgicheskie printsipy Aristotelya," *Literaturny kritik*, No. 10 (October, 1935), pp. 52–74.

"stretching," only physical extinction, which the hero confronts unflinchingly.[9] And it has nothing to do in the end with Sholokhov, or the Russian past, or for that matter with Hegel or Aristotle, or any one else who has thought seriously about tragedy.

II

Leonov's *Road to the Ocean* (1935) also ventures toward a tragic statement and then withdraws when it approaches the boundary between socialist realism and the larger world of art's undirected possibilities. Leonov is a gifted writer, literate in his craft, and aware of those possibilities which lie just beyond his reach. As a result of his knowledge of forbidden areas, Leonov is forced to expend a great deal of energy devising ingenious compromises between the requirements of the formula and what he might really like to say. Thus the two obligatory situations of the literature of industrialization, the exposure of the hidden wrecker-enemy and the celebration of the achievements of the Communist hero, are both in Leonov's novel, though they are disguised and set in the background. On the other hand, Leonov's pursuit of his genuine interests is clearly evident in the novel, and though he stops short of real tragic revelation, the work is permeated with a sense of the permanence, the dignity, and the value of human suffering.

His hero, Kurilov, is an old Bolshevik who holds high office in the Volga-Revizan railway, and has dedicated the whole of his life to the service of the cause. His life can be summarized, Leonov tells us, "in one infinite word: work." [10]

[9] The title of one of the plays under discussion, Vishnevsky's *Optimistic Tragedy*, gives the game away.

[10] Leonid Leonov, *Road to the Ocean*, trans. Norbert Guterman (New York, copyright 1944, by A. A. Wyn, Inc., formerly L. B. Fischer Publishing Corp.), p. 4.

The costs of this existence are fully acknowledged by Leonov, and more frankly than by any other latter-day Soviet writer. Moreover, they are not presented as wistful sidelights on the character, as in Sholokhov's Davidov, but are brought into the foreground and incorporated in the hero's image as an ingredient of his greatness. Solitude and barrenness are the consequences of the dedicated, politicalized life, as we have come to know it. None the less so in Kurilov's case.[11] He is denied any intimacy with his subordinates whom he encounters primarily as incompetents, liars, or worse, and treats accordingly. His private life is equally solitary. Marriage has been a bleak, bloodless failure, and children have been denied him, first by the urgency of events, and then by the prolonged illness of his wife. His two fumbling efforts to have affairs with younger women after her death are failures. The friendship of an odd crew of fellow-Bolsheviks and others, including "a poet and heretic" and an old steelworker, is the only nourishing relationship he has with other human beings, and it is denied him most of the time because of their physical separation. The quality of these relationships is conveyed in Kurilov's remarks at a birthday party that has brought them together. He is answering an earlier speech by the poet-heretic, Kutenko, who has proposed a toast to the younger generation which will survive to populate the future, "which certainly neither you nor I will see!" Kurilov replies:

And so, Kutenko, in your opinion, socialism is for those who will survive. You even spoke of friendship from the point of view of our fate, rather than of our community of social interests. . . . But now, as I look at your faces, those dear familiar old

[11] Leonov is sometimes called "Dostoevskyan." The remark of one of Kurilov's colleagues suggests that his solitude has its origins in a rebellion against God similar to Ivan Karamazov's: "Atheism means ignoring God. But you negate him, fight against him, disrespectfully take the universe away from him." (Ibid., p. 463.)

beans, I see myself multiplied in them. All of you are fragments of my own life; that is because we made our lives together, guided by the same purpose. Each of you separately is my friend. I did not bring you together, I did not introduce you to each other, and yet you are each other's friends, too. And if I fall out of this circle, your friendship will remain unchanged. It binds you by an iron and rational discipline, it does not spoil or disintegrate— let us not even mention those who betrayed it! Of this friendship you should have spoken, not of the dead or the unborn ones, Kostia.[12]

Inadequate as these friendships are as a source of emotional sustenance, they are all that matters outside the cause. But the onset of death, which first announces itself by a sharp pain at the moment he finishes this speech, is to cut him off from whatever comfort these politically rationalized relations provide. Kutenko, it turns out, is right: Kurilov's work ends, the "community of social interests" loses its value for him, and he enters a more human plane of existence, from which he contemplates "the common human fate" and the immensely ironic fact that he will never live to see the future he has given his life to build.

In this new state he falls back on a strange, poetic, often incoherent apprehension of the place he and his society occupy in the perspective of history. He is oddly well informed about the human past. He is, for example, an occasional student of the history of religions, for the record he finds there of human fears and aspirations. At the same time he is a dreamer and a prophet. Large sections of the novel are taken up with his explorations, in fantasy, of Ocean, the city of the socialist future. His effort to locate himself in history is the primary intellectual activity of his final months of life. Kurilov's own history is rooted, not surprisingly, in the Marxian view of progress, but there is a very un-Soviet aware-

[12] *Ibid.*, p. 100.

ness of the enormous human suffering that accompanies, and
will continue to accompany, its unfolding.

Kutenko, the poet-heretic, has been right on another
point, we are told, and has stated indirectly part of Leonov's
design for the novel:

He had once been attacked for maintaining that the social maturity of a class in art is acquired through tragedy, and he assumed that the tragedy of the future might consist in biological
extinction.[13]

Kurilov reenacts this "tragedy of the future" as he dies. But
his fate has the other dimension indicated by Kutenko: the
awareness generated in the tension between the imperfect
present, in which he will expire, and the unattained future,
which has called forth all the deprivations in his private life.

This is a most sympathetic recognition of the condition of
the "interim man," and a complete transposition into Soviet
terms of Marx's formula for the premature revolutionary,
the man whom death forces to realize that he is a discarded
means, not an end, whose personal claims on life are forcibly
disconnected from the continuum of society's progress, since
he is not ready to die and his aspirations are not yet realized
in society.[14] Several images convey the sense of Kurilov's
interim position. At one point he is described thus: "Kurilov,
the great hunter, the seeker after human happiness, the man
mountain, from the summit of which we see the future." [15]
The girl, Liza, who is closest to him at the end of his life, and
is most influenced by him as a human being, sees him in
similar terms. "Yes," she says after his death, "he was like a

---

[13] *Ibid.*, p. 99.
[14] Leonov emphasizes this point by his extraordinary frankness about
the dirt, disorder, and breakdown of Soviet life, and the vanity, dis-
honesty, and selfishness of the people Kurilov encounters. The present
is indeed imperfect if not unbearable.
[15] Leonov, *Road to the Ocean*, p. 453.

bridge, and people passed over him into the future." [16]
Kurilov sees himself and the men of his time in the process
of development toward the new, whole man. He is as imperfect and uncompleted as his society: "We ourselves are only
rough drafts of giants, who in their own time will learn that
they are only dwarfs." [17]

Kurilov is engaged in striking the balance of his life in the
months before his death, but as he counts out the human
cost in full detail, he never brings himself to challenge the
cause of it all, his allegiance to the revolution. He is finally
more concerned with justifying than with questioning the
value of his life. Here Leonov has missed the opportunity to
transcend the tragic *fact* of death, and, by stretching Kurilov
another degree, to comment on the tragic *nature* of experience. The novel ends, rather, on a note of muffled affirmation, although it is uttered in an atmosphere heavy with
grief, and Leonov has swerved back at the last moment and
by the skin of his teeth into the confines of socialist realism.

The positive, life-giving word is not pronounced by Kurilov, himself, but is communicated through the effect
the example of his life has had on Liza. But Liza, herself,
apprehends the meaning of his life through her own suffering
at his death. The fact that maturity and self-mastery come
to her through sorrow brings us finally to the matter of Soviet
criticism of Leonov's novel. In general the reception was
chilly. The consensus of a number of critics was that the
novel was "abstract," "unreal," and "weak." One article
represents the lowest common denominator of these opinions, and is very helpful in bringing to light, though in
reverse, as it were, a number of my own general conclusions.

I. Grinberg devoted a large part of an article, called "The
Hero of the Soviet Novel," to an attack on *Road to the*

[16] *Ibid.*, p. 362.   [17] *Ibid.*, p. 262.

Ocean as an example of the way Soviet writers should *not* handle the fusion of the social and the human in Soviet experience.[18] Grinberg's principal objection is that Leonov seems dedicated to the pointless celebration of sorrow and suffering. Liza's path to understanding is a case in point. Because of his treatment of this and other situations the novel is denounced as "false." [19] But the implication is unmistakable that it is also harmful, and in this charge there is much that is instructive.

Kurilov has the "stamp of sorrow, the shadow of an undefined grief" on him. The young people in the novel are unhappy, too. As Leonov sees it, men's interest in their leaders is in the suffering the latter undergo in the name of the common cause. Even the Utopian future he sketches is marked not only by its joyousness, but by the purity and

[18] I. I. Grinberg, "Geroi sovetskogo romana," in *Obraz bolshevika* (Leningrad, 1938), pp. 3–93. This book, an obvious response to the purge trials, is concerned with proving that loyalty to the Party of Lenin and Stalin is the noblest of *human* virtues. The qualities of Leonov's questioning individualist Bolshevik, Kurilov, prompt the speculation that if he had been real, he might well have ended in the dock with Bukharin, Radek, and others, from whose mold he seems, in some respects, to have been cast. Grinberg's definition of the monolithic Bolshevik "new man" contrasts sharply with Kurilov. It has the additional virtue of standing for hundreds of other such pronouncements. "The Bolshevik, the hero of our literature and of our epoch, is a man who is changing the world, an active man, strong-willed, whose actions are full of a high Leninist-Stalinist ideology, a man who grows in struggle, a man for whom the happiness of the whole people is a vital matter, the happiness of our beautiful and happy motherland, for the defense of which he has given, is giving, and is ready to give all his strength, abilities, and talents." (*Ibid.*, p. 79.)

[19] Grinberg may be right in one sense. It is possible that Kurilov's extraordinary capacity for speculation and fantasy are a "falsification" of the literal human reality. It may be that by humanizing the Bolshevik, Leonov has sentimentalized him out of all recognition. It seems more likely that Leonov has dramatized his own idiosyncratic terms for making peace with the painful, disorderly revolutionary reality, and has projected them into the figure of the political commissar.

dignity of its grief.[20] All this is wrong, Grinberg insists, and partakes of a misguided "worship of sorrow," inherited from the diseased capitalist past. Leonov should be reminded that folklore from the most wretched periods is "optimistic" in its effects, and that the best of written literature from the past (he does not cite any) is distinguished by its message of hopeful joy about the human future. Leonov's misreading of the past has betrayed him into harmful practices:

All the harm the "soothers" and "glorifiers" of suffering bring is clearly seen. . . . It is necessary not to sing the sufferings, but to hate them, to destroy them, to struggle with them, it is necessary to show that the popular mass can deliver itself from them—and is delivering itself from them.[21]

The too frank recognition of suffering, quite apart from its celebration, might contradict the certain assurances that the removal of all known causes of human suffering was next on the Party agenda. Leonov had been misled, as had others, by relying too heavily on the classical past: "Some of our writers . . . still think they can find the key to the new man by using the old traditions of the literature of suffering." [22] Leonov's sin is made perfectly clear, and his kinship with

[20] Leonov, with Marx clearly in mind, says of the inhabitants of Ocean: "The people stood more erect, seemed more assured—whether because each one was aware of his neighbor at his side and did not fear him, or because the clean air of the new time did not contain the bacillus of falsehood. . . . I expected them to boast of the perfection of their social order and I should not have condemned their pride, but actually they took no notice of the social order. Here, man's natural state had at last been attained—he was free, he was not exploited, and he rejoiced in the work of hand and brain. But although everything was in reach—bread, work and fate itself—we often saw people with careworn faces. We understood that sadness dwelt among them, and that they, too, knew tragedy, though of a kind more worthy of man's dignity." (Leonov, *Road to the Ocean*, p. 365.)

[21] Grinberg, "Geroi sovetskogo romana," in *Obraz bolshevika*, p. 19.

[22] *Ibid.*, p. 18.

the tradition, as Grinberg remarks it, does him greater honor than his earnest but confused novel.

This is the last time we shall observe the two phases of Russian realism in conflict with each other, and it is permissible to draw from it certain conclusions about the political attack on literature. Experience must be viewed optimistically at all times because the Party program offers nothing but joy, hope, and positive achievement. Suffering is irrelevant, uninteresting, and obstructive, whenever it is brought to public attention. In this way political agitation performs its final act of emasculation on the artist's traditional view of mankind. Let there be nothing but the solid joy of public successes. Let man be measured and known by this alone, and let him be ashamed of his broken heart—unless it can somehow be made to increase production. Whatever makes man suffer—his weakness, his illusions, his miscalculations, his progress toward senility and death, his commitments to unrealizable goals—is without efficacy and without general interest for that reason. Such is the burden of Grinberg's attack on Leonov's statement of the prevalence of human sorrow. Soviet man is not even to have his suffering as a measure of his joy. A blank-faced optimism, decreed by officialdom, is the only mood permitted him, encompassing his setbacks and illuminating his next day's triumph. Even his dreams must submit to the same kind of censorship. Kurilov's vision of Ocean is false and harmful when it is set against Klychkov's dream of controlling Chapaev or Davidov's dream of the happy kolkhoz meeting its production norms with the help of electric plows.[23]

Grinberg's attack on suffering is not the same as Chernyshevsky's repudiation of tragedy. But the same bleakly pro-

[23] See *ibid.*, p. 25, and see above, pp. 236–37 and p. 286.

grammatic optimism and the same simplified, politicalized view of man underlie it. Grinberg concludes his criticism of Leonov by quoting Gorky's definition of "complexity": "Complexity is the sad and deformed result of the . . . disintegration of the 'soul' under the living conditions of petit-bourgeois society." [24] All else is clear, simple, unilinear, disciplined.

In the new Soviet Babbitry, suffering is simply inefficient, and when it does make itself felt it is seen as a phenomenon that can be reduced or assimilated by ideological ministrations.[25] For the writer who is forced to abide by these definitions this is an irreparable loss. The image of man he is required to work with (and accept on his own terms) has a small, politically bound view of experience which is proof against all shocks. He cannot be dragged forth from his political casing and exposed to the temptations or trials of the human universe. He is limited, compact, smug, and unbreakable. The writer may acknowledge suffering but he may not show its effects. Deprived by his political masters of the

[24] Quoted in *ibid.*, p. 23.

[25] A recent Soviet novel had this to say on the question: "Great historical events are accompanied not only by general excitement, finding expression in elation or dejection of the human spirit, but also by suffering and deprivations far from the ordinary and beyond the power of man to prevent. For one who recognizes that the events taking place are part of the general movement of history, as well as for one who is consciously guiding the course of history, this suffering does not cease to exist any more than physical suffering ceases to exist when the disease causing it is known. But such a person reacts differently to the suffering than one who does not appreciate the historical significance of events, knowing only that life today is harder or easier, better or worse, than it was yesterday or will be tomorrow. For the former, the logic of history lends meaning to his suffering; for the latter, the suffering seems to have been imposed only to be suffered, as life itself seems to have been granted only to be lived." (Konstantin Fedin, *No Ordinary Summer* [Moscow, 1950], pp. 9–10.) The belief that there are political inoculations against the destructive effects of suffering is undoubtedly one of the positive sources of Soviet morale.

full "awareness" of suffering, he has lost a fundamental tool
of definition and illumination.[26]

Leonov's world-view has one other important aspect: the
heavy influence it shows of the humanist strain in the Marxian inheritance. The entire novel is set against the large
perspective of men's progress toward wholeness, and the central dramatic situation of the inopportune revolutionary is
translated into Soviet terms without major alteration from
Marx's and Engels's correspondence with Lassalle.[27] The
attack on *Road to the Ocean* by Grinberg and others suggests
the growing estrangement in orthodox Soviet circles of the
late thirties from those aspects of Marxism which bear most
closely on imaginative literature.

III

The publication, section by section, of Alexei Tolstoy's
The Road to Calvary spans the full era between the wars;
the first volume appeared in 1920, the last in 1940. For this
reason it is a laboratory specimen of the important changes
in Soviet writing, most notably in the matter of the writer's
control over his material. It may be that Alexei Tolstoy
simply changed his mind, but it must be pointed out, also,
that in doing so he has betrayed the vital interests of his
profession and capitulated to the political invaders.

The novel has no hard center of moral purpose, nor any
strong inner necessity of development. The mass of material
might have been shaped to many ends; individual destinies,
since they are not closely interlocked, might have been
worked out in a number of ways. Only one thing is certain:
the final solution Tolstoy did impose on the novel is extremely questionable, because it is introduced in the last
third of the book in total disregard of what has gone before.

---

[26] See above, p. 108.   [27] See above, pp. 166–67.

Despite its shortcomings, in its first two-thirds the work exhibits a number of the traditional attributes of the novel as an independent comment on experience. Tolstoy's interest in his material seems largely documentary. Thus, Part I stands as a vivid sketch of the St. Petersburg intelligentsia on the eve of the revolution; Part II is an attempt, like many others, to reflect the chaos of civil war itself. In his investigation on this not too profound level, Tolstoy has assembled a large group of sharply individualized characters, who embody, among other things, a number of contrasting attitudes toward the revolution. As an illustration of the variety of character and the honesty of presentation, consider Sapozhkov, the ex-Futurist, who fights on the Bolshevik side, but without illusions about the future: "The bourgeois world is vile, and it bores me stiff. . . . And if we win, the Communist world will be just as boring and grey, virtuous and boring." [28] In a disconnected speech he analyzes with pity and irony the dilemma of the pampered intelligentsia in the violence of civil war:

Our tragedy, my dear fellow, is that we, the Russian intelligentsia, have been cradled in the peaceful lap of serfdom, and the Revolution has terrified us out of our wits; it has given us a kind of vomiting of the brain. It's not right to frighten delicate people like that, is it? We used to sit in a quiet country arbor, with birds singing around us, and think to ourselves: Really, it would be very nice indeed to fix things up so that everybody would be happy. . . . What silly fools we are—serve the people indeed! It's a tragicomedy. We wept so much over the sufferings of the people that our tears ran dry. And when those tears were taken away we found we had nothing to live for. . . . It all comes from our gentle nurture; we're too squeamish, we can't understand without nice little books. . . . In the nice little books the Revolution is described very attractively. . . . But our peo-

[28] Alexei Tolstoy, *Road to Calvary*, trans. Edith Bone (New York, 1946), p. 350.

ple simply deserts from the front, drowns officers, lynches the
Commander-in-Chief, burns manors, hunts the merchants' wives
on the railways, and digs their diamond ear-rings from all sorts of
places under their petticoats. No, we say, we don't want to play
with this nasty people, there's nothing written in our books
about such a people. . . . What's to be done? Shed an ocean
of tears at home in our flats. . . . There's nothing left to live
for. And so out of horror and disgust, some of us stick our heads
under the pillow; others slink away to foreign parts; and those
who are angriest take up arms.[29]

Sapozhkov is among the latter, though it is clear that he
does so without hope, under a crushing and well-informed
sense of his own and his country's doom. At the end of his
tirade, Gymsa, the regimental security officer, enters and
tells him, in a voice like the grinding of millstones, to keep
quiet: "You've started your philosophical chatter again,
your idiotic rigmaroles; hence I infer that you are drunk."
Gymsa has just come from an execution. Sapozhkov says to
him: "All right, I'm drunk. All right, shoot me!" To which
Gymsa answers readily: "You know quite well I'd shoot you
soon enough. If I don't it's because I take your fighting
qualities into account." [30] Gymsa goes out a moment later
and Sapozhkov mocks him:

Here's the whole secret: to give a straight answer to a straight
question. . . . Does God exist?—No. May one kill a man?—
Yes. What is the immediate objective?—The world revolution.
. . . Just like that, brother, without any high-falutin' emotions.[31]

If this episode reveals little else, it demonstrates that Tolstoy is still working from an independent vantage, from
which he is prepared to consider ambiguities, to explore conflicting points of view, and to set humane considerations
against political loyalties.

[29] *Ibid.*, pp. 351–52.   [30] *Ibid.*, p. 353.   [31] *Ibid.*, p. 355.

It is precisely this independence of judgment that is sacrificed in Part III. The results are striking. Characters are
interrupted in the more or less plausible drift of their careers,
are hurried to improvised destinies, are hastily converted and
refurbished as moral political beings. A highly questionable
series of coincidences reunites separated lovers and scattered
families.

That the blight of socialist realism is on the book becomes
evident first when iron-jawed, clear-eyed Communists appear
from nowhere and take over the direction of events. (Up to
now the Communists have been indistinguishable as people
from the other characters. These new men are of a higher
moral order.) An imperturbable, pipe-smoking Stalin outwits
Denikin at Tsaritsyn and crushes him, and the traitorous
Trotsky issues orders which are properly disobeyed and unmasked.

The disintegration of the entire fabric of the novel is
clearest in the last ten pages. Two quite ordinary characters,
who have been hurriedly made up on the model of positive
heroes, are united with their wives in Moscow and troop off
to a political meeting in the Bolshoi Theater. Before they
go Roshchin, the converted White, talks intimately with his
Katia:

Katia, our task is immense. We never dreamt that we would accomplish it. Remember, we often talked about it—the whirlpool
of history, the destruction of great civilizations, ideas transformed
into pitiful parodies of themselves—it all seemed so meaningless to us. Under the starched dress-shirt still the same hairy
chest of the *pithecanthropos!* All lies! But now the veil has been
torn from our eyes. All our past life was a lie and a crime! Russia
has borne a new man and this man demands the right for men
to live like men. . . . A dazzling light has fallen on the half-
ruined arches of the past. Everything has a meaning; everything
is governed by the same laws. We have found a goal, a goal

every Red Army man knows. Katia, can you understand me a
little better now? I wanted to give myself to you, all of myself,
my darling, my heart, my beloved, my star.[32]

With such a political resolution fastened on the novel, it is
not surprising that political rhetoric permeates even the love-
making.

At the meeting Katia asks Roshchin: "Which is Lenin?"
Roshchin answers:

Over there, in the black overcoat—he is writing quickly . . .
now he is throwing the note across the table. That's Lenin. And
that thin one, with the black mustache, at the end of the row, is
Stalin, the man who destroyed Denikin.[33]

Against this historical tableau, the two couples listen to a
speech on the industrialized future and make their declaration of solidarity with Party, state, and the official blueprint
of the future. Telegin, the engineer, engages in this dialogue
with his wife:

Dashenka, I'm just wild to get to work again. If they build a
network of electric power there is nothing we can't do. We
have a devil of a lot of natural resources; once we get down to
using them properly America can watch our smoke! . . . We'll
go to the Urals together, you and I.

Dasha takes it up:

Yes, we'll live in a log cabin with large windows, beautifully
clean, with pearls of resin coming out of the wood. In the winter
we'll have a huge fire flaming in the hearth.[34]

Roshchin addresses his Katia in the same vein ("Can you
see now how purposeful our efforts, all the blood we shed
. . . have become . . . ? And this is happening here, in my
country, and this is Russia!" [35]). And there the novel ends.
The banality of the situation has penetrated the emotions

[32] Ibid., p. 877.   [33] Ibid., p. 884.   [34] Ibid.
[35] Ibid., pp. 884–85.

of the characters and the very texture of the language.[36]

We do not know whether Alexei Tolstoy made his surrender cynically or from conviction. In any case, he has
provided a perfect case-study within the limits of a single
work of the damages that result when rough political hands
are laid on an imaginative work of more than average vitality.
We may view this novel as marking one more instance of
the conclusion of the long quarrel between the writers and
the revolutionaries. The final consequences of Chernyshevsky's attempt to capture Russian realism are again made
clear. Alexei Tolstoy's capitulation has this melancholy advantage.

IV

In our descent down the scale of literary value there is
one more level we must plumb to bring the journey to an
end. If we address some of the questions we have used before
to one more novel, Ostrovsky's *The Making of a Hero*, we
shall find, first of all, a sameness of pattern. But that is not
all and that would not be reason enough for taking the
trouble. We shall find, in addition, a progressive deteriora-
tion in insight and an increase in fictional disorganization
that brings us finally to the level of juvenilia which Chernyshevsky first established as a norm in *What Is to Be Done?*
We shall find final confirmation, too, of the close kinship
between the heroes of the two novels, as psychological and
moral beings. Finally, this novel set the standards for much
of the writing that followed the Zhdanov blackout.

[36] It is comforting to discover that Grinberg is in complete disagreement with my evaluation of the two halves of the novel. He finds a
lack of ideological clarity in the first two parts, and condemns them,
therefore, as bad writing. In those sections of Part III which were
published by the time he wrote his article, he found vast improve-
ment on all levels. (Grinberg, "Geroi sovetskogo romana," in *Obraz
bolshevika*, pp. 80–86.)

Pavel Korchagin, the hero of Ostrovsky's *The Making of a Hero*, carries the notion of the moral monolith to the limits of plausibility or beyond, to absurdity. To the extent that the novel is autobiographical, the author has sacrificed the essential remove from his protagonist that enabled Sholokhov, for example, to exercise a measure of control over his Davidov, to trace the outline, at least, of his fallibilities, and to suggest that there are values in life not easily given up. For Korchagin the universe is completely demarcated into blacks and whites, according to his simplicistic political morality. The bourgeois girl's lips twitch for cocaine; the Communists' eyes are clear and steady.

From the moment Korchagin joins the Komsomol, his only guiding principle is to serve: service is happiness; happiness, service. Since there are no other large choices, since there can be no question of moral fallibility, the only genuine tests he can undergo involve his capacity to stand physical suffering. Korchagin's body endures a severe beating in prison; in the civil war he incurs a hip wound, a head wound, a spinal wound, and a smashed knee; in addition, he contracts typhus, pneumonia, and rheumatic fever. When the cumulative effect of these afflictions result in paralysis and blindness, his "tempered" Bolshevik will responds to this ultimate challenge: he learns to become a writer and continues his life of service to the cause.

Korchagin's personal moral code is indistinguishable from the Party program. The habits of service and leadership in its name, we are led to believe, have become basic *character traits*. From this total absorption in Party work he derives whatever spiritual nourishment his intense if dehydrated nature requires. Thus powered, his actions are always successful (although it should be pointed out that the successes are never magically easy), whether he is tracking down a mur-

derer on the frontier or discouraging kissing games among
the youth. From his central fund of belief he, like Davidov
and all the others, develops problem-solving virtues as required by the situation. He is endowed with technical skill,
civic initiative, administrative subtlety, and military resourcefulness. As a leader he displays a range of qualities appropriate to the many roles he plays: patience, tact, indignation,
courage, or, if the presence of the class enemy is sensed, intolerance and ruthlessness.

We must recall that we are always viewing Korchagin
from within, as he justifies his own behavior to himself. No
attention is paid to the likelihood that the people he manipulates or clashes with might regard him as a prig, a busybody,
or a fanatic.[37] Since he is not seen at all from an outside
vantage, we are only able to guess at the degree of the costs
of his alienation from the rank-and-file members of the various communities he inhabits, or from the normal human
experiences he has voluntarily foregone. We note, with a
few exceptions, not the absence so much as the unimportance
of friendship, love, or family ties. His personal attachments,
such as they are, have an invariable political cast: they are
with members of his own elite, or they are initiated, sustained, or ended on political grounds. In Korchagin's case,
the question of rewards and costs must be changed to: What
are the costs of *non*participation? As it happens, they are
very nearly fatal. His deepest spiritual crisis is brought on by

[37] An episode is revealing: "There was not much to learn, but these
things were noted: Razvalikhin drinking and gathering all the rotters
around him and keeping the better comrades out of things. Pavel
reported all this to the Bureau. The other comrades . . . were all for
reprimanding Razvalikhin severely, when Pavel surprised them by saying: 'I am for expelling him without the right to apply for member-
ship again.' Everybody thought this much too severe, but Pavel said
again: 'This scoundrel must be expelled.'" (Nikolai Ostrovsky, *The
Making of a Hero* [New York, 1937], pp. 377–78.) He was.

a doctor's decision that his multiple injuries have ended his usefulness to the Party. If he cannot serve it, life is without meaning and he has no alternative but to succumb to his wounds. But by overcoming the handicaps he wins through to a new kind of service, hence to a renewal of his life.

In this extraordinarily naive and incomplete human image the myth of the monolithic, functional, political man as it was first set forth in the nineteenth century has reached some kind of apotheosis. His author would have us believe that he has made the move from life as it is with its challenges, temptations, and ambiguities, to a fabricated, self-contained universe of ideology, and anchored himself within it. Doctrine has replaced life.[38] His activist political faith "permeates" his entire being as it does with Insarov in Turgenev's *On the Eve*, and like him, if he is denied participation in his cause, he will die. In the same way, Rakhmetov's bed of nails (in Chernyshevsky's *What Is to Be Done?*) forecasts Korchagin's terrible physical battering. By accepting the total commitment of the totally political man, Korchagin has placed himself beyond the last frontier of the human habitat. He does not, like Kurilov, accept death as a release from duty, but fights against it as an inexplicable nuisance. Both men are contemporaries and members of the same Party, but beyond that a world separates them. Their respective situations measure the gap between the old Bolshevik with his memory of other standards and other worlds,

[38] Consider this passage: "He was in a constant hurry to *live*; not only in a hurry himself, but anxious to urge others on too. . . . Often a light could be seen in his window late into the night, and people there gathered round a table—reading and studying. In two years they had worked through the third volume of *Capital*, and had gained an understanding of the delicate mechanics of capitalist exploitation." *Ibid.*, p. 377.

and the new Stalinist man who knows nothing but what he
needs to know.

V

With this novel the work of the literary investigator comes
to an end. So long as Soviet writing remains on this level it
is more usefully investigated by social scientists or propaganda analysts. In bequeathing the literary tradition to them,
certain tentative conclusions about the angle of refraction
at which reality is reflected, about the inner workings of the
literary mechanism, and about literature's function in times
of social crisis may be useful. The hero, it may be assumed,
will be a Party member on the level of tactical command,
that is, where actual day-to-day leadership is exercised. The
problem he is ordered to solve will doubtless be a widespread
one, and the description of the problem will be a more or
less frank account of some point of friction, breakdown, or
disorganization in the social or economic structure. Or, if it
is a story of new construction, the peculiar problems of terrain, technology, etc., will be carefully set forth.

Beginning on this level of *is*, the hero, by a process of
engineering—human, technological, or administrative—lifts
the entire situation to the level of *should be* and provides
in that process minute instructions for the solution of similar
problems. In addition to instruction there will be inspiration
and the assurance of success provided everybody does what
he should. In this last transaction with the reader, there is
a kind of primitive process of wish fulfillment, as in the
savage's war dance in which the imagined victory of the dance
strengthens him for the next day's battle. But the Soviet
citizen is not given magic assurances. His active, conscious,
dedicated participation is an indispensable ingredient in the
success of the project. The Soviet fictional dream does not

endow him with false fantasies of his strength, but a moral blueprint accompanied by detailed instructions for its use.

The above description is a rough summary of the lowest level of Soviet writing as it existed on the agitational level in the days of RAPP, and as it has dominated the postwar years. It is a literature entirely shaped by didactic needs. And it is a literature which, I should say, is characteristic of a certain kind of crisis in Soviet life—not the *crisis of event,* such as the Nazi invasion—but the induced crisis or the crisis of anticipation in which invisible future menaces—imagined or real—are evoked to drive men to work. The latter is a time of the greatest constriction, regimentation, and coercion.[39] And it is reflected in the kind of fictional design I have just described. The hero, in this context, can be read as a kind of temperature gauge measuring the degree of crisis. When the crisis is considered greatest he will tend to be most infallible, most monolithic, most parental, most mythic, and most closely identified with the Party. As and if the crisis eases we may expect to see him resume more humane dimensions, although his quotient of virtue will probably be unacceptably high and unreal for Western readers for an indefinite period.

More rewarding here than a cataloguing of the virtues and vices of the positive hero, it seems to me, is a broad charac-

---

[39] Oddly enough, this is not necessarily so in wartime, when the enemy is tangibly present on Soviet soil and every blow against him is a socially useful act. The literature reflects this *relaxation* of attitude and exhibits a greater concern with the heroism and the human problems of the humble, non-Party citizens. There is no large body of war literature, partly because there was little time to write during the war, and partly because Zhdanovism ruled it out shortly after the war. But novels like Simonov's *Days and Nights,* Panova's *Train,* or Leonov's *Chariot of Wrath* exhibit a more than minimal concern with the problems of being human, and a consequent diminution of the political strain. Nation, army, state, or people are the objects of primary allegiance, not the Party, since they are the institutions that conduct the struggle.

terization of him as an *alienated* man, as that concept has
been communicated by the great writers of the Russian past.
There is a pathos in the fact that a tradition which has since
its inception called for wholehearted engagement in history
should play itself out with heroes who are disengaged from
life, cut off even from a recognition of their own suffering.
Soviet writers, with the few exceptions we have noted, will
not, or are not permitted to, accord him that recognition.

The positive hero, unlike the estranged, "superfluous,"
or alienated man of the nineteenth century, is not rejected
by, or denied participation in, society. The Soviet hero is
promised fulfillment only through his acceptance of the institutions and values of his status quo. In the very act of
conformity significant losses are registered.

He is, first of all, entirely politicalized, with his needs
and aspirations defined by his political allegiances. Although
he is expected to respond with *inner* enthusiasm to grandiose
public goals, the real locus of judgment in these matters is
outside his own conscience. He makes decisions, so to speak,
but no choices. He lives in a world of rationalized deprivations, subsisting on reduced rations of love, friendship, and
family happiness because, he is always told, of the terrible
urgencies besetting his community. Finally, he is manipulated from above and in turn manipulates those beneath
him: he lives in a hierarchy of these relationships.

Is his "incompleteness" envisioned as eternal? History
will give the actual answer, of course, but we should note
that the framers of the old and the new versions of his moral
code did expect an end to his estrangement. The children,
Chernyshevsky said, were to grow up in their parents' image.
Few could belong to Rakhmetov's elite which would soon
disappear, but, on a lower level, the number of new men was
expected to increase by arithmetic progression, through the

power of example, until they composed the whole population.[40] The extension of the Leninist ethic since 1930 to all levels of the population through every channel of communication seems to contemplate the same eventual reunion of the leaders and the led. Obviously, this "solution" raises additional troubling problems: the leaders, the exemplars, it should be remembered, are interim men. The life of the interim man has been long—it is a century since he was first conceived, a third of a century since he inherited the Russian earth—but, in theory, at least, it is not expected to last forever. And if it ends, one wonders, will anyone remember how to live, as Marx hoped men would, as a "total man" in his full "human reality," "seeing, hearing, smelling, tasting, feeling, thinking, contemplating, willing, acting, loving?" [41] Or will the alienation of the incomplete, inopportune socialist man have become universalized? "Too long a sacrifice," as Yeats said in "Easter 1916," "can make a stone of the heart./ O when may it suffice?"

The pathos of the positive hero, as we have said, is that he does not know his sacrifice. Ostrovsky's novel *The Making of a Hero*, which with Chernyshevsky's *What Is to Be Done?* and Gorky's *Mother* is recognized as a major work in the tradition, provides us with a classic instance. Ostrovsky's hero, Pavel Korchagin, is often linked with Rakhmetov and Vlasov, and he stands before us today as the most celebrated example of the new Soviet man, heading the company of latter-day heroes. By the same token he presents himself to us as the apotheosis of the politicalized man and the clearest example of the official literary treatment of the Communist "emasculate." The writer's attitude toward his hero's wound is central in the whole aesthetic tradition we have explored.

[40] See *Chto delat?* (Moscow, 1947), pp. 55–56 and 191.
[41] *Literature and Art* (New York, 1947), p. 61.

Should it be celebrated, confronted, assimilated, deprecated, concealed, or denied? If the governing type is Ostrovsky's hero, and not Sholokhov's or Leonov's, the question is closed. The fact that we know so much of the aridity of Korchagin's life suggests that Ostrovsky does not even know of his hero's deprivations. His identification with him is so thorough (in this case the novel is autobiographical) that the last pretense of fiction has evaporated. The hero's blindness coincides with the author's. It is as if we had been given a nihilist's view of Bazarov, or an atheist's view of Ivan Karamazov. The emasculated Myshkin goes mad, but the Soviet saint writes with abandoned admiration about himself.

The image of the hero as it has been cast from Belinsky to Zhdanov and the treatment of that image in literature has falsified the very values which the new man and the new literature were supposed to realize. The aesthetic of radicalism is self-defeating, if indeed it is not a contradiction in terms, when considered in the light of the tradition we have examined. It has led finally to the incomplete portraiture of incomplete men.

APPENDIX [1]

A rt for art's sake," "art as an end in itself"—a false and harmful theory prevalent in bourgeois studies of art and literature. It rests upon the assertion that art is not dependent upon social life, and is not called upon to serve the people.

Depriving art of its ideological content and social significance, the champions of this theory disguise the fact that they actually serve the ruling classes in bourgeois society. They demand that the artist be concerned solely with the form of an artistic work.

The great revolutionary democrats, V. G. Belinsky, N. A. Nekrasov, N. G. Chernyshevsky, and N. A. Dobrolyubov, stood opposed to this interpretation of the goal and function of art, an interpretation which runs counter to the interests of the people. In their view the function of art was to serve the people. They believed that the artist participated actively and effectively in the people's struggle, since artistic works not only reflect reality and reproduce life, but also explain life and "have the force of judgments upon the phenomena of life" (N. G. Chernyshevsky).

All decadent currents in the literature of the nobility and the bourgeoisie used the slogan "art for art's sake" to disguise in one way or another their antipopular nature. In his report on the magazines *Zvezda* and *Leningrad* A. A. Zhdanov offered a devastating critique of the theory of "art for art's sake."

[1] The glossary included here is taken from an important postwar dictionary of literary terms (L. I. Timofeev, *Kratki slovar literaturovedecheskikh terminov* [Moscow, 1952]). The entire range of Soviet thinking about art is set forth here with devastating clarity. The connections with the Russian past and the deflation of the Marxian legacy are also quite evident. Timofeev's work is intended as a text for middle-school students. This fact gives it a semi-official character, and it does not diminish the validity of these definitions that they are intended for school children. This is perhaps the most instructive thing about Timofeev's work: the USSR has perfected not only a national literature but a universal aesthetic for juveniles.

Hero of a literary work, one of the main characters in a work, possessed of distinct characteristics and behavior traits and of a definite attitude to the other characters and situations shown in the work.

The term hero is often applied to any personage in a work who is treated thoroughly. It would be more correct if the term hero were reserved for the positive hero of a work, the character whose actions, thoughts, and emotions, in the writer's opinion, set an example for the reader's behavior.

Just such heroes in the minds of an entire generation were Vera Pavlovna and Rakhmetov, the heroes of N. G. Chernyshevsky's novel *What Is to Be Done?* In Gorky's novel *Mother* the heroes are Pelageya Nilovna and Pavel Vlasov; the heroes of N. Ostrovsky's novel *How the Steel Was Tempered* (The Making of a Hero) are Pavel Korchagin, Seryozha and Valya Bruzzhak, and Zhukhrai.

In contradistinction to the positive heroes, it would be more appropriate to call the other people portrayed in the work characters or personages.

Idea, a thought concerning an experience, individual, object, etc., which expresses a reaction to these phenomena, the conception, that is, which people entertain regarding them.

"Idea is (a person's) cognition and aspiration (wanting)," V. I. Lenin teaches.

A given idea is always determined by the social order in which people live and by the material conditions in the life of the society.

In class society ideas—people's views of and attitudes toward experiences, and their aspirations—express the point of view of a given class and its material interests in this society. . . .

The idea of an artistic work is the dominant thought regarding the fundamental complex of phenomena portrayed in the work. A writer's idea is the thought which he expresses in artistic images, that is, in the pictures of life in a work—the behavior of the characters, their actions and emotional experiences.

The writer, in portraying persons and events, expresses his attitude toward them and tries to rouse the same attitude toward them in the reader. The writer's thinking and his attitudes reflect the interests of the class with which he is in sympathy, whose side he takes in the people's struggle.

Thus, it was in the interests of the people struggling against the exploiting classes that N. Ostrovsky told of the life and struggle of Pavel Korchagin and his comrades. With convincing artistry and fidelity to life he showed that there are no difficulties which a man cannot overcome if he is inspired by a great goal, the happiness of mankind, the building of Communism. This is the fundamental idea, the chief thought of the novel *How the Steel Was Tempered* (The Making of a Hero), the idea which inspired N. Ostrovsky himself to a great artistic achievement. . . .

Ideinost',[2] the trend of the ideas in a work which is determined by the profundity and the truthfulness of a writer's world view and in turn determines the importance of the work's content. The more progressive are the ideas which the writer has used as his premise in reflecting life and in selecting and evaluating experiences, the more significant, truthful, and profound is the work of art.

Erroneous ideas lower the significance of art; progressive ideas, which express the interests of the working people, give the writer the greatest opportunities to produce a fully realized work.

"The only literary trends which achieve brilliant development are those which arise under the influence of ideas which are powerful and vibrant and which meet the real requirements of an age," wrote the great revolutionary democrat N. G. Chernyshevsky.

Soviet writers, who reflect in their works a "higher order than any bourgeois-democratic order" (A. A. Zhdanov), are guided by the ideas of Marxism-Leninism, which are the most advanced ideas of our time and are bringing happiness to toiling mankind. The greater the extent to which Soviet writers are inspired by the ideas of Communism, are committed to these ideas, the loftier their successes.

[2] This term may be translated variously as "ideological orientation," "commitment to a given ideology," or "the nature of an ideology."

Partiinost' [3] signifies in literature and art that in class society any artist, as a participant in social life and the class struggle, expresses, in his attitude to experience, the interests of a given class and of a given party. In this respect any ideological activity, including literary, is always identified with party, and has a definite class tendency.

Pretending that they represent the interests of the whole nation, interests which they allege to be above and beyond class, bourgeois writers hypocritically conceal their party identification.

Lenin teaches us: "The absence of *partiinost'* in bourgeois society is nothing but hypocritically camouflaged, passively expressed affiliation with the party of the full-bellied, the party of the rulers and of the exploiters."

Hence "freedom from party identification is a bourgeois idea. *Partiinost'* is a socialist idea" (V. I. Lenin).

The highest form of party identification is the identification of socialist art and literature with the Bolshevist Party.

V. I. Lenin for the first time in history [in "Party Organization and Party Literature"] presented an exhaustive justification of the principle of identification with the Bolshevist Party as the basis of a socialistic literature, genuinely identified with the people, genuinely revolutionary, and the only free literature, resting upon the premise of a scientific, Marxist-Leninist understanding of life. . . .

The *partiinost'* of Soviet literature lies in its Bolshevist idea-content, as a result of which its works are genuinely identified with the people. It is characteristic of both Party and non-Party Bolsheviks, of all writers whose works are identified with the Bolshevist Party. It determines the basic features of the artistic method of Soviet literature—socialist realism.

Realism, the basic method of art and literature. Its fundamental principle is fidelity to life. The artist is guided by this in his efforts to produce the fullest and most truthful reflection of life.

Friedrich Engels wrote that "realism means, in addition to truthfulness of detail, truthfulness in the reproduction of typical

[3] May be translated as "party spirit" or "party identification."

characters in typical circumstances," having in mind that that is typical which is most true and characteristic, in which the laws of life are revealed with the greatest fullness.

Realism achieved its greatest development in the nineteenth century, as a result particularly of the activity of the great Russian realist writers.

It was so-called critical realism which was developed to a greater extent in the art of the past. The critical realists (for example, N. V. Gogol) with profound truthfulness portrayed chiefly the negative phenomena of life in an effort to rouse a protest against them in the readers. They defended their ideals and showed those negative phenomena in life which prevented those ideals from being realized, in order to evoke in the reader a desire to combat everything negative in life. For this reason it was the critical portrayal of life which was most important in their works. But critical realism rested on positive ideals—patriotism, sympathy with the oppressed masses, the quest for life's positive hero, and faith in a bright future for Russia (Gogol's *Dead Souls*, for instance).

A new and higher type of realism, socialist realism, has come into being in socialist society, where the ideal of the progressive writer is being realized.

Romanticism is an artistic method in art and literature employed by many artists of the past. It represents an attempt to confront a life which did not satisfy them with unusual images and plots. These images were generated by the artists' dreams and were prompted in them by experiences which for specific historical reasons do not at the present time play a decisive role in life. The term romanticism itself derives from this notion, that is, from the adjective "romanic"—"as in a novel (roman), in a book," and not as in life. The romantic artist seeks to express in his images what he wants to see in life, what should, in his opinion, be fundamental and decisive in life. . . .

Romanticism takes on a different character in different historic conditions.

If the circumstances nurturing the artist's dream are obsolescent in life, and if the artist defends them in his dream, it is reactionary romanticism which his work is manifesting.

If these are progressive aspects of life, born in the struggle of the new with the old, but not yet having become firmly entrenched in life, and if the artist fights in his dream for forward movement—the romanticism of his art is progressive.

If in his art the artist calls for a struggle against the old, for the remaking of society, then his is the method of revolutionary romanticism.

Hence in the history of literature romanticism in each given instance demands its historical interpretation: the romanticism of V. Hugo, the romanticism of V. A. Zhukovsky, the romanticism of M. Yu. Lermontov—these are all historically different types of romanticism.

Revolutionary romanticism reached its highest form in the early work of A. M. Gorky, whose dream fully corresponded to the revolutionary struggle of the working class, directed by the Party of Lenin and Stalin.

In Soviet literature, in which the best aspirations of the writer coincide with the trend of development of Soviet society and with its movement to Communism, romanticism no longer exists separately. Reflecting the revolutionary romanticism of socialist reality, it has become a part of socialist realism. A. A. Zhdanov defined it as a component part of a literary work, which does not develop independently as it did in the art of the past. . . .

For our literature, which has both feet planted firmly in a materialist foundation, romanticism cannot be alien. But it is a romanticism of a new type, it is revolutionary romanticism. When we say that socialist realism is the basic method of Soviet literature and criticism, we assume that revolutionary romanticism must become a component part of literary creation. For the entire life of our Party, the entire life of the working class and its struggle, consists in a combination of the most exacting and sober kind of practical work with the greatest of heroism and with grand prospects.

Socialist realism. In his talk with writers in 1932 J. V. Stalin defined it as the artistic method of Soviet literature.

The Charter of the Union of Soviet Writers declares that "Socialist Realism is the basic method of Soviet literature and literary criticism. It demands of the artist a truthful, historically concrete depiction of reality in its revolutionary development. Truthfulness and historical concreteness in the artistic depiction of reality must be combined with the task of reforming the ideas of the toilers and of educating them in the spirit of socialism."

The main features of this artistic method were indicated by V. I. Lenin in 1905 in his historic work, "Party Organization and Party Literature," in which he foresaw the creation and flowering of a free socialist literature when socialism should have been victorious.

This method was applied for the first time by A. M. Gorky in his novel *Mother* and in other works. In poetry the most vivid expression of socialist realism is the work of V. V. Mayakovsky (the poems *Vladimir Ilich Lenin, Good,* the lyric poetry of the twenties).

While continuing the best artistic traditions of the literature of the past, socialist realism at the same time represents a qualitatively new and higher artistic method, since its fundamental characteristics have been determined by completely new social relations in socialist society.

Socialist realism reflects life realistically, deeply, truthfully; it is socialist because it reflects life in its revolutionary development, that is, in the process of the creation of socialist society on the way to Communism. It differs from the methods which preceded it historically in that the foundation of the idea for which the Soviet writer appeals in his art is the movement toward Communism under the leadership of the Party of Lenin and Stalin. This ideal is embodied in the new type of positive hero created by Soviet literature. His characteristics are determined primarily by the unity of the individual and society which was impossible in the preceding periods of social development and by the enthusiasm of free, collective, creative, constructive labor which in the Soviet land has become "a thing of honor, a thing of glory, a thing of valor and of heroism" (J. V. Stalin). They are determined by the lofty emotion of Soviet patriotism, love for one's Socialist homeland, by his identification with the Party, and by the Communist attitude to life instilled in Soviet people by the Party of Lenin and Stalin.

Also qualitatively new in socialist realism is the way in which

life's processes are portrayed, resting on the fact that the difficulties in the development of Soviet society are difficulties of
growth which bear in themselves the possibilities of being overcome, and of the victory of the old over the new [*sic!*], and of
what is being born over what is dying. The Soviet artist thereby
receives an opportunity to portray the present in the light of the
future, that is, to depict life in its revolutionary development, to
portray the victory of the new over the old, to show the revolutionary romanticism of socialist reality. "Soviet literature must be
able to portray heroes and to look ahead into the future," said
A. A. Zhdanov. "This will be no utopia, for our future is being
prepared by today's planned, conscious work."

. . . .

The Communist ideal, the new type of positive hero, the depiction of life in its revolutionary development on the basis of
the victory of the new over the old—these fundamental traits of
socialist realism are manifested in infinitely diversified artistic
forms. . . .

Tendency in a work of art is the idea or conclusion to which the
author strives to lead the reader as he portrays life and characters
in a work.
    "The tendency should emerge by itself from the situations
and actions, without being pointed out in any special way" (F.
Engels).
    Bourgeois literature strives, by distorting the truth of life, to
effect in the reader a reconciliation with social injustice, to dis-
tract him from the idea that capitalism must be fought, and to
instill in him the conviction that such a struggle is hopeless. Its
tendency is often concealed. Soviet literature, on the other hand,
portraying life truthfully, not only does not conceal its Communist tendency, but seeks in every way to have the work of art
set an example of how an actual individual should behave, to inspire the people to fight for their happiness, and to help build a
Communist society.[4]
    "Yes, our Soviet literature is tendentious, and we are proud of
its tendentiousness, because our tendency lies in liberating the

    [4] Notice how this sentence contradicts Engels's definition just above it.

toilers—all mankind—from the yoke of capitalist slavery" (A. A. Zhdanov).

Tragedy, one of the types of dramatic works in which the hero is shown in a hopeless situation, in an unequal, intense struggle in which he is doomed.

Tragedy is one of the most ancient forms of drama. It arose in ancient Greece and derived its name from the popular performances during the celebrations in honor of the god Dionysus. A goat was sacrificed to him (the Greek word for goat is *tragos*). This ritual was accompanied by dances, recitations concerning the sufferings of Dionysus, and songs about the sacrificial goat.

Having lost its primal character, tragedy later became an independent form of theatrical spectacle.

We know the tragedies of Aeschylus, Sophocles, Euripides (fifth century B.C.), and of other great tragedians.

With its picture of the sufferings of a man, ancient classical tragedy had a powerful emotional impact, and aroused an awareness that it was hopeless to struggle against unknown, supernatural powers imagined to be directing human fate.

The tragedies of William Shakespeare, the great English dramatist of the end of the sixteenth and the beginning of the seventeenth century, became world famous. His works contain a profound picture of the sharply contradictory psychological world of his heroes which reflected the traits of the society which produced these heroes (*King Lear, Macbeth, Romeo and Juliet, Hamlet, Othello*).

A. S. Pushkin also wrote in this genre, producing his immortal "little tragedies" (*The Stone Guest, Mozart and Salieri*), and the tragedy *Boris Godunov.*

In Soviet literature tragedy, unlike the tragedy of the past, has quite a different, affirmative meaning. The hero of such a tragedy fights not for his personal destiny, divorced from the destiny of the people, but for the general cause of the people. If necessary, he knowingly sacrifices his life on behalf of this victory. The death of the hero thus becomes his spiritual triumph, his victory.

We realize and feel this when we view, for example, Vs.

Vishnevsky's *Optimistic Tragedy* depicting the death of a group of sailors in the struggle for Soviet power during the civil war, or when we read works on the exploits of the heroes of the great patriotic war (A. A. Fadeev's *The Young Guard,* etc.).

Tragedy in Soviet literature arouses a feeling of pride for the man who has accomplished a great deed for the people's happiness; it calls for continued struggle against the things which brought about the hero's death.

BIBLIOGRAPHY

Altman, Iogann. "Dramaturgicheskie printsipy Aristotelya," *Literaturny kritik*, No. 10 (October, 1935), pp. 52–74.
Antonovich, M. A. Izbrannye stati; filosofiya, kritika, polemika. Edited by V. Evgenev-Maksimov. Leningrad, Gosizdat, 1938.
Averbakh, L., ed. S kem i pochemu my boremsya. Moscow-Leningrad, Zemlya i fabrika, 1930.
Babel, Isaac. The Collected Stories. Edited by Walter Morison. Introduction by Lionel Trilling. New York, Criterion Books, 1955.
—— Konarmiya. Moscow-Leningrad, Gosizdat, 1926.
Bauer, Raymond A. The New Man in Soviet Psychology. Cambridge, Harvard University Press, 1952.
Belinsky, V. G. Polnoe sobranie sochinenii. 12 vols. Moscow, Izdatelstvo Akademii Nauk SSSR, 1953–56.
—— Selected Philosophical Works. Edited by M. T. Yovchuk. Moscow, Foreign Languages Publishing House, 1948.
Berlin, Isaiah. "A Marvellous Decade," *Encounter*, IV, No. 6 (June, 1955), 27–39.
—— "A Marvellous Decade (II), 1838–48: German Romanticism in Petersburg and Moscow," *Encounter*, V, No. 5 (November, 1955), 21–29.
—— "A Marvellous Decade (III), Belinsky: Moralist and Prophet," *Encounter*, V, No. 6 (December, 1955), 22–43.
—— "A Marvellous Decade (IV), Herzen and the Grand Inquisitors," *Encounter*, VI, No. 5 (May, 1956), 20–34.
Bolshaya sovetskaya entsiklopediya. 65 vols. Moscow, 1926–47; 2d ed., 46 vols. Moscow, 1950–57.
Borland, Harriet. Soviet Literary Theory and Practice during the First Five-Year Plan. New York, King's Crown Press, 1950.
Bowman, Herbert E. Vissarion Belinski, 1811–1848; a Study in the Origins of Social Criticism in Russia. Cambridge, Harvard University Press, 1954.

Brown, Edward J. The Proletarian Episode in Rusian Literature, 1928–1932. New York, Columbia University Press, 1953.

Bukharin, N. Etyudy. Moscow-Leningrad, Gosizdat, 1932.

Bursov, B. Mat M. Gorkogo i voprosy sotsialisticheskogo romana. Moscow, Gosizdat, 1951.

Butcher, Samuel Henry. Aristotle's Theory of Poetry and Fine Art. 4th ed. New York, Dover, 1951.

Camus, Albert. L'homme revolté. Paris, Gallimard, 1952. Translated as The Rebel. New York, Knopf, 1954.

Carr, Edward Hallet. The Bolshevik Revolution, 1917–1923. 3 vols. New York, Macmillan, 1951–53.

Caudwell, Christopher. Further Studies in a Dying Culture. London, Bodley Head, 1950.

—— Illusion and Reality; a Study of the Sources of Poetry. London, Lawrence and Wishart, 1946.

—— Studies in a Dying Culture. London, John Lane, 1938.

Chekhov, Anton Pavlovich. Letters on the Short Story, the Drama, and Other Literary Topics. Edited by Louis S. Friedland. New York, Minton, 1924.

—— Polnoe sobranie sochinenii i pisem A. P. Chekhova. Edited by S. D. Balukhaty, A. M. Yegodin, V. P. Potemkin, N. S. Tikhonov. 20 vols. Moscow, Gosizdat, 1944–51.

—— Selected Letters. Edited by Lillian Hellman. Translated by Sidonie Lederer. New York, Farrar, Straus, 1955.

—— Three Plays: The Cherry Orchard, Three Sisters, Ivanov. Translated by Elizaveta Fen. Harmondsworth, Middlesex, Penguin, 1951.

Chernyshevsky, N. G. Chto delat? iz rasskazov o novykh lyudyakh. Moscow, Gosizdat, 1947.

—— Estetika. Edited by N. G. Bogoslovsky. Moscow-Leningrad, Gosizdat, 1939.

—— Estetika i literaturnaya kritika. Edited by B. I. Bursov. Moscow-Leningrad, Gosizdat, 1951.

—— Polnoe sobranie sochinenii. 16 vols. Moscow, Gosizdat Khudozhestvennaya literatura, 1939–51.

—— Selected Philosophical Essays. Moscow, Foreign Languages Publishing House, 1953.

Conrad, Joseph. The Secret Agent. New York, Doubleday, 1955.

—— Under Western Eyes. New York, New Directions, 1951.

Dobin, E. "Voinstuyushchi optimizm," *Literaturny kritik*, No. 6 (June, 1935), pp. 3–31.

Dobrolyubov, N. A. Izbrannye filosofskie proizvedeniya. Edited by M. T. Yovchuk. Moscow, Gosizdat, 1946–48.

—— Polnoe sobranie sochinenii. 6 vols. Moscow, Gosizdat, 1937.

—— Selected Philosophical Essays. Edited by M. T. Yovchuk. Translated by J. Fineberg. Moscow, Foreign Languages Publishing House, 1948.

Dostoevsky, F. M. The Brothers Karamazov. Translated by Constance Garnett. New York, Modern Library, 1937.

—— Crime and Punishment. Translated by Constance Garnett. New York, Modern Library, 1932.

—— The Idiot. Translated by Constance Garnett. New York, Modern Library, 1935.

—— Iz arkhiva F. M. Dostoevskogo. Prestuplenie i nakazanie: neizdannye materialy. Edited by I. I. Glivenko. Moscow-Leningrad, Gosizdat, 1931.

—— Polnoe sobranie sochinenii F. M. Dostoevskago. St. Petersburg, Prosveshchenii, 1896.

—— The Possessed. Translated by Constance Garnett. New York, Modern Library, 1936.

—— The Short Novels of Dostoevsky. Translated by Constance Garnett. Introduction by Thomas Mann. New York, Dial, 1945.

Eastman, Max. Artists in Uniform; a Study in Literary Bureaucratism. New York, Knopf, 1934.

Ehrenburg, Ilya. Den Vtoroi. Paris, Dom Knigi, 1933. Translated by Alexander Bakshy as *Out of Chaos*. New York, Henry Holt, 1934.

Eikhenbaum, Boris. Lev Tolstoy. Kniga pervaya. Pyatidesyatye gody. Leningrad, Priboi, 1928.

—— Lev Tolstoy. Kniga vtoraya. Shestidesyatye gody. Moscow-Leningrad, Gosizdat Khudozhestvennaya literatura, 1931.

Engels, Friedrich. Herr Eugen Dühring's Revolution in Science. Translated by Emile Burns. Edited by C. P. Dutt. New York, International Publishers, 1939.

—— *See also* Marx, Karl, and Friedrich Engels.

Fadeev, A. Molodaya gvardiya. Moscow, Goslitizdat, 1946.

Fadeev, A. (*Continued*)
—— "Na kakom etape my nakhodimsya," *Na literaturnom postu*, Nos. 11–12 (June, 1927).
—— Razgrom. Moscow, Gosizdat, 1932. Translated as *The Nineteen*, in *Russian Literature since the Revolution*. Edited by Joshua Kunitz. New York, Boni and Gaer, 1948.
Fedin, Konstantin. Goroda i gody. Moscow, Gosizdat, 1926.
—— Neobyknovennoe leto. Moscow, Sovetski pisatel, 1949. Translated by Margaret Wettlin as *No Ordinary Summer*. Moscow, Foreign Languages Publishing House, 1950.
—— Pervye radosti. Moscow, Sovetski pisatel, 1954. Translated as *Early Joys*. Moscow, Foreign Languages Publishing House, 1950.
Fischer, Louis. Machines and Men in Russia. New York, Harrison Smith, 1932.
Forster, E. M. Aspects of the Novel. New York, Harcourt, Brace, 1927.
Fox, Ralph. The Novel and the People. New York, International Publishers, 1945.
Friche, V. M. Zametki o sovremennoi literature. Moscow-Leningrad, Moskovski Rabochi, 1928.
Frohock, Wilbur Merrill. André Malraux and the Tragic Imagination. Stanford, Stanford University Press, 1952.
Furmanov, Dmitri. Chapaev. Moscow, Sovetski pisatel, 1947. Translated by A. M. Anichkova as *Chapayev*. Moscow-Leningrad, Co-operative Publishing Society of Foreign Workers in the USSR, 1934.
Gifford, Henry. The Hero of His Time; a Theme in Russian Literature. London, Edward Arnold, 1950.
Gladkov, Feodor. Tsement. Moscow, Zemlya i fabrika, 1927. Translated by A. S. Arthur and C. Ashleigh as *Cement*. New York, International Publishers, 1929.
Goffensheffer, V. "Den vtoroi I. Erenburga," *Literaturny kritik*, Nos. 7–8 (July–August, 1934), pp. 103–17.
—— Mikhail Sholokhov; kriticheski ocherk. Moscow, Gosizdat, 1940.
—— "Mirovozzrenie i masterstvo," *Literaturny kritik*, No. 4 (September, 1933), pp. 57–77.
—— "Tikhii Don zakonchen . . . ," *Literaturny kritik*, No. 2 (February, 1940), pp. 86–105.

Gogol, Nikolai. Dead Souls. Translated by Constance Garnett. New York, Modern Library, 1936.
—— Polnoe sobranie sochinenii. 14 vols. Leningrad, 1937–52.
Goncharov, I. A. Oblomov. Translated by Natalie Duddington. New York, Everyman's Library, 1946.
Gorbov, D. "A. Fadeev," Pechat i revolyutsiya, No. 6 (September, 1928), pp. 159–69.
Gorky, Maxim. The Artamanov Business. Translated by Alec Brown. New York, Pantheon, 1948.
—— Autobiography of Maxim Gorky. Translated by Isidor Schneider. New York, Citadel, 1949.
—— Best Short Stories. Edited by Avrahm Yarmolinsky and Baroness Moura Budberg. New York, Grayson, 1947.
—— Culture and the People. New York, International Publishers, 1939.
—— Days with Lenin. New York, International Publishers, 1932.
—— Literaturno-kriticheskie stati. Edited by S. M. Bretburg. Moscow, Gosizdat, 1937.
—— Mat. Moscow, Pravda, 1952. Translated by Isidor Schneider as Mother. New York, Citadel, 1947.
—— O literature; stati i rechi, 1928–1936. 3d ed. Edited by N. F. Belchikov. Moscow, Sovetski pisatel, 1937.
—— Reminiscences. Translated by S. S. Koteliansky, Leonard Woolf, and others. New York, Dover, 1946.
—— Seven Plays of Maxim Gorky. Translated by Alexander Bakshy and Paul S. Nathan. New Haven, Yale University Press, 1947.
—— Sobranie sochinenii. 25 vols. Moscow-Leningrad, Gosizdat, 1933–34.
Gurvich, A. V poiskakh geroya; literaturno-kriticheskie stati. Moscow, Gosizdat "Iskusstvo," 1938.
Haimson, Leopold H. The Russian Marxists and the Origins of Bolshevism. Cambridge, Harvard University Press, 1955.
Hecker, Julius Friedrich. Moscow Dialogues; Discussions in Red Philosophy. London, Chapman and Hall, 1934.
Herzen, A. I. Polnoe sobranie sochinenii i pisem. Edited by M. K. Lemke. 21 vols. Petrograd, Literaturno-izdatelski otdel Narodnogo kommissariata po prosveshcheniyu, 1919.

History of the Communist Party of the Soviet Union (Bolsheviks). New York, International Publishers, 1939.

Hyman, Stanley Edgar. The Armed Vision; a Study in the Methods of Modern Literary Criticism. New York, Knopf, 1948.

James, Henry. The Princess Casamassima. Introduction by Lionel Trilling. New York, Macmillan, 1948.

Kataev, V. Rastratchiki. Moscow, Zemlya i fabrika, 1928. Translated by Leonide Zarine as The Embezzlers. New York, Dial Press, 1929.

—— Vremya vpered! Moscow, Gosizdat, 1935. Translated by Charles Malamuth as Time, Forward! New York, Farrar and Rinehart, 1933.

Kaun, Alexander. Maxim Gorky and His Russia. New York, Jonathan Cape and Harrison Smith, 1931.

Khmelnitskaya, Tamara. "Konets 'lishnego cheloveka,'" Literaturny sovremennik, No. 3 (1937), pp. 251–62.

Koestler, Arthur. Darkness at Noon. New York, Macmillan, 1941.

—— The Yogi and the Commissar. New York, Macmillan, 1945.

Konstantinov, F. V., ed. Istoricheski materializm. Moscow, Gosizdat, 1950.

Korabelnikov, V. G. "Konets chekhovskoi temy," Literaturni kritik, No. 1 (June, 1933), pp. 80–99.

Kosarev, A. "Pokazhite geroya nashego vremeni," Oktyabr, No. 9 (October, 1933), p. 6.

Krupskaya, Nadezhda K. Memories of Lenin (1893–1917). London, Lawrence and Wishart, 1942.

Kruzhkov, V. S. Mirovozzrenie N. A. Dobrolyubova. Moscow, Gospolitizdat, 1952.

Kunitz, Joshua, ed. Russian Literature since the Revolution. New York, Boni and Gaer, 1948.

Lavretsky, A. Belinsky, Chernyshevsky, Dobrolyubov v borbe za realizm. Moscow, Gosizdat, 1941.

Lebedev, G. "Individualnoe i tipicheskoe, Podnyataya tselina Mikh. Sholokhova," Literaturny kritik, No. 1 (June, 1933), pp. 57–70.

Lebedev-Polyansky, P. I. N. G. Chernyshevsky. Moscow, Khu-
dozhestvennaya literatura, 1939.
—— V. G. Belinsky, literaturno-kriticheskaya deyatelnost.
Moscow-Leningrad, Izdatelstvo Akademii nauk SSSR, 1945.
Lenin, V. I. "Left-Wing" Communism, an Infantile Disorder;
a Popular Essay in Marxian Strategy and Tactics. New York,
International Publishers, 1940.
—— Materialism and Empirio-Criticism; Critical Comments on
a Reactionary Philosophy. Moscow, Foreign Languages Pub-
lishing House, 1952.
—— Sochineniya. 4th ed., 35 vols. Moscow, Gosizdat, 1941–52.
Leonov, Leonid. Izbrannoe. Moscow, Gosizdat, 1946.
—— Road to the Ocean. Translated by Norbert Guterman.
New York, L. B. Fischer, 1944.
—— Skutarevsky. Moscow, Khudozhestvennaya literatura, 1935.
Translated by Alec Brown as Skutarevsky. New York, Har-
court, Brace, 1936.
—— Sobranie sochinenii v pyati tomakh. 6 vols. Moscow, Go-
sizdat Khudozhestvennaya literatura, 1953–55.
—— Sot. Moscow, Zemlya i fabrika, 1930. Translated by Ivor
Montagu and Sergei Nalbandov as Soviet River. New York,
Dial Press, 1932.
—— Vor. Riga, Izdatelstvo Literatura, 1928. Translated by
Hubert Butler as The Thief. New York, Dial Press, 1931.
—— Vzyatie velikoshumska. Moscow, Gosizdat, 1944. Trans-
lated by Norbert Guterman as Chariot of Wrath. New York,
L. B. Fischer, 1946.
Lermontov, M. A Hero of Our Time. Translated by Martin
Parker. Moscow, Foreign Languages Publishing House, 1947.
Levin, F. "Kak zakalyalas stal," Literaturny kritik, No. 10 (Oc-
tober, 1935), pp. 75–82.
Levin, Harry. "From Priam to Birotteau," Yale French Studies,
No. 6 (1950), pp. 75–82.
Libedinsky, Yurii. Generalnye zadachi proletarskoi literatury.
Moscow-Leningrad, Gosizdat, 1931.
—— Rozhdenie geroya. Leningrad, Priboi, 1930.
Lifshitz, Mikhail. Lenin o kulture i iskusstve; sbornik statei i
otryvkov. Moscow, Gosizdat, 1938.

Lifshitz, Mikhail (*Continued*)
—— The Philosophy of Art of Karl Marx. Translated by Ralph B. Winn. Edited by Angel Flores. New York, Critics Group, 1938.
Literaturnaya entsiklopedia. Vols. I–IX, XI. Moscow, 1929–39.
Lukačs, George. Literaturnye teorii xix veka i marksizm. Moscow, Gosizdat Khudozhestvennaya literatura, 1937.
—— "Marks i Engels v polemike s Lassallem po povodu Zikingen," *Literaturnoe nasledstvo*, No. 3 (1932).
—— Studies in European Realism. Translated by Edith Bone. London, Hillway, 1950.
Lunacharsky, A. V. Kritika i kritiki; sbornik statei. Edited by N. F. Belchikov. Moscow, Gosizdat, 1938.
—— "Mysli o kommunisticheskoi dramaturgii," *Pechat i revolyutsiya*, No. 2 (August–October, 1921).
Lyons, Eugene, ed. Six Soviet Plays. Boston, Houghton Mifflin, 1934.
Makedonov, A. "Problema geroya v estetike Belinskogo," *Literaturny kritik*, No. 6 (June, 1936), pp. 107–37.
Malraux, André. La Condition humaine. Paris, Gallimard, 1933. Translated by Haakon Chevalier as *Man's Fate*. New York, Modern Library, 1936.
"Marksizm-Leninizm i khudozhestvennaya literatura," *Literaturny kritik*, No. 3 (August, 1933), pp. 3–11.
Marshall, Herbert, ed. Mayakovsky and His Poetry. London, Pilot, 1945.
Marx, Karl. Capital; a Critique of Political Economy. Edited by Friedrich Engels. Translated by Samuel Moore and Edward Aveling. Chicago, Charles H. Kerr and Company, 1906–9.
Marx, Karl, and Friedrich Engels. The German Ideology. Edited by R. Pascal. New York, International Publishers, 1939.
—— Handbook of Marxism. Edited by Emile Burns. New York, International Publishers, 1935.
—— Historische-Kritische Gesamtausgabe; Werke, Shcriften, Briefe. Edited by D. Ryazanov. Frankfort am Main, 1927–35.
—— The Holy Family; or, Critique of Critical Critique. Moscow, Foreign Languages Publishing House, 1956.
—— Literature and Art; Selections from Their Writings. New York, International Publishers, 1947.
—— Literaturnoe nasledstvo. Edited by Franz Mehring. Trans-

lated from German by E. A. Gurvich and M. G. Lunts. Moscow, 1907.
—— Marks i Engels ob iskusstve. Edited by A. V. Lunacharsky. Compiled by F. P. Shiller and M. A. Lifshitz. Moscow, Sovetskaya literatura, 1933.
—— Selected Correspondence, 1846–1895. Marxist Library, Vol. XXIX. New York, International Publishers, 1942.
—— Selected Works in Two Volumes. 2 vols. Moscow, Foreign Languages Publishing House, 1951.
—— Sur la littérature et l'art. Edited by Jean Frèville. Paris, Editions Sociales Internationales, 1936.
Mead, Margaret. Soviet Attitudes toward Authority; an Interdisciplinary Approach to Problems of Soviet Character. New York, McGraw-Hill, 1951.
Meilakh, B. Lenin i problemy russkoi literatury kontsa XIX–nachala XX vv. 2d ed. Moscow-Leningrad, Gosizdat, 1951.
Merleau-Ponty, Maurice. Humanisme et terreur; essai sur le problème communiste. Paris, Gallimard, 1947.
Milosz, Czeslaw. The Captive Mind. Translated by Jane Zielonko. New York, Knopf, 1953.
Mirsky, D. S. A History of Russian Literature. Edited by Francis J. Whitfield. New York, Knopf, 1949.
Nedoshivin, G. "Lenin and Soviet Art," Soviet Literature, No. 1 (1952).
Novich, I. Zhizn Chernyshevskogo. Moscow, Gosizdat, 1939.
Noyes, George Rapall, ed. Masterpieces of the Russian Drama. New York, Appleton-Century, 1933.
Nusinov, I. Vekovye obrazy. Moscow, Gosizdat, 1937.
Obraz bolshevika; sbornik kriticheskikh statei. Leningrad, Gosizdat, 1938.
Olesha, Yu. K. Envy; with V. Kaverin, Unknown Artist. Translated by P. Ross. 2 vols. in 1. London, Westhouse, 1947.
—— Zavist. 2d ed. Moscow, Zemlya i fabrika, 1930.
Ostrovsky, Nikolai. Kak zakalyalas stal. Moscow, Sovetski pisatel, 1947. Translated by Alec Brown as The Making of a Hero. New York, Dutton, 1937.
Ovsyaniko-Kulikovski, D. N. Istoriya russkoi intelligentsii; itogi russkoi khudozhestvennoi literatury XIX veka. 2 vols. Moscow, V. M. Sablin, 1906.

344   BIBLIOGRAPHY

Ovsyaniko-Kulikovski, D. N., ed. Istoriya russkoi literatury XIX v. 5 vols. Moscow, Izdanie T-va "Mir," 1908–10.

Panova, Vera. Sputniki. Moscow, Sovetski pisatel, 1953. Translated by Marie Budberg as The Train. New York, Knopf, 1949.

Pavlenko, P. Izbrannoe. Moscow, Sovetski pisatel, 1949.

Pertsov, V. Etyudy o sovetskoi literature. Moscow, Gosizdat, 1937.

—— Podvig i geroi; etyudy o sovetskoi literature. Moscow, Sovetski pisatel, 1946.

Pervyi vsesoyuznyi s'ezd sovetskikh pisatelei, 1934; stenograficheski otchet. Moscow, Gosizdat, 1934.

Plamenatz, John. German Marxism and Russian Communism. New York, Longmans Green, 1954.

Plekhanov, George. The Role of the Individual in History. New York, International Publishers, 1940.

—— V. G. Belinski; sbornik statei. Moscow-Petrograd, Gosizdat, 1923.

Polevoi, Boris. Povest o nastoyashchem cheloveke. Moscow, Sovetski pisatel, 1947. Translated as A Story about a Real Man. Moscow, Foreign Languages Publishing House, 1949.

Polonsky, Vyacheslav. Na literaturnye temy; stati kriticheskie i polemicheskie. Leningrad, "Krug," 1927.

—— Ocherki literaturnogo dvizheniya revolutsionnoi epokhi. Moscow-Leningrad, Gosizdat, 1929.

Pospelov, G. N. Teoriya literatury. Moscow, Uchpedgiz, 1940.

Praz, Mario. The Hero in Eclipse in Victorian Fiction. Translated by Angus Davidson. London and New York, Oxford University Press, 1956.

Protiv bezideinosti v literature; sbornik statei zhurnala Zvezda. Leningrad, Sovetski pisatel, 1947.

Pushkin, A. S. Evgeny Onegin. Translated by Oliver Elton. London, Pushkin Press, 1946.

Raglan, Fitz Roy Richard Somerset, 4th baron (Lord Raglan). The Hero; a Study in Tradition, Myth, and Drama. London, Watts, 1949.

Read, Herbert. Art and Society. 2d ed. London, Faber and Faber, 1945.

Reavey, George. Soviet Literature Today. London, Lindsay Drummond, 1946.

Reeve, Franklin. "Politics and Imagination," *American Slavic and East European Review*, XVI, No. 2 (April, 1957), 175–89.

Report of Court Proceedings in the Case of the Anti-Soviet "Bloc of Rights and Trotskyites." Moscow, People's Commissariat of Justice of the USSR, 1938.

"Resolution on Political and Creative Questions of International and Revolutionary Literature," *Literature of the World Revolution*, Special Issue, 1931.

Rozental, M. "Partiya i literatura," *Literaturny kritik*, No. 10–11 (October–November, 1937), pp. 9–36.

Rozental, M., ed. O sovetskoi literature; kriticheskie stati. Moscow, Gosizdat, 1936.

Sartre, Jean-Paul. What Is Literature? Translated by Bernard Frechtman. New York, Philosophical Library, 1949.

Serafimovich, A. Zheleznyi potok. Moscow, 1926. Translated as *The Iron Flood*. New York, International Publishers, 1935.

Sholokhov, Mikhail. Podnyataya tselina. Moscow, Federatsiya, 1932. Translated by Stephen Garry as *Virgin Soil Upturned*. London, Putnam, 1948.

—— Tikhii Don. Leningrad, Gosizdat, 1945. Translated by Stephen Garry as *The Silent Don*. New York, Knopf, 1946.

Shub, David. Lenin; a Biography. New York, Doubleday, 1951.

Simmons, Ernest J. Continuity and Change in Russian and Soviet Thought. Cambridge, Harvard University Press, 1955.

—— Dostoevski; the Making of a Novelist. New York, Oxford University Press, 1940.

—— Leo Tolstoy. Boston, Little, Brown, 1946.

—— Pushkin. Cambridge, Harvard University Press, 1937.

Simmons, Ernest J., ed. Through the Glass of Soviet Literature; Views of Russian Society. New York, Columbia University Press, 1953.

Simonov, Konstantin. Dni i nochi. Moscow, Gosizdat, 1946. Translated by Joseph Barnes as *Days and Nights*. New York, Simon and Shuster, 1945.

Sokolov, Yu. M. Russki folklor. Moscow, Uchpedgiz, 1938.

Somerville, John. Soviet Philosophy, a Study of Theory and Practice. New York, Philosophical Library, 1946.

Sovetskaya literatura; sbornik statei. Moscow, Gosizdat, 1948.

Soviet Linguistic Controversy, The. Translated by John V.

Murra, Robert M. Hankin, and Fred Holling. New York, King's Crown Press, 1951.

Soviet Scene; Six Plays of Russian Life. Translated by Alexander Bakshy. New Haven, Yale University Press, 1946.

Stalin, Joseph. Leninism; Selected Writings. New York, International Publishers, 1942.

Struve, Gleb. Twenty-five Years of Soviet Russian Literature, 1918–1943. London, Routledge, 1944.

Timofeev, L. I. Kratki slovar literaturovedcheskikh terminov; posobie dlya uchashchikhsya srednei shkoly. Moscow, Uchpedgiz, 1952.

—— Sovremennaya literatura; uchebnoe posobie dlia 10-go klassa srednei shkoly. 3d ed. Moscow, Uchpedgiz, 1947.

—— Teoriya literatury; osnovy nauki o literature. Moscow, Uchpedgiz, 1938.

Tolstoy, Alexei. Khozhdenie po mukam. Moscow, Gosizdat, 1943. Translated by Edith Bone as Road to Calvary. New York, Knopf, 1946.

Tolstoy, L. N. Anna Karenina. Translated by Constance Garnett. New York, Modern Library, 1950.

—— Polnoe sobranie sochinenii. Edited by V. G. Chertkov. Moscow, Khudozhestvennaya literatura, 1934–56.

—— War and Peace. Translated by Louise and Aylmer Maude. New York, Simon and Schuster, 1942.

—— What Is Art? and Essays on Art. Translated by Aylmer Maude. London, Oxford University Press, 1950.

Tomašič, Dinko. The Impact of Russian Culture on Soviet Communism. Glencoe, Illinois, Free Press, 1953.

Tretyakov, V. S. "Lef i NEP," Lef, No. 2 (April–May, 1923), pp. 70–78.

Trilling, Lionel. The Liberal Imagination; Essays on Literature and Society. New York, Viking, 1950.

Trotsky, L. D. Literatura i revolyutsiya. 2d ed. Moscow, Gosizdat, 1924. Translated by Rose Strunsky as Literature and Revolution. New York, International Publishers, 1925.

Turgenev, Ivan Sergeevich. The Borzoi Turgenev. Translated by Harry Stevens. New York, Knopf, 1950.

—— A Nest of Gentry. Translated by Bernard Isaacs. Moscow, Foreign Languages Publishing House, 1947.

—— Polnoe sobranie sochinenii. 6th ed., 10 vols. St. Petersburg, Glazunov, 1913.

—— Sobranie sochinenii. Edited by N. L. Brodski, I. A. Novikov, A. A. Surkov. Moscow, Izdatelstvo *Pravda,* 1949.

Usievich, E. Cherty geroya nashei literatury. Moscow, Gosizdat, 1941.

—— Pisateli i deistvitelnost. Moscow, Gosizdat, 1936.

—— Za chistotu Leninizma v literaturnoi teorii. Moscow-Leningrad, Gosizdat, 1932.

Valentinov, N. "Chernyshevsky i Lenin," *Novy zhurnal,* No. 26 (1951), pp. 193–216.

—— "Chernyshevsky i Lenin," *Novy zhurnal,* No. 27 (1951), pp. 225–49.

—— "Lenin v Simbirske," *Novy zhurnal,* No. 37 (1954), pp. 211–35.

—— "Rannie gody Lenina, brat lenina—A. Ulyanov," *Novy zhurnal,* No. 40 (1955), pp. 200–216.

—— "Rannie gody Lenina, Lenin v Kokushkine," *Novy zhurnal,* No. 36 (1954), pp. 220–37.

—— "Rannie gody Lenina, prevrashchenie Vladimira Ulyanova v Lenin," *Novy zhurnal,* No. 41 (1955), p. 176–87.

—— "Vydumki o rannei revolyutsionnosti Lenina," *Novy zhurnal,* No. 39 (1954), pp. 212–31.

Venable, Vernon. Human Nature; the Marxian View. New York, Knopf, 1946.

Vischer, Friedrich Theodor. Aesthetik oder Wissenschaft des Schoenen. Leipzig, 1846–58.

Vishnevsky, Vsevolod. Sobranie sochinenii v pyati tomakh. 5 vols. Moscow, Khudozhestvennaya literatura, 1954.

Voronsky, A. K. Literaturnye portrety. Moscow, "Federatsiya," 1929.

—— Na styke; sbornik statei. Moscow-Petrograd, Gosizdat, 1923.

—— Ob iskusstve. Moscow, *Pravda,* 1925.

V sporakh o metode; sbornik statei o sotsialisticheskom realizme. Leningrad, Leningradskoe oblastnoe izdatelstvo, 1934.

Wilson, Edmund. "The Historical Interpretation of Literature," in The Triple Thinkers; Twelve Essays on Literary Subjects. New York, Oxford University Press, 1948.

Wilson, Edmund (*Continued*)
—— To the Finland Station. New York, Doubleday, 1940.
Yarmolinsky, Avrahm Tsalevich. Turgenev; the Man, His Art and His Age. New York, Century, 1926.
Yudin, P. "Lenin i nekotorye voprosy literaturnoi kritiki," *Literaturny kritik*, No. 1 (June, 1933), pp. 11–33.
Yuzovsky, Yu. "Osvobozhdennyi Prometei," *Literaturny kritik*, No. 10 (October, 1934), pp. 113–39.
Zhdanov, A. A. "Doklad o zhurnalakh *Zvezda* i *Leningrad*," *Literaturnaya gazeta*, September 21, 1946.

INDEX

Lenin, Nikolai (*Continued*)
idea, 326; and socialist realism,
331-32
"Lenin and Soviet Art" (Nedoshivin), 171
Leningrad (journal), 325
Leonardo da Vinci, Engels on,
177
Leonov, Leonid: literary heroes
of, 260, 301-6, 308, 323; literary quality of, 282; and socialist realism, 296, 301, 305; and
Dostoevsky, 302*n*; Soviet criticism of, 305-10
Lermontov, Mikhail, 14, 62, 330
Lessing, Gotthold, 288
Levin (*Anna Karenina*), 14, 17-
18, 114
Levinson (*The Nineteen*), 243-
53, 272*n*
Libedinsky, Yurii, 279, 280
Liberals: writers as, 110-17, 119-
25; and audience, 119-20;
views on universal values in art
of, 121-23; and principles, 131-
32; break with radical democrats, 145-46; and Marxism,
170; see also Turgenev
Lifshitz, Mikhail, 158, 168*n*-69*n*;
on art in Communist society,
182
Linguistic controversy (1950),
157
Literary criticism, *see* Criticism,
literary
Literary Encyclopedia, 224, 230*n*,
241, 276
Literary hero, *see* Hero, literary
Literary Reminiscences (Turgenev), 109*n*, 110
Literary truth, *see* Truth, literary
Literature: and politics, 1-2, 22-
23, 51-56, 103-25, 200-26,
232-67, 309-10, 322; and cult
of heroism, 2-3; and Com-
munist Party, 3-4, 7-8, 111;
and leisure, 7; moral claims on,
8-9, 36, 85-87, 95-107; Belin-

sky's views of, 31-56; Dobrolyubov's views of, 57-79; and social consciousness, 75; Chernyshevsky's views of, 80-107, 118-
19, 141; Turgenev's views of,
110-17, 121, 135-42, 144; Tolstoy on, 111, 123-25; Chekhov's views of, 119-20, 122,
143-44; Marxism and, 119,
122, 147-99; conflict of, with
revolution, 209-10; *see also*
Hero, literary; Positive hero;
Soviet literature; Truth, literary
Literature and Revolution (Trotsky), 299
Litfront, 273, 275
Liza (*Road to the Ocean*), 304-6
Lopukhov (*What Is to Be
Done?*), 96, 99*n*, 106
Lukačs, George, on literature,
156*n*
Lukeria (*Virgin Soil Upturned*),
286
Lunacharsky, Anatoli, 189, 299
Luther, Martin, 41; Engels on,
177

Macbeth (Shakespeare), 333
Machiavelli, Engels on, 177
Makedonov, A., 49
Making of a Hero, The (Os-
trovsky): and civil war, 227-28;
as journalistic mythology, 241;
as type of Soviet novel, 296,
315-19; positive hero in, 322,
326
Malraux, André, 9, 11-12, 291,
292; on heroes, 9
Man's Fate (Malraux), 11-12
Margulies (*Time, Forward!*), 279
Marriage, in Chernyshevsky's
work, 96
Marx, Karl: attitude of, toward
literature, 7, 153, 155, 157-68;
Lenin on, 105; on philoso-
phers, 119, 150; influence of, in
Russia, 127; on motion, 147;

Stakhanovites, and cult of heroism, 2

Stalin, Joseph: on writer, 4, 107; Zhdanov on, 24; extension of theory of conscious political partisanship by, 149-50; and Soviet criticism, 156-57, 172, 273-74; in Soviet literature, 283, 313-14; and socialist realism, 330-31

Stavrogin (*The Possessed*), 15-16, 141

Stolz (*Oblomov*), 68-69

Stone Guest, The (Pushkin), 333

Storm (A. Ostrovsky), 72-75, 79

Story of a Real Man, The (Polevoi), 241

Strachey, John, 147

Subjectivity, of writer, Belinsky's view of, 37; *see also* Writer

Suffering: Dostoevsky's view of, 19; Chernyshevsky's view of, 44; Soviet view of, 307-10; *see also* Tragedy

Suicide, Dobrolyubov's view of, 67, 73, 79

Superfluous man: radical democratic criticism of, 15-16, 62-64, 91-92; Turgenev's version of, 16; and alienation, 16-17, 321; Goncharov's version of, 44; in 1920s, 231; Gorky's view of, 293

"Superfluous Men and the Men with a Grudge, The" (Herzen), 134

Surovin, A. S., 119

Tatyana (*Eugene Onegin*), 72

Telegin (*Road to Calvary*), 314

Tendentiousness, Engels on, 161, 162

Thief, The (Leonov), 260

Third Thesis on Feuerbach (Marx), 148

Time, Forward! (Kataev), 279

Timofeev, L. I.: and radical

democrats, 24n; on socialist realism, 26, 328, 330-32; on the artist, 53n; on Aristotle, 82n; view of literary creation, 90n; on Soviet art, 169; on Gorky's Pavel Vlasov, 214; on *Mother*, 225; glossary of, 325-34

Tolstoy, Alexei, 296, 310-15

Tolstoy, Leo: and literature, 7-9, 207-8, 270, 293; literary heroes of, 14, 15, 17-18, 114; and Soviet criticism, 25-26, 125, 276n; as a new voice, 58; and politics, 108-9; on audience, 110; and radical democrats, 110-11; on literature, 111, 123-25, 145, 270; and writer, 111, 189, 204; and history, 130-31; and Gorky, 144; on heroes, 144; positive hero of, 145-46; aesthetic theory of, 169; and Soviet literature, 279

Tragedy: Chernyshevsky's view of, 88-94, 299; and Soviet literature, 299-301; Timofeev on, 333-34; *see also* Suffering

Trilling, Lionel: on politics and literature, 108; on creation, 113

Trotsky, Leon: on Belinsky, 30, 31; on literature, 31; and Party, 197; and literary heroes, 230; and proletarian literature, 231; and tragedy, 299; in Soviet literature, 313

Truth, literary: Belinsky and, 39, 43-44, 51; radical democrats and, 60-61, 83-84, 98-100, 116-17; Tolstoy and, 112; Turgenev and, 112, 116; Chekhov and, 113; Marxists and, 150-51, 160, 162-63; in Soviet criticism, 270-71, 275-76; *see also* Realism

Turgenev, Ivan: and radical democrats, 4, 76, 81, 83-84, 87-88, 110, 118, 135-42, 144-45; literary heroes of, 11, 14, 16, 20, 57, 63-64, 69-73, 75,

Yovchuk, M. T., on Belinsky, 48
Yuzovsky, Yuri, 300

Zatochnik, Daniel, 134n
Zhdanov, Andrei A.: and Party
control of literature, 4, 8, 36,
212, 279, 315; on nineteenth-
century heritage, 23-24; on art,
54; on fine writing, 118; and
Marx and Engels, 171; and

Lenin, 201n, 202; on socialist
realism, 288, 290; on Soviet
literature, 289, 332-33; on positive hero, 290n, 323; Timofeev
on, 325, 330; on Soviet writers,
327
Zhukhrai (*The Making of a
Hero*), 326
Zhukovsky, V. A., 330
Zoshchenko, Mikhail, 118, 258
Zvezda (journal), 325